Dublin Castle Art

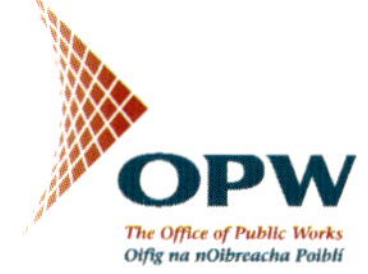

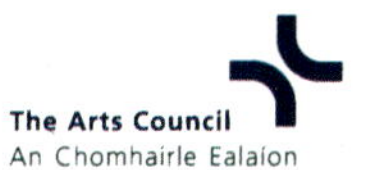

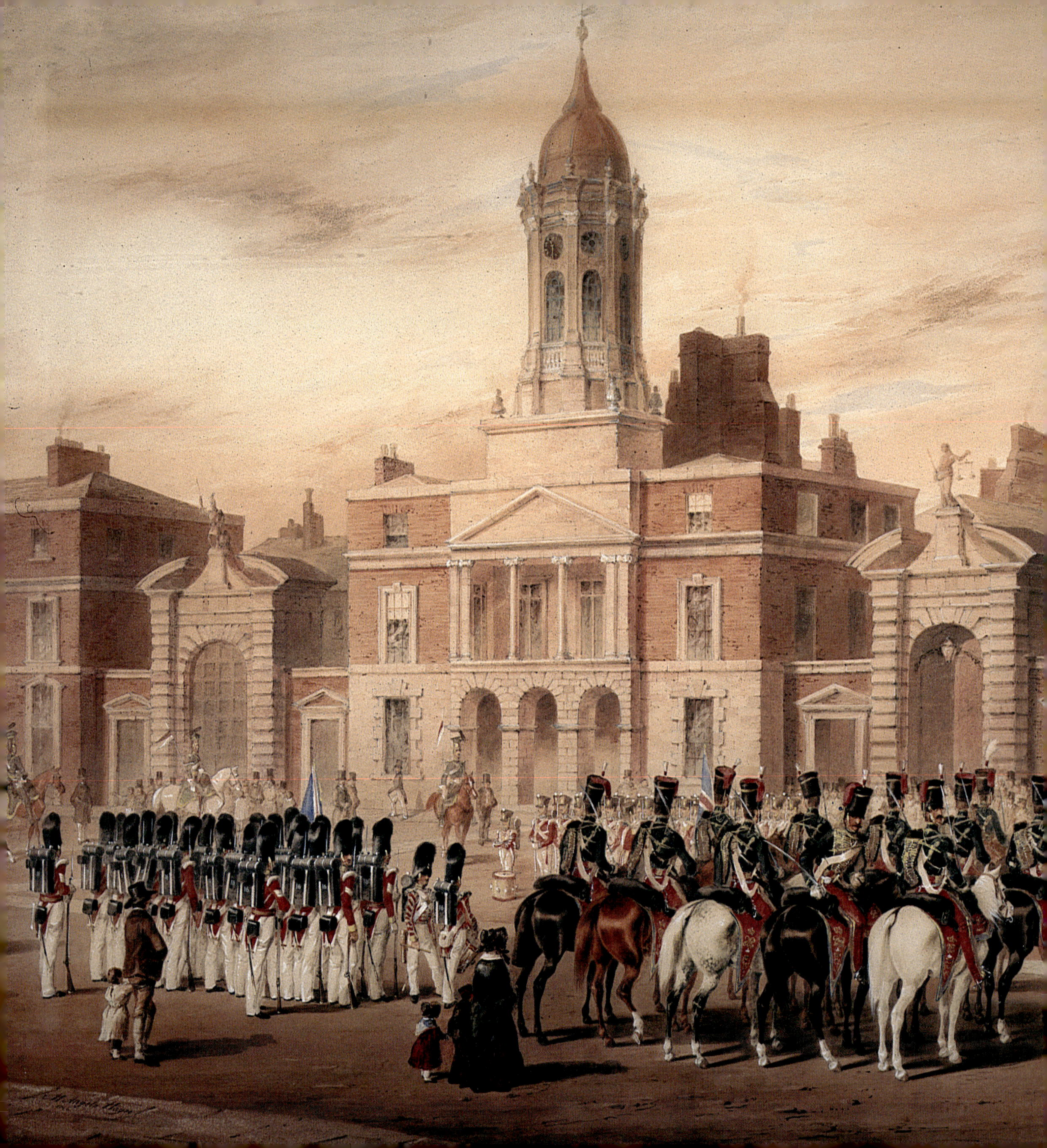

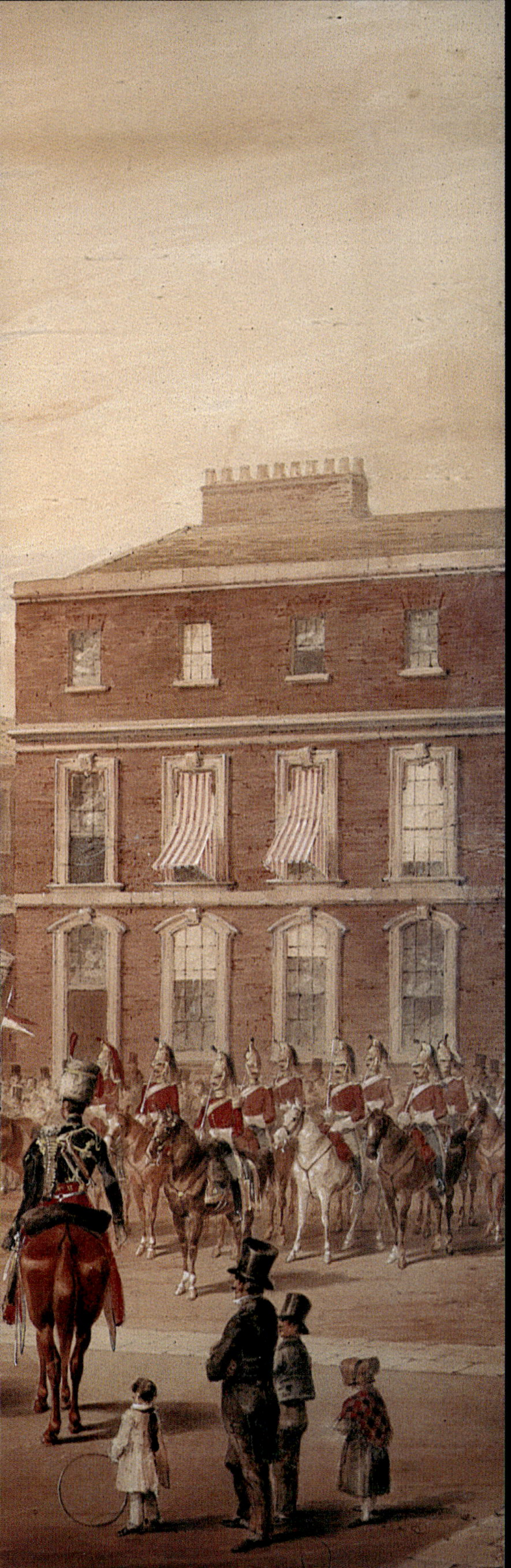

Dublin Castle Art

THE HISTORICAL AND CONTEMPORARY COLLECTION

BY RÓISÍN KENNEDY

OFFICE OF PUBLIC WORKS

DUBLIN CASTLE ART
The Historical and Contemporary Collection

ISBN 07076 6280 X

Dublin: Published by the Stationery Office

Author Róisín Kennedy

Design John O'Regan (© Gandon Editions, 1999)
Production Nicola Dearey
Gandon Editions, Kinsale
Text editor Elizabeth Mayes
Photography Dennis Mortell, Dublin
Printing Nicholson & Bass, Belfast

cover Vincenzo Waldré, St Patrick's Hall ceiling, c.1787-1802 (detail)
back cover Vivienne Roche, *Plumbline*, 1995 (detail)
frontispiece Michelangelo Hayes, *St Patrick's Day Military Parade at Dublin Castle*, 1844 (detail)

to be purchased directly from the
Government Publications Sale Office
Sun Alliance House, Molesworth Street, Dublin 2
or by mail order from
Government Publications, Postal Trade Section,
4-5 Harcourt Road, Dublin 2 – tel: 01-647 6000 / fax: 475 2760
or through any bookseller
price: £15

Minister for Finance:
Charlie McCreevy, TD

Minister of State at the Department of Finance with responsibility for the Office of Public Works:
Martin Cullen, TD

OPW Art Management Group:
Brian (Barry) Murphy, Chairman
Michael O'Doherty
Noel de Chenu
Angela Rolfe
Mary Heffernan
Jacquie Moore
Jennifer Lonergan, Secretary

Project Co-ordinator:
Mary Heffernan

The Arts Council / An Chomhairle Ealaíon:
Brian Farrell, Chairman
Patricia Quinn, Director
Oliver Dowling, Visual Arts Officer
Sheila Gorman, Visual Arts Executive

Illustration credits

Dúchas, The Heritage Service — 18, 30, 123t
Pat Flaherty, Narrowcast — 16b
The Illustrated London News — 12
Seamus Kearns Collection — 13m
Lensmen & Associates — 13b
National Library of Ireland – Lawrence Collection — 13t, 23, 89
Pieterse-Davison International — 11, 12t, 16t
All other illustrations courtesy of the Office of Public Works

Contents

Foreword

In 1998, the Bursary in Visual Arts Curation was jointly funded by the Office of Public Works and the Arts Council / An Chomhairle Ealaíon, and was awarded to Róisín Kennedy.

The Arts Council / An Chomhairle Ealaíon introduced the Bursary in Visual Arts Curation in 1996 in order to encourage high standards in all aspects of curatorial practice in the contemporary visual arts in Ireland. The Office of Public Works became involved in the bursary scheme so as to further its objective of continuing research on the State's collection.

The goal of the 1998 bursary was to offer an individual the opportunity to curate works from one of the major collections in Ireland over a one-year period. The culmination of the project is a re-hang of Dublin Castle's permanent collection and the publication of this book.

Róisín Kennedy, the bursary winner, has been researching the OPW's historical and contemporary collections housed in Dublin Castle since September 1998. She has made significant and exciting discoveries, and has increased the accessibility of the Castle collection – a long-term aim of the Office of Public Works. This book will be a source of useful information for professional art historians and the wider public, and a valuable contribution to the OPW's art management and maintenance programme.

The Office of Public Works and the Arts Council / An Chomhairle Ealaíon are delighted with the outcome of this project, and it is hoped that it will lead to further links between them. Both organisations warmly congratulate Róisín Kennedy on the success of the project and thank her for the professional approach, enthusiasm and commitment she brought to the work.

MARTIN CULLEN, TD
Minister of State at the Dept of Finance
with responsibility for the Office of Public Works

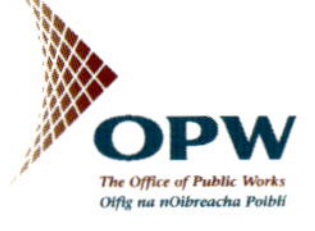

BRIAN FARRELL
Chairman
The Arts Council / An Chomhairle Ealaíon

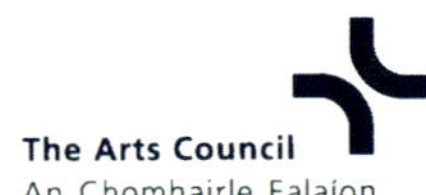

Author's Foreword

Dublin Castle features regularly in the media on the occasion of State visits to Ireland, presidential inaugurations, and public enquiries, and is one of the most popular tourist attractions in Ireland. In spite of its fame and notoriety, little attention has been paid to the collection of artworks housed within its walls. This book provides the first guide to the painting and sculpture of the State Apartments and to the other artworks located throughout the complex. Many of the historical paintings and sculpture have not been published before, and are attributed here to an artist for the first time. A discussion of the contemporary artworks and their commissioning is also included. All the works of art, both old and new, have become part of the fabric of Dublin Castle, and they provide a unique way of understanding this intriguing place.

The text aims to highlight the importance of the artwork to Dublin Castle's past and present, and to give the reader a sense of its context. Details of the provenance and commissioning of the works, and biographical details of the sitters in the many portraits of the collection will, it is hoped, make this a useful guide to the Castle for the general visitor. Readers with a particular interest in art will find that the Castle houses an impressive collection of paintings and sculpture, particularly of the 18th and 19th centuries, as well as one of the most interesting groups of contemporary site-specific artworks in the country.

The publication is the outcome of a one-year bursary in curatorship administered by the OPW and the Arts Council / An Chomhairle Ealaíon. This bursary provided the impetus and support for the research and writing of the book, and gave the author a unique opportunity of working in one of the country's most prestigious locations. I hope that this book will generate further research into the State collections, and that it will provide a useful and interesting guide to Dublin Castle and its art collection.

RÓISÍN KENNEDY
November 1999

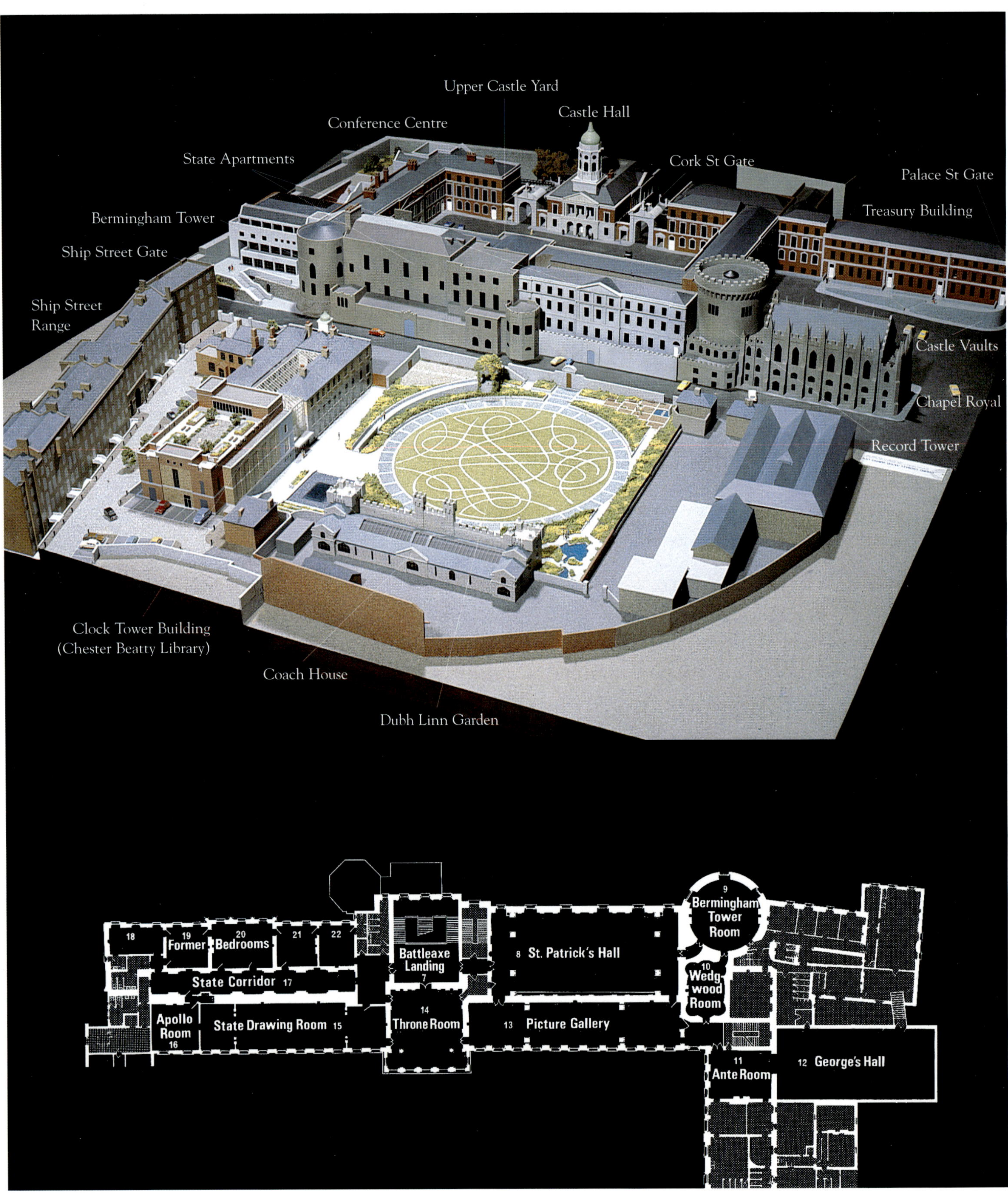
Upper Castle Yard
Castle Hall
Conference Centre
State Apartments
Cork St Gate
Palace St Gate
Treasury Building
Bermingham Tower
Ship Street Gate
Ship Street
Range
Castle Vaults
Chapel Royal
Record Tower
Clock Tower Building
(Chester Beatty Library)
Coach House
Dubh Linn Garden
18
19 Former
20 Bedrooms
21
22
State Corridor 17
Apollo Room 16
State Drawing Room 15
Battleaxe Landing 7
14 Throne Room
8 St. Patrick's Hall
13 Picture Gallery
9 Bermingham Tower Room
10 Wedgwood Room
11 Ante Room
12 George's Hall

Author's Acknowledgements

opposite

Model of Dublin Castle complex
[model by Pat Flaherty and Denis McCarthy]

Plan of State Apartments, Dublin Castle

This book would never have been written or published without the generosity and initiative of the Government and the Arts Council / An Chomhairle Ealaíon. I would like to thank both the OPW and the Arts Council for giving me the opportunity of producing it. I thank Barry Murphy and the members of the OPW Art Management Group for their comments and advice. I am grateful to Angela Rolfe for assisting with information on the commissioning of contemporary artworks, and for her comments on my text, and to Sharon Doyle and Jenny Lonergan for their administrative skill. My particular thanks to Mary Heffernan and Jacquie Moore, who have both put a tremendous amount of work and energy into this project. Oliver Dowling and Sheila Gorman of the Arts Council have given me their continuous encouragement and support throughout the past year.

The staff of Dublin Castle have been both helpful and accommodating, particularly Tommy O'Shaughnessy, Manager of Dublin Castle, Denis McCarthy, Paddy Herbert, and the staff of the conference office, Tom Doyle, Barry Flynn, and the staff of the State Apartments. David Byers and Patricia Woods have kindly answered many of my queries.

Many individuals and institutions have assisted in research and been generous with their time and information: Bibliotheque des Arts Decoratifs, Paris, Dr Eileen Black, Edwin Buijsen of the Netherlands Institute for Art History, Dr Lorne Campbell, Hugh Carey, Mary Clark, Maud Cotter, Prof Anne Crookshank, Dean Nicholas Cummins, Pauric Dempsey, Dr Judy Egerton, Jason Ellis, Susan Em and the staff of the National Archives, Elaine Fallon of Designyard, Dr Jane Fenlon, Andrew Folan, Goethe Institute Library, Dublin, the staff of the Heinz Archive at the National Portrait Gallery, London, Anne Hodge of the National Visual Arts Library, Roland Hulme-Beaman, David Griffin and the staff of the Irish Architectural Archive, Mary Kelleher, Vincent Kinane, David Lambert, Jack Maguire, Prof Michael McCarthy, Eileen McDonagh, Catherine Marshall and the staff of IMMA, Roxanne Moorhead, Margaret Morrisson, the staff of the National Library, Dr Ann Neville, Freddie O'Dwyer, Registry of the Office of Public Works, Jack Pakenham, Niall Parsons, Peter Pearson, Caroline Pegum, Vivienne Roche, Oscar Richardson, Dr Wendy Roworth, Sculpture Society of Ireland, Dr Philip Smyly of the National Maritime Museum, Ann Stewart, Lavinia Wellicome, David White. The contribution of Dr John Loughman to the entries on Ambrosius Francken and de Saive, and those of Joseph McDonnell, Dr Lynda Mulvin, Dr Paula Murphy and Philip Ward-Jackson to the sculpture section have been of enormous help. I warmly acknowledge the support and interest of Dr Michael Wynne, who is more familiar than anyone with the collection at Dublin Castle. I would also like to thank Elizabeth Mayes for editing the catalogue at short notice, and David O'Mara for helping with photography and research.

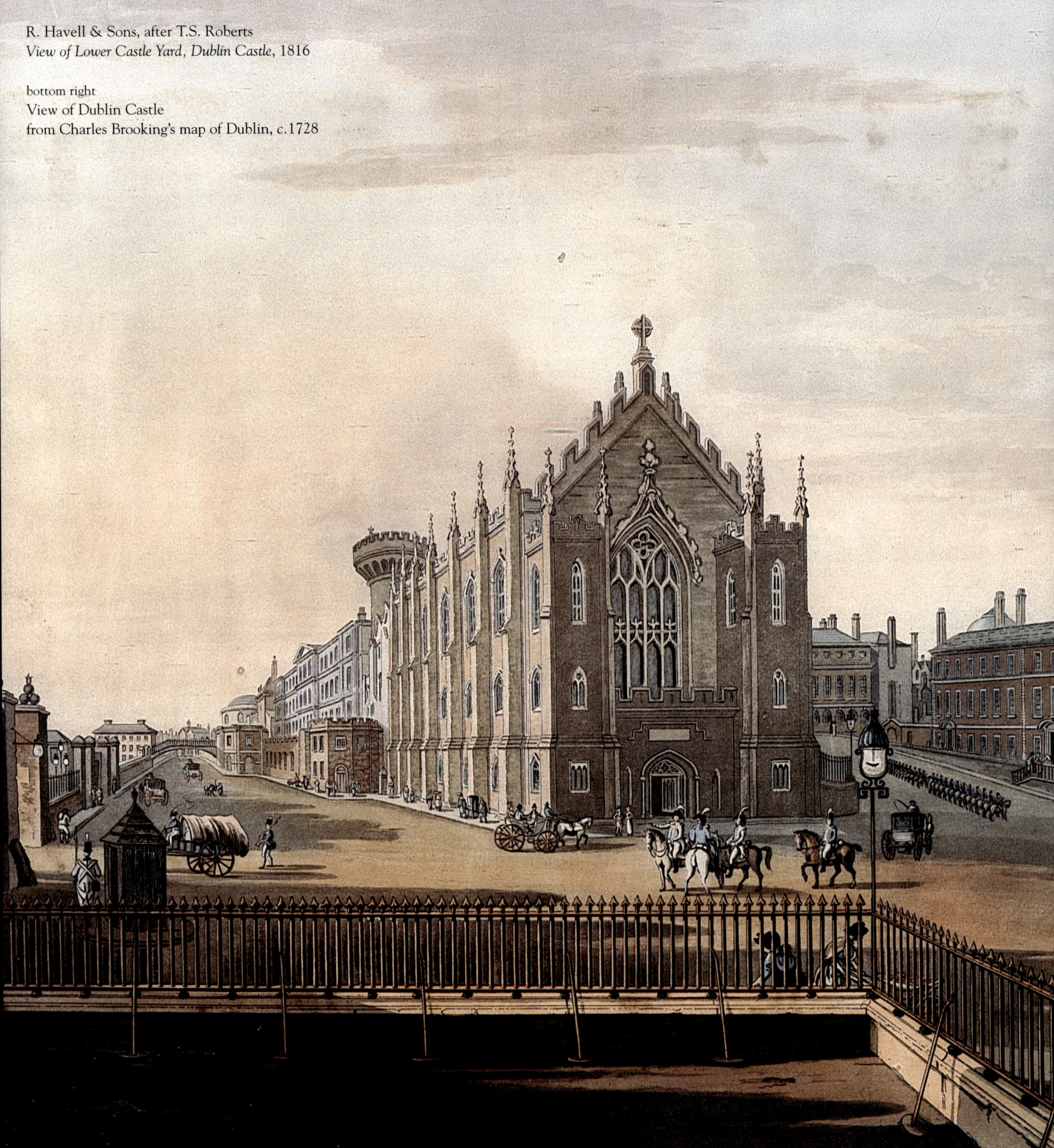

R. Havell & Sons, after T.S. Roberts
View of Lower Castle Yard, Dublin Castle, 1816

bottom right
View of Dublin Castle
from Charles Brooking's map of Dublin, c.1728

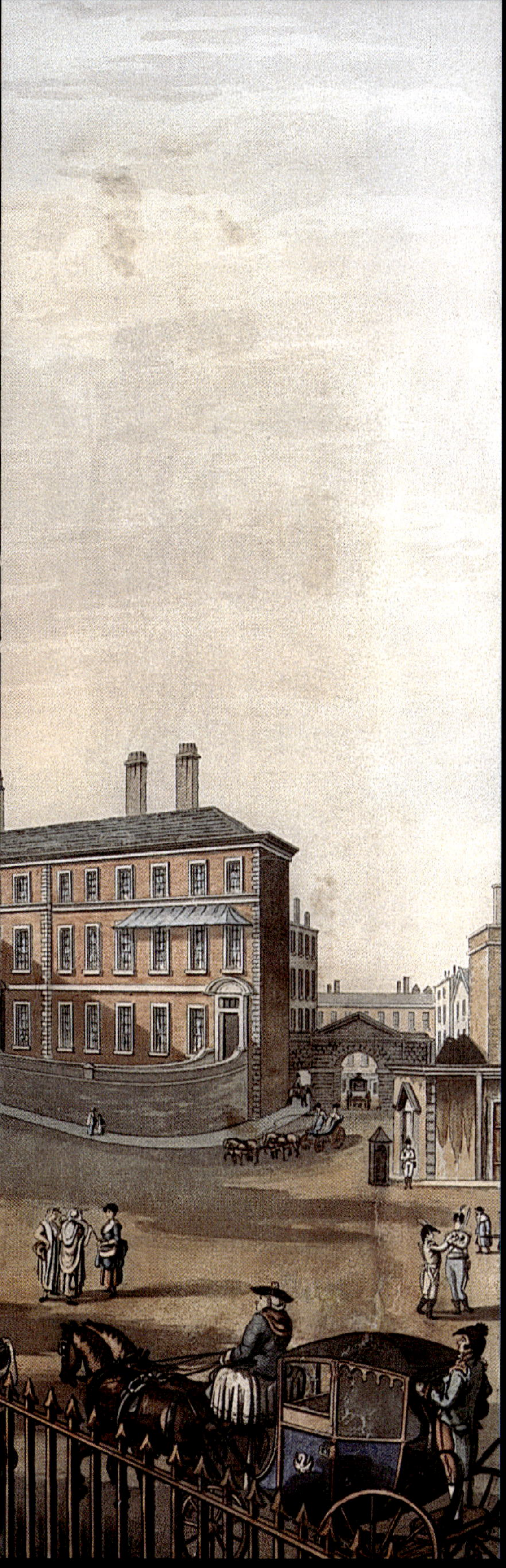

Introduction

WITH NOTES ON THE FURNISHINGS OF THE STATE APARTMENTS AND THE CHAPEL ROYAL

Brief history of Dublin Castle and its artworks

The history of Dublin Castle goes back to its foundation by King John in 1204. The site has an even older history, which makes it central to the foundation and development of the early settlement of Dublin. The Black Pool (Dubh Linn), a large pool formed by tidal movements in the estuary between the rivers Poddle and Liffey, was situated where the present Castle gardens are now. In the 8th and 9th centuries, a large fort or rath was situated on the site of the Castle, and in the medieval period the fortress of the Castle occupied the south-east corner of the city. A 'proper' stone castle, with walls, towers and moat, was built on the site in the 13th century, and was occupied by early Norman settlers in Ireland. Archaeological excavations carried out during the major building work of the 1980s have revealed the enormous extent of the occupation of the site throughout these periods.

In the middle of the 16th century, the Lord Lieutenant, Sir Henry Sidney, was responsible for the building of a residence on the present site of the State Apartments. In this period, and later, the core of the administration of government was located in the Castle. Parliament met here, prisoners were held within its walls, and the State records were stored in one of the towers (the Bermingham Tower). A massive fire which broke out in 1684 destroyed the State Apartments, and William Robinson, the Surveyor-General and architect of the Royal Hospital Kilmainham, drew up plans for their rebuilding. James II stayed in the newly finished apartments in 1688, and two years later his victor at the Battle of the Boyne, William III, also visited them.

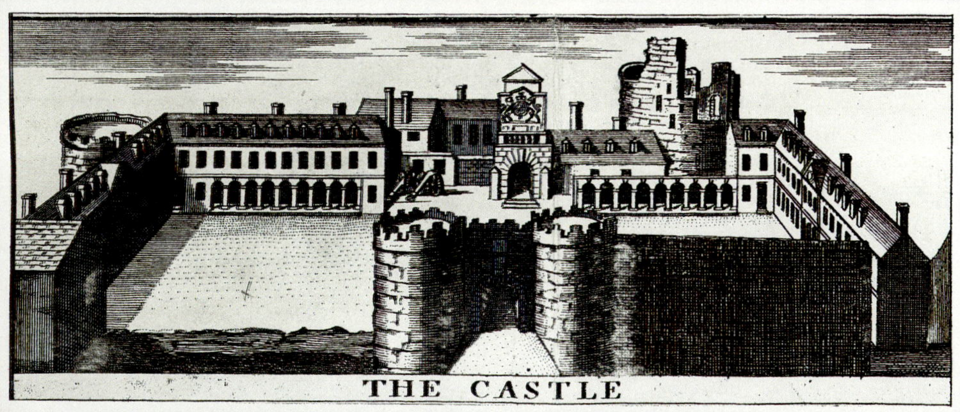

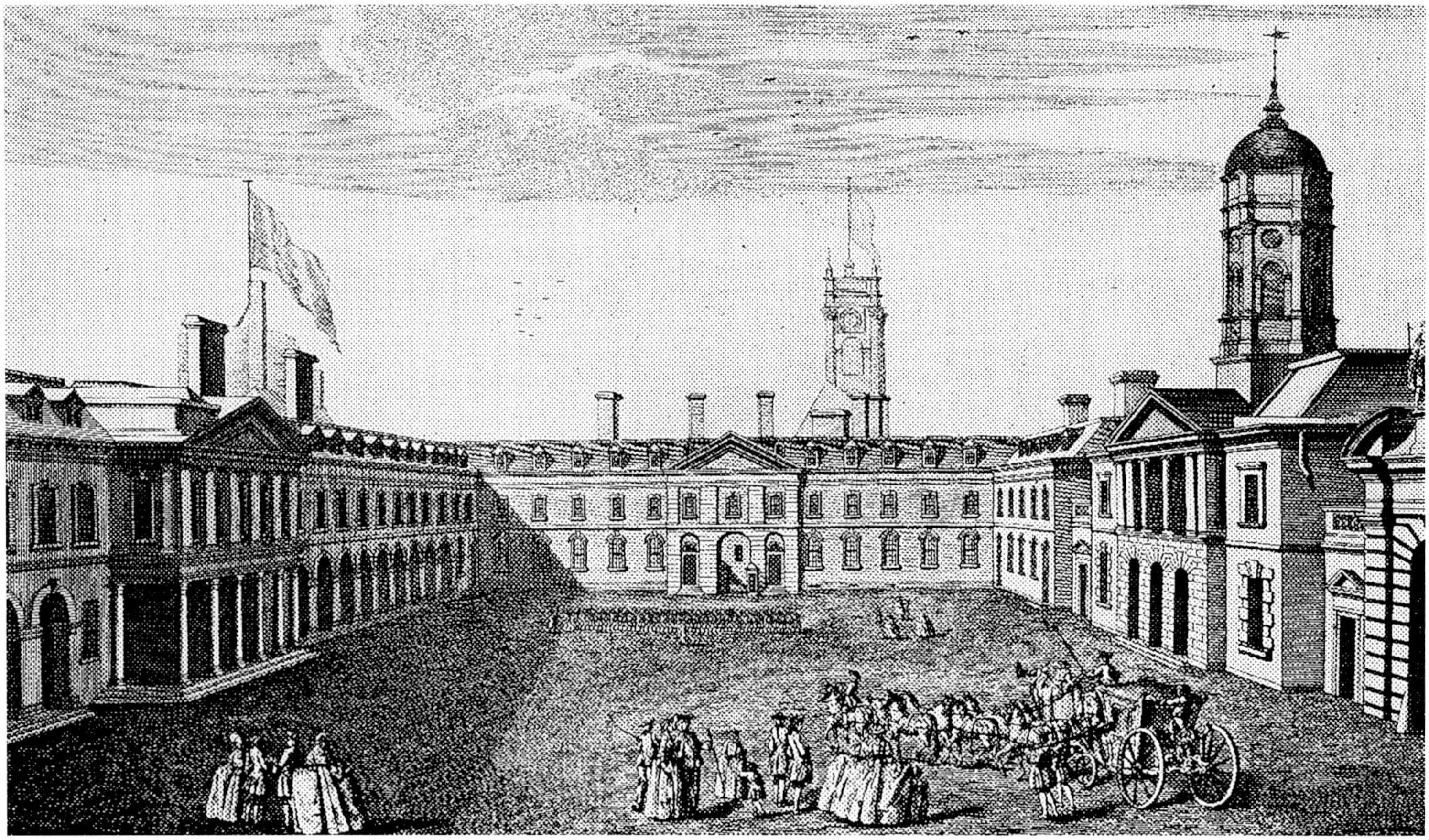

J. Tudor
A Prospect of the Upper Castle Court from the council chamber, Dublin (c.1750)

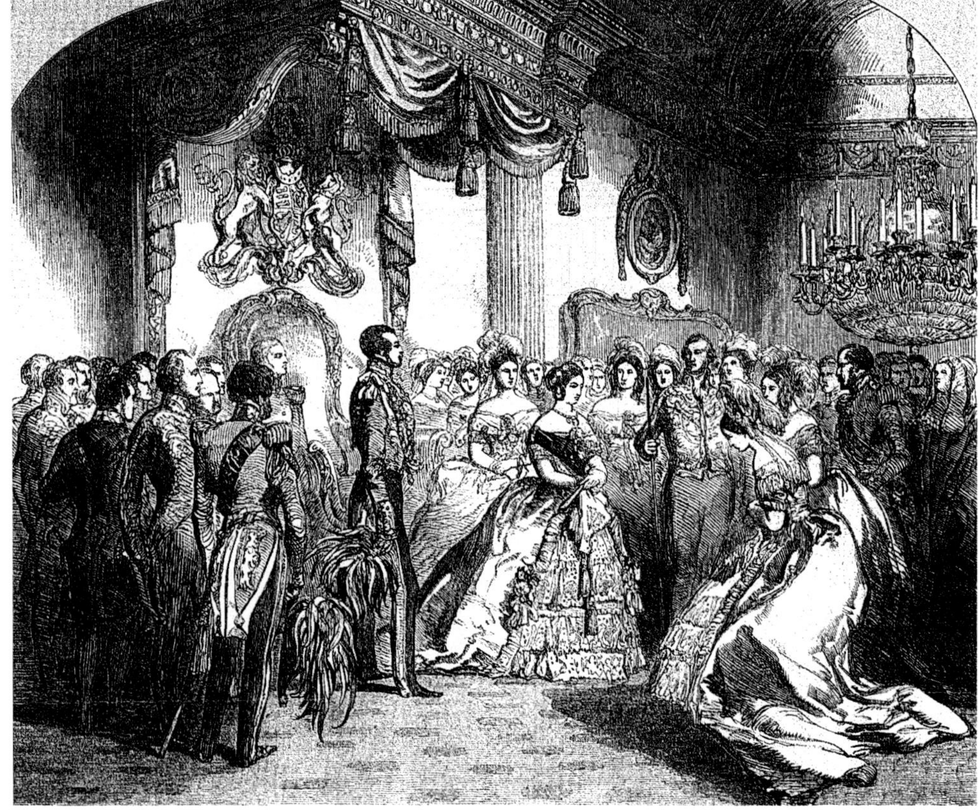

Illustration of Queen Victoria and Prince Albert in the Throne Room, Dublin Castle, from *Illustrated London News*, 1849

By the time Lord Chesterfield came to Ireland as Lord Lieutenant in 1746, the State Apartments had fallen into a dilapidated state. Chesterfield instigated a major programme of rebuilding, which continued throughout the mid-18th century, and gave the Upper Castle Yard its present appearance. The main rooms in the State Apartments, the ballroom (St Patrick's Hall), the Throne Room, and so on, date to this period. It is from this time that works of art began to be acquired for the Castle. The two van Nost sculptures above the gateways to the Upper Yard were erected in 1753. A bronze bust of Lord Chesterfield was certainly in the State Apartments by 1777, and was probably acquired at the time of, or shortly after, his lord lieutenancy. A large carved wooden overmantle also survives from the refurbishment of the presence chamber (now part of the State drawing room) in 1751. The most spectacular artwork of the 18th century is the Waldré ceiling paintings in St Patrick's Hall, which George Grenville, Marquis of Buckingham, commissioned in 1787 to commemorate the foundation of the Order of St Patrick in 1783. These latter two works of art are indicative of the formality of the viceregal court in the second half of the 18th century, and the importance of appropriate works of art and furnishings.

In the 19th century this formality continued, possibly spurred on by the Act of Union (1801) which reinforced the importance of the Castle as the centre of political power in Ireland. By this time, the lords lieutenant lived in Dublin all year round, and many of the post-union lieutenants spent large sums of money on the refurbishment of the Viceregal Lodge (their recently acquired residence in the Phoenix Park), and on works in the State Apartments. In the 1830s, the Throne Room was largely rebuilt, and it was as part of this scheme that the set of mythological paintings by the Bolognese painter Gaetano Gandolfi was acquired. It was probably also around this period that the idea of a series of portraits of the lords lieutenant came about. These portraits were hung in the State dining room, or Picture Gallery, as it became known. By the end of the 19th century, a small group of paintings, in the care of the OPW, was in existence. These works, some of which are in this catalogue, were scattered throughout the State Apartments, the Viceregal Lodge, the Chief Secretary's Lodge, and the Under Secretary's Lodge (the latter were located in the Phoenix Park). A small number of pieces of sculpture had also become part of the furnishings of the State Apartments. How exactly these came to be part of the collection is not certain; some may have been presented by lords lieutenant or chief-secretaries, but it is more likely that the OPW acquired them as part of the furnishing of particular rooms or for particular occasions.

During the First World War, the State Apartments were used as a Red Cross hospital – the beginning of a chaotic period which was to last for many years. In 1922 the Castle was handed over to the provisional government of the new state. A long period of readjustment followed in which works of art were of the

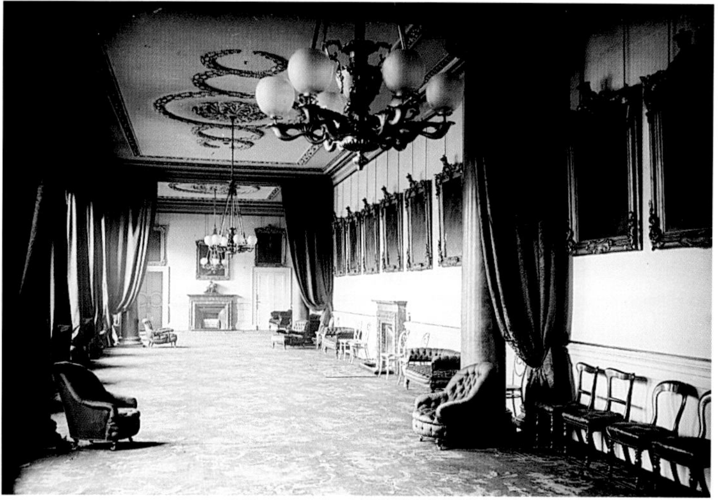

The Picture Gallery (State Dining Room), Dublin Castle

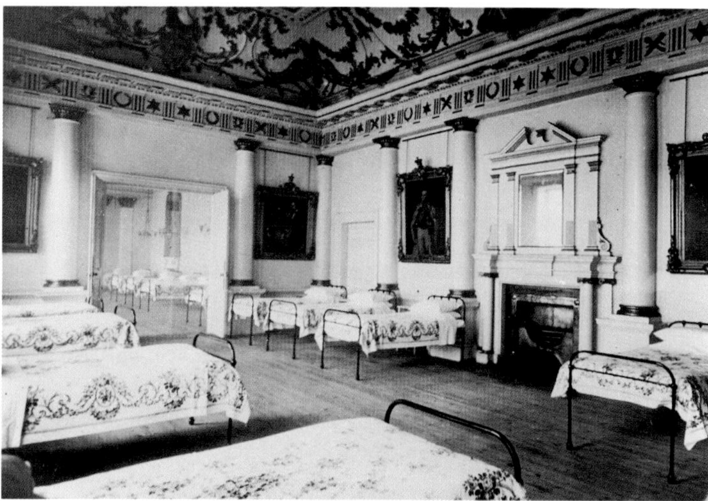

State Drawing Room being used as a Red Cross hospital during World War I

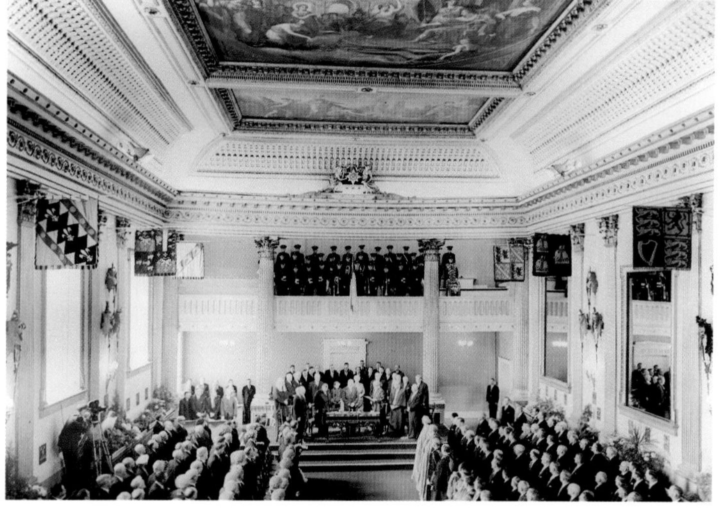

The inauguration of Eamon de Valera as President, St Patrick's Hall, 1959

least concern. After the burning of the Four Courts in the Civil War, the High Court of Justice was held in the State Apartments (1924-1931), the lion and unicorn having been removed from above the viceregal throne. (They were returned in 1955.) When Douglas Hyde became the first President of Ireland in 1938, his inauguration took place in St Patrick's Hall. This was symbolic of the State's acceptance of the historical importance of the Castle. Eamon de Valera is credited with the pragmatic decision to use the State Apartments for such functions.[1] He also recognised the importance of accepting its history as part of the story of modern Ireland, and is said to have wanted the OPW to keep the banners of the Knights of St Patrick hanging in the Castle.

In 1941 a fire in the State drawing room destroyed four of the portraits of the lords lieutenant, as well as part of the State Apartments. Reconstruction work was carried out by OPW architects in the late 1950s and 1960s. Three 18th-century stuccowork ceilings were incorporated into rooms in the bedroom suite and the newly created Apollo Room. This was the impetus for a refurbishment of the entire State Apartments. A number of paintings were taken out of storage, and a number of new works acquired.[2] The latter include some of the most interesting paintings in the Castle, and details of their acquisition are known only from a later memo. A group of five paintings was purchased from the Dublin art dealer, Henry Naylor. These include two fine 16th-century Flemish paintings and a very fine copy of a work by the 18th-century painter Angelica Kauffmann, who, coincidentally, was a guest at the Castle in 1771. In 1962 the Castle acquired an important group of neoclassical marble sculpture at the sale of Lord Cloncurry's collection at Newcastle Lyons.

In 1973 the State Apartments received another important boost to its collection of artworks when the 9th Earl of Granard, on the wishes of his mother, donated a number of paintings and sculpture in memory of his father. These included three fine paintings by the late 18th-century Irish artist, Matthew William Peters, and a portrait by van Dyck, which research has shown has a fully documented provenance. Two very interesting pieces of sculpture and a 17th-century-style French marble pedestal were also part of this gift.

In the late 1980s the Castle underwent a further period of major refurbishment. In preparation for the EC presidency in 1990, most of the paintings hanging in the State Apartments were restored and their frames repaired and regilded. Since the building of the conference centre in 1988, and the conversion of the Bedford Tower to Castle Hall and the adjoining offices, the residual paintings are gradually being taken out of storage, and an ongoing programme of restoration is in progress. As will be seen in the catalogue, the latter works are mainly portraits of the royal family, perhaps not surprisingly the last to be reincorporated into the collection.

From the late 1980s onwards, the commissioning and acquisition of contemporary artworks has become important. The role of these works is outlined in the second part of the catalogue, but in the context of a history of the Castle, these relate to the opening up of the complex to the public and to the users of such diverse venues as the conference centre, the Coach House, the Revenue Commission, and the new Chester Beatty Library. Like some of the 18th and 19th century works, they elucidate the history and architectural space of the Castle, but in a more personal and less didactic way.

The historical collection is still being added to when an appropriate work is available. A 19th-century watercolour view of the Upper Castle Yard by Michelangelo Hayes was purchased as recently as 1997. The paintings on the Battleaxe stairs and in the State drawing room are on loan, mainly from the National Gallery of Ireland, which has acted in an advisory capacity to the OPW when required.

Furniture

The furniture, like the paintings and sculpture, comes from a variety of sources. The lords lieutenant tended to bring some of their furnishings with them when they came to Ireland, and take them back with them when they left. Occasionally they made a gift of some pieces to the Castle, such as the Waterford chandelier for the Throne Room (replaced in the 19th century), which was presented by the Duke of Rutland in the late 18th century. The 19th-century letterbooks and accounts of the OPW record the names of cabinet makers, upholsterers and pierglass makers who were being paid to do work for the Castle or the Viceregal Lodge. Most of the furnishings were produced in Ireland by local craftsmen. One of the most successful firms was that of Mack, Williams and Gibton, who worked for the viceregal court in the early 19th century.[3] Their fine regency-style work can be seen in the two sideboards now in the marble hall near the entrance to the State Apartments. They also made the Gothic Revival pews, which were originally in the Chapel Royal but which are now in the entrance hall of the State Apartments. Other original pieces are the mirrors and the throne in the Throne Room, and the inlaid table known as the Prisoner's Table due to an unsubstantiated story that it was made by a prisoner in one of Dublin's debtor prisons for Queen Victoria. The name plates and flags in St Patrick's Hall date to the late 19th and early 20th century, and were put in place after the disestablishment of the Church of Ireland in 1869 when the Knights were no longer able to hold their installation ceremonies in St Patrick's Cathedral. Some of the nameplates were designed by Sir Neville Wilkinson (1869-1940), the Ulster King of Arms. (Two of them were made by the Irish Arts and Crafts metalworker, Oswald Reeves.)[4]

After independence, many pieces of furniture from the

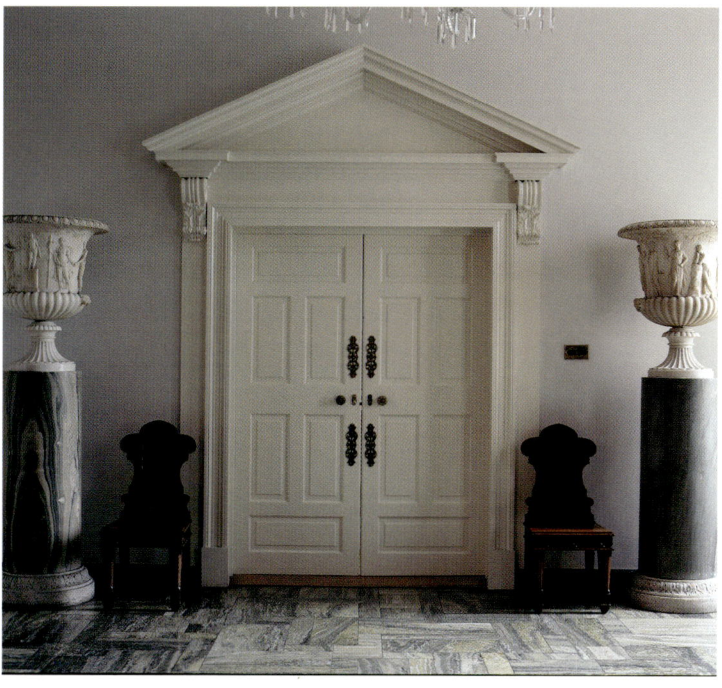

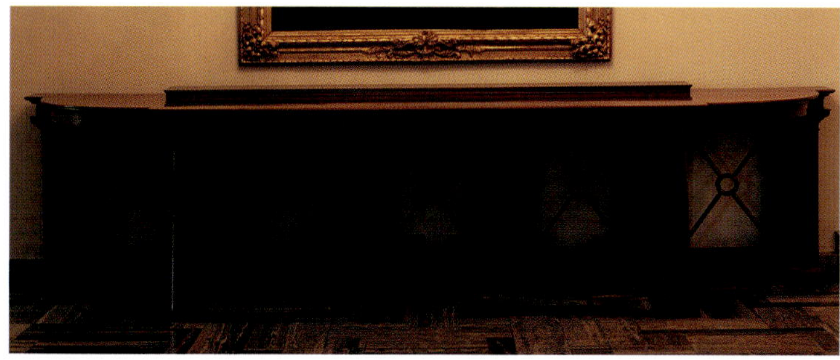

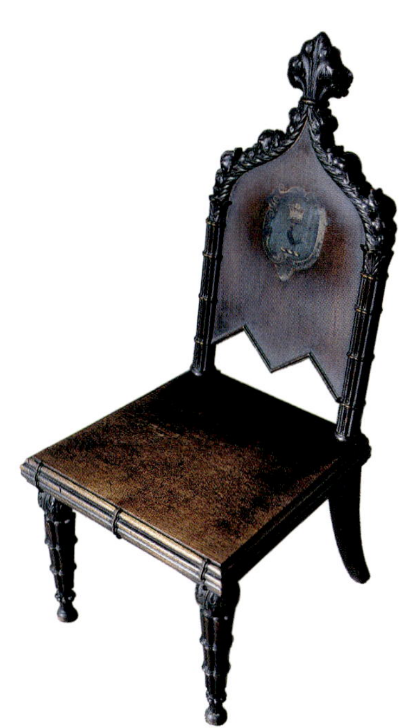

top
Marble Hall, Dublin Castle – two marble urns from Newcastle Lyons, and two hall chairs from Dromoland Castle

middle
Marble Hall, Dublin Castle – Mack, Williams & Gibton serving table

bottom
Gothic Revival chair, originally made for Thomastown Castle, Co Tipperary

Royal Hospital Kilmainham and the Viceregal Lodge were moved to the Castle. Finding appropriate furniture for the State Apartments seems to have been a problem for the OPW, and from the late 1930s onwards, schemes for its decoration were being made by successive OPW architects. Files in the OPW suggest that the Taoiseach and his officials took a close interest in this aspect of the Castle, particularly as it was now the established setting for the inauguration of the President and for State visits. With the refurbishment of the State drawing room and the bedroom suite in the late 1950s and 1960s, numerous pieces of furniture and decorative art were acquired at house auctions all over the country. Two of the most impressive purchases are the hall chairs from Dromoland Castle (marble hall), and the Gothic-style seats at the bottom of the Battleaxe stairs, which came from Dunsandle, Co Galway (now demolished), but which were originally made for the Richard Morrison designed library (*c.*1812) in Thomastown Castle, Co Tipperary. The blue and red Chinese-style bowl which is now the centrepiece of the State drawing room was purchased at a sale at Kenure Park, Rush, Co Dublin, in 1964. Also dating to this period of refurbishment are the Donegal carpets, which were designed by the principal architect of the OPW, Raymond McGrath (1903-1977). The Granard gift, which contained furniture as well as artworks, was a major contribution to the decor of the State Apartments; the French 18th-century carved gilt chairs in the Granard Room are now a highlight of the Castle's collection.

The Chapel Royal

The Chapel Royal, situated in the Lower Castle Yard, is a work of art in its own right. It was designed by an architect of the Board of Works and Civil Buildings, Francis Johnston (1760-1829), who was also the architect of the GPO, and was built on the site of an earlier chapel. It is one of the finest examples of Gothic Revival architecture in Ireland.

The foundation stone of the building was laid by the Lord Lieutenant, the Duke of Bedford, in February 1807, and it was first used for worship on Christmas Day, 1814. The exterior is of Tullamore limestone, and has numerous carvings of heads of saints and historical figures, including St Peter and Jonathan Swift, over the modest entrance, which is at the side of the building because the construction of a west façade was prevented by the situation of the medieval record tower.

Over the eastern door, which leads into the crypt, there are carved heads of St Patrick and Brian Boru, the last High King of Ireland. These carvings are by Edward Smyth (1749-1812), who carried out the famous *River Heads* and the other stone carvings on the Customs House for the architect James Gandon. Smyth died before the interior of the building was complete, and his son,

John Smyth (*c*.1773-1840), was mainly responsible for the stuccowork heads inside the Chapel Royal. These dominate the chancel end of the interior, and depict the four evangelists and Moses with the Commandment tablets, as well as the figures of Faith, Hope and Charity over the east window. The remainder of the delicate stuccowork which imitates Gothic stone vaulting and tracery was made by George Stapleton.

The original pulpit, which, because of it height, allowed the dean to preach to the lord lieutenant and the peers assembled in the upper galleries is now in St Werburgh's Church, behind the Castle. This and the other woodwork in the chapel is by Richard Stewart (fl.1807-1819), a rather temperamental but otherwise very capable craftsman. A passageway connects the upper storey of the chapel with the State Apartments.

In 1823 Francis Johnston wrote a memorandum of the building and the design of the chapel, which was published in *The Irish Builder* in 1869, and which gives a full account of the windows and the carved interior.[5] He was proud of the fact that the entire building except the organ was made by local craftsmen.

While this introduction will give some sense of the importance and history of the Chapel Royal and the furniture of the State Apartments, the book will concentrate on the artworks – the historic collection of paintings and sculpture, and the contemporary artworks which are located throughout the Castle's gardens and buildings. Dublin Castle is an unusual context within which to find such a diverse range of art. It is not a museum or a stately home, but a busy complex of offices and meeting places, and it has always been liable to modernisation and change. This has resulted in a certain amount of chance and accident in the acquisition of artworks and in their survival. It is hoped that this book will demonstrate the strong connections between works of art and the historical and architectural context in which they exist, and provide the reader with an insight into one of the most fascinating aspects of the past and present uses of Dublin Castle.

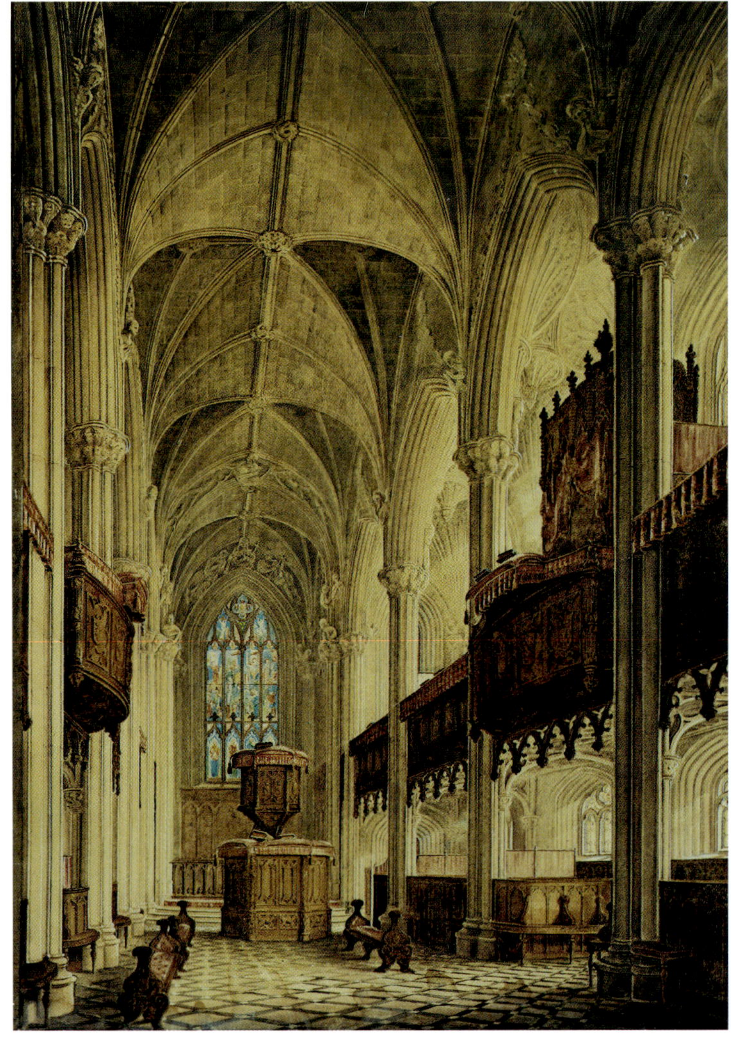

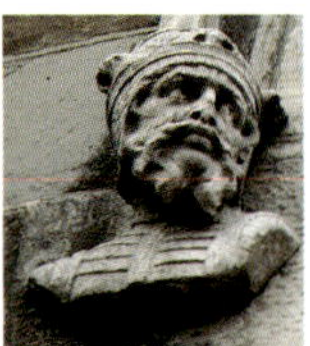

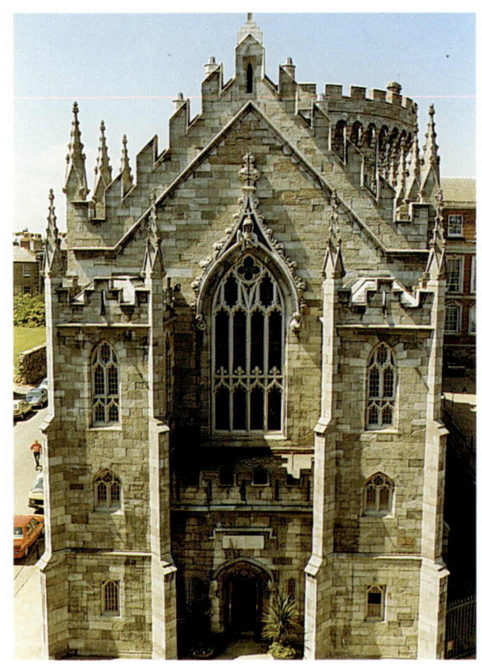

Chapel Royal, Dublin Castle

top
19th-century watercolour of interior with original pews and pulpit

middle
Brian Boru

bottom
Restored façade

1 The State Apartments were used for the Eucharistic Congress in 1932.
2 The State visit of the King and Queen of Belgium in 1968, and Ireland's Presidency of the EEC in 1975, were added incentives for the improvements.
3 Angela Alexander, 'A Firm of Dublin Cabinet-makers, Mack, Williams and Gibton', *Irish Arts Review Yearbook 1995*, vol. 11 (Dublin, 1994)
4 Paul Larmour 'The Works of Oswald Reeves (1870-1967)', *Irish Architectural and Decorative Studies: The Journal of the Irish Georgian Society*, vol. 1 (Dublin, 1998) 49
5 Francis Johnston, 'The Chapel Royal' (May 1823), published in *The Irish Builder* (Dublin, 1869) 48-51; reprinted in Patrick Henchy 'Francis Johnston, Architect, 1760-1829', *Dublin Historical Record,* xi, no. 1 (1949-50) appendix c, 14-16

Guide to using the catalogue

The catalogue follows the conventional approach of most standard art catalogues. An alphabetical index of artists is found at the back of the book. It is divided into two parts. The first deals with the historic collection – that is, with works made before 1922. The second part concentrates on contemporary artworks – works which have been acquired since 1987. While artworks were being acquired throughout the 20th century, they tended to be historical works until the refurbishment of the Castle in the 1980s and 1990s.

The historical collection has been divided into a number of sections. The first three parts are closely linked with specific rooms in the State Apartments – St Patrick's Hall, the Throne Room and the Picture Gallery. The rest of the catalogue is divided into sections based on the kind of works contained within them, i.e. the Granard Gift, Royal Portraits, Miscellaneous Paintings, Prints, Sculpture, and Stuccoed Ceilings.

A brief biography of the artist is followed by a catalogue entry on the work.

The catalogue entries are arranged as follows:

Title of work (dates of sitter, if portrait)	
Date	
Medium / support	
Measurements	Given in centimetres (height before width). Unframed measurements for painting, and, unless specified, for height only in sculpture.
Signed or inscribed	
Account of the work (and sitter, if portrait)	
Provenance	This is given as fully as possible. In many cases it has not been possible to establish one for the work.
Literature	Works or Office of Public Works (OPW) files which contain direct references to the work.
Comparative literature	Key items of literature which refer to the artist or to related works.
Exhibited	All recorded exhibitions of the work are listed.

Please note the following abbreviations:

ARA	Associate of the Royal Academy
BI	British Institution
DNB	Dictionary of National Biography
NCAD	National College of Art & Design
OPW	Office of Public Works The terms Board of Works and Office of Public Works are synonymous.
RA	Royal Academy
RHA	Royal Hibernian Academy
ARHA	Associate of the Royal Hibernian Academy

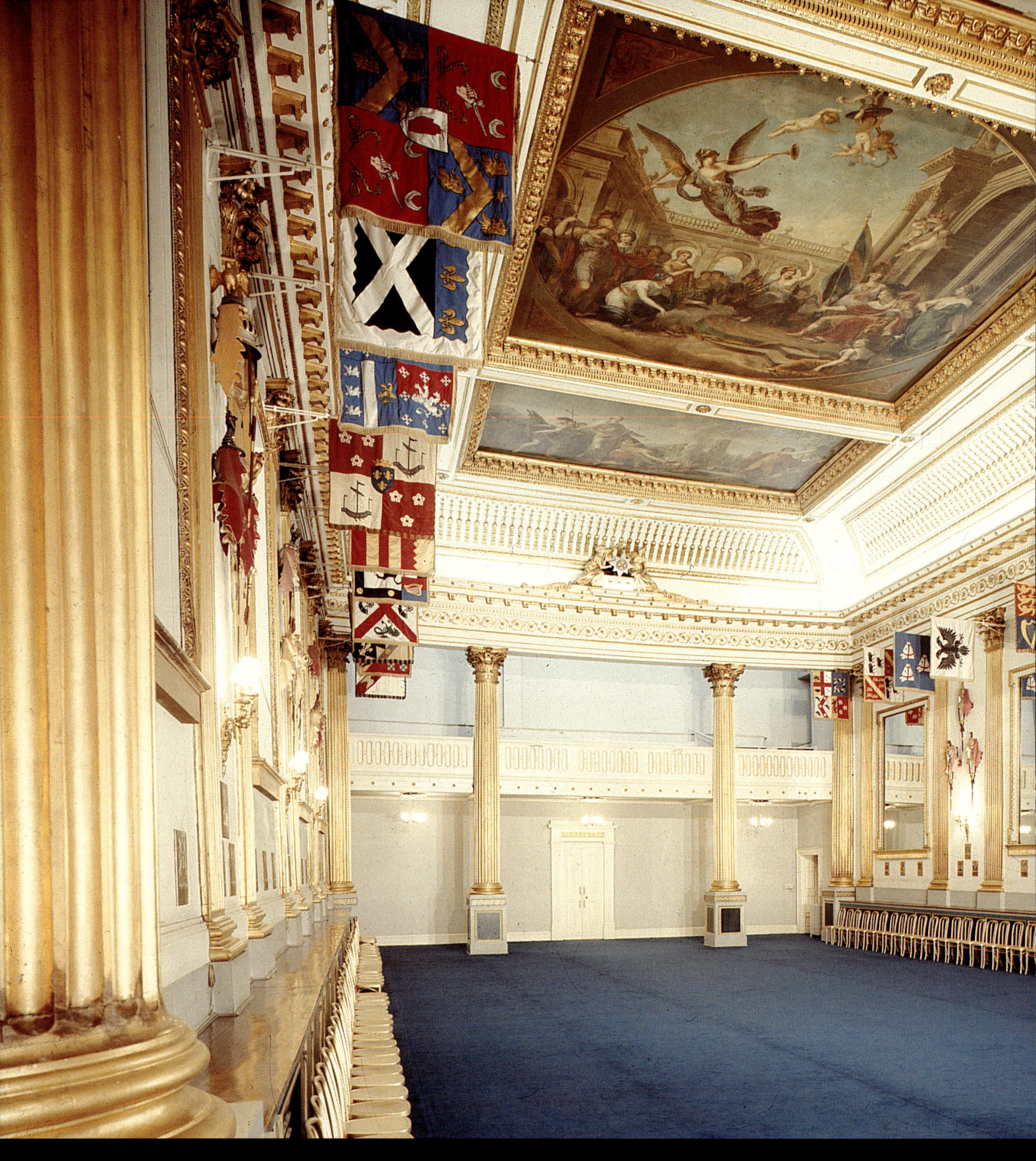

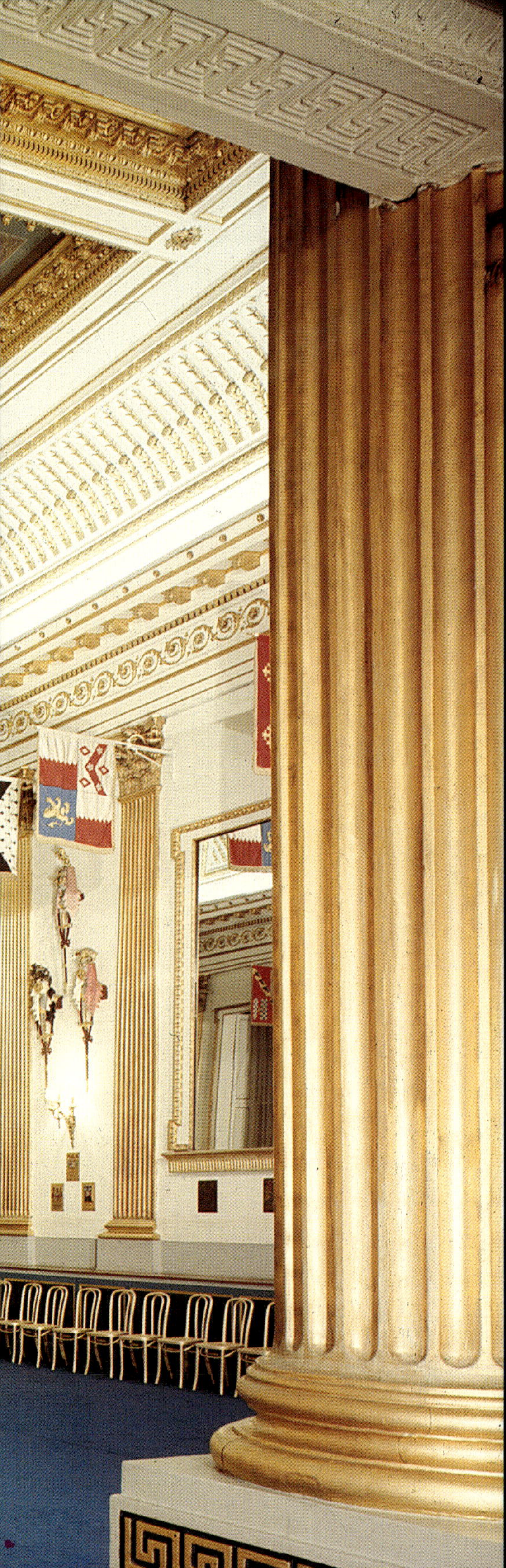

HISTORICAL COLLECTION

Ceiling Paintings, St Patrick's Hall

Vincenzo Waldré (1742-1814)

Vincenzo Waldré was born in Faenza but educated and brought up at Parma, completing his art training at the French Academy in Rome *c*.1768. In the mid 1770s, he came to London and worked as a scene painter in the Italian opera. At the same time, he came to the attention of George Grenville, the future Marquis of Buckingham, who employed him at his country seat, Stowe in Buckinghamshire, and subsequently brought him to Ireland in 1787 to decorate the ceiling of St Patrick's Hall. Waldré was appointed chief architect to the Board of Works in the early 1790s, and settled in Ireland at this time.

Apart from his architectural work, which included work on the Castle itself, Waldré also designed decorations for festivities at the viceregal court and carried out scene-painting for Dublin theatres. He appears to have been a colourful character who led an eventful life. He apparently met his wife at a wedding near Stowe, at which Waldré was a guest. The day was almost ruined when the bridegroom failed to arrive, but Waldré good humouredly stepped into the breach and married the bride instead. Later when Waldré was living in Leixlip, Co Kildare, he underwent an ordeal at the hands of thieves who broke into his house, tied him up and beat him. According to Strickland, the leader of the gang was subsequently convicted and hanged.

The Dublin Castle paintings are Waldré's most accomplished works, and are unique in Irish art history as an example of a major decorative scheme of painting still in its original context. Waldré worked in a transitional style, between late baroque and the newer, more fashionable neoclassical style – both of which can be seen in his work in St Patrick's Hall.

Henry II receiving the submission of the Irish chieftains
c.1787-1802, oil on canvas, 683 x 325 cm

George III, supported by Justice and Liberty
c.1787-1802, oil on canvas, 687 x 687 cm

St Patrick converting the Irish to Christianity
c.1787-1802, oil on canvas, 683 x 325 cm

St Patrick's Hall is one of the most impressive rooms in the State Apartments. Formerly the ballroom and the official Hall for the Knights of St Patrick, it is still

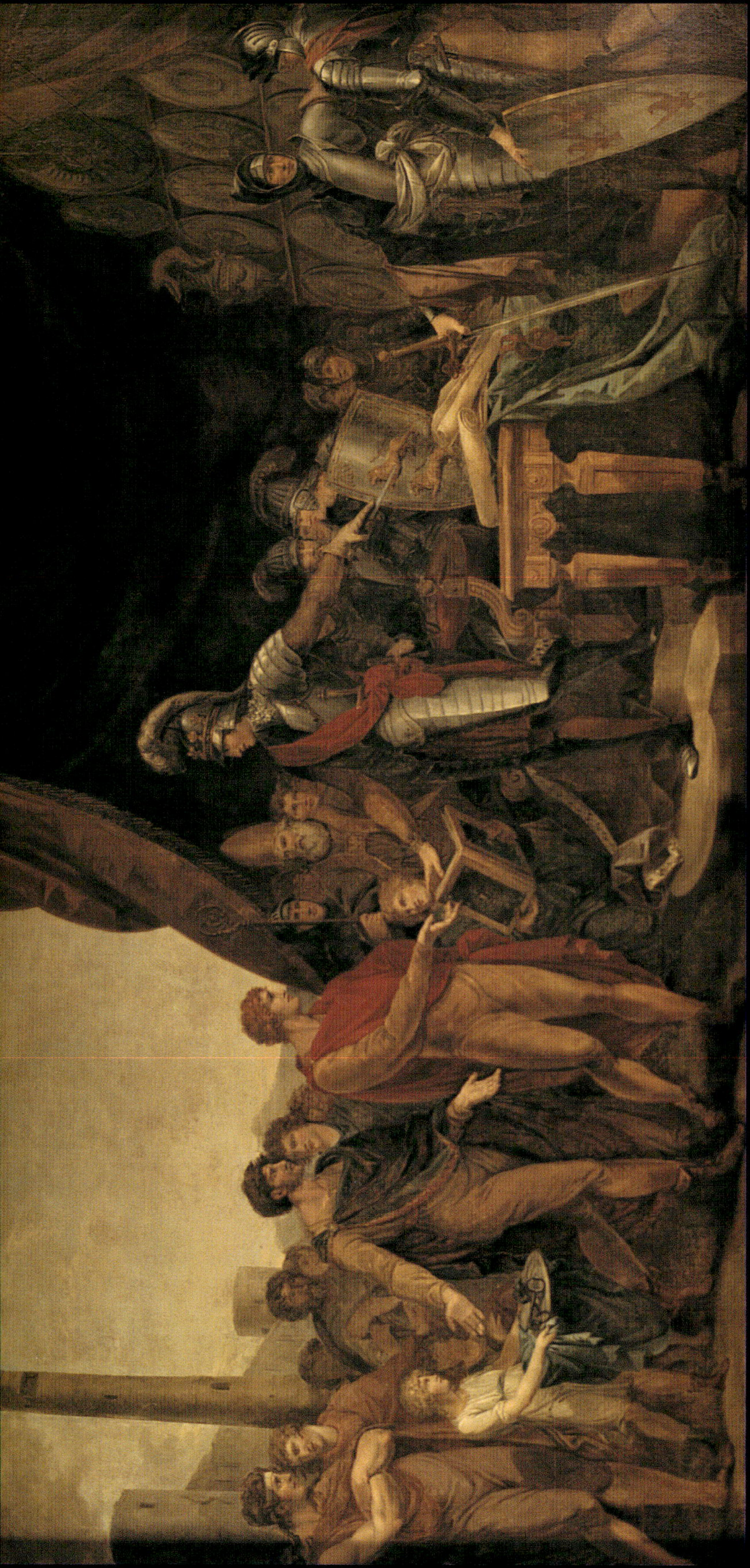

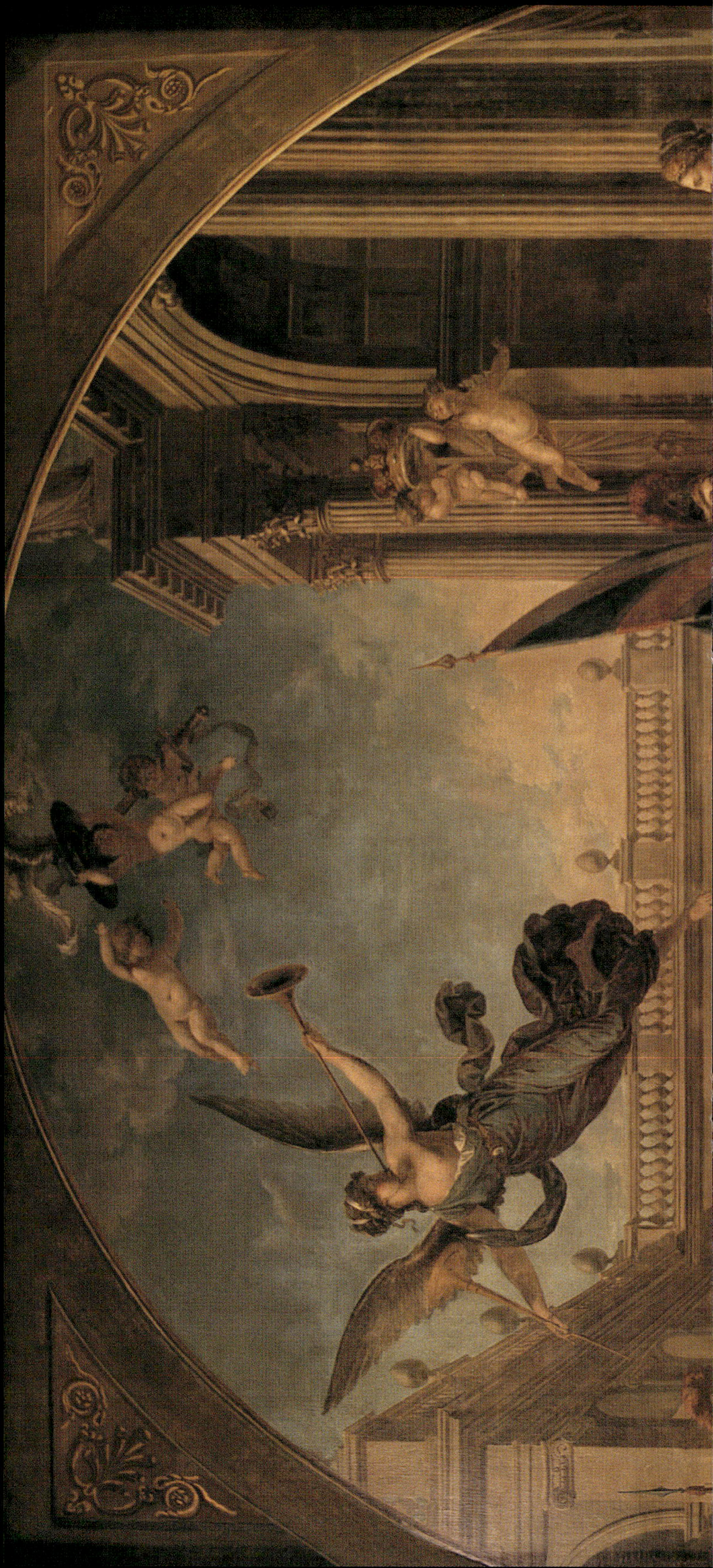

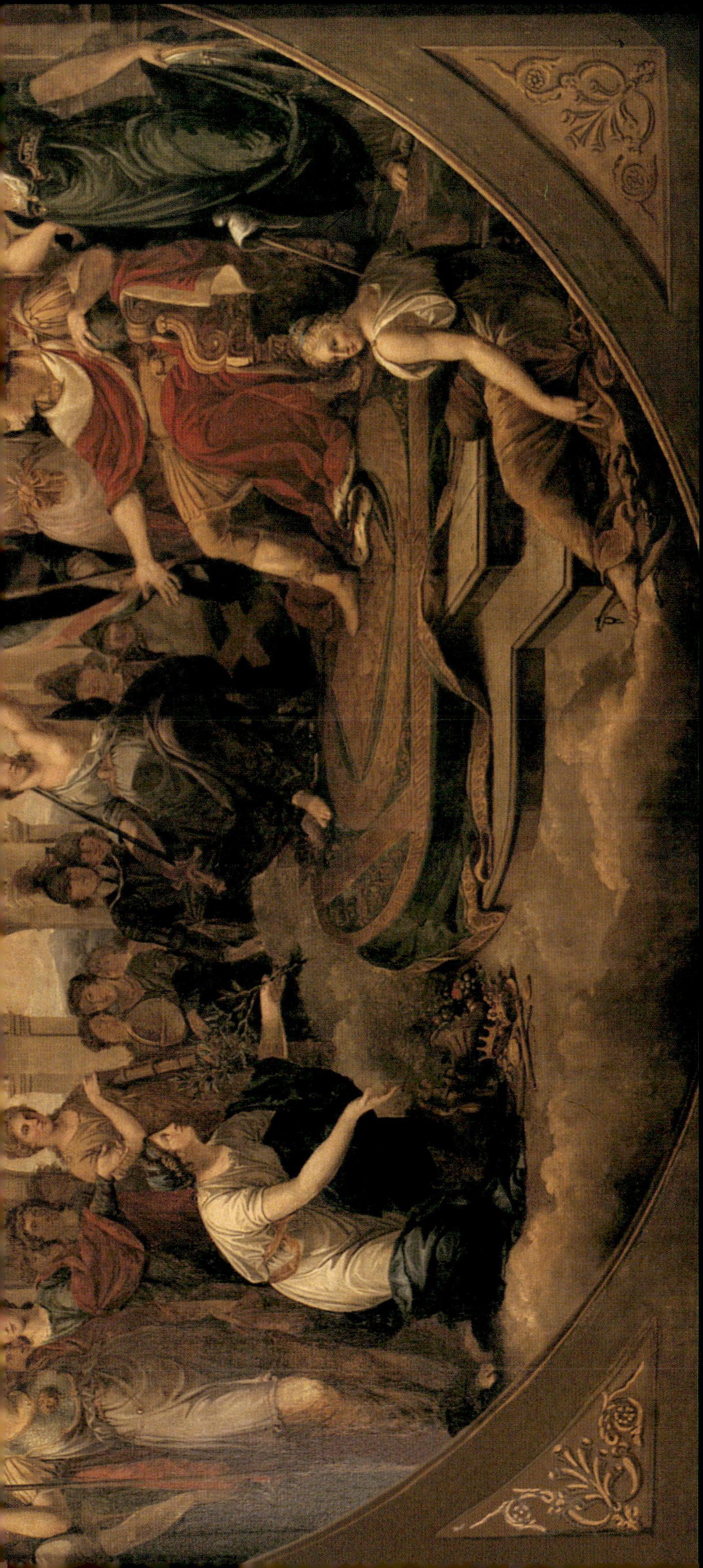

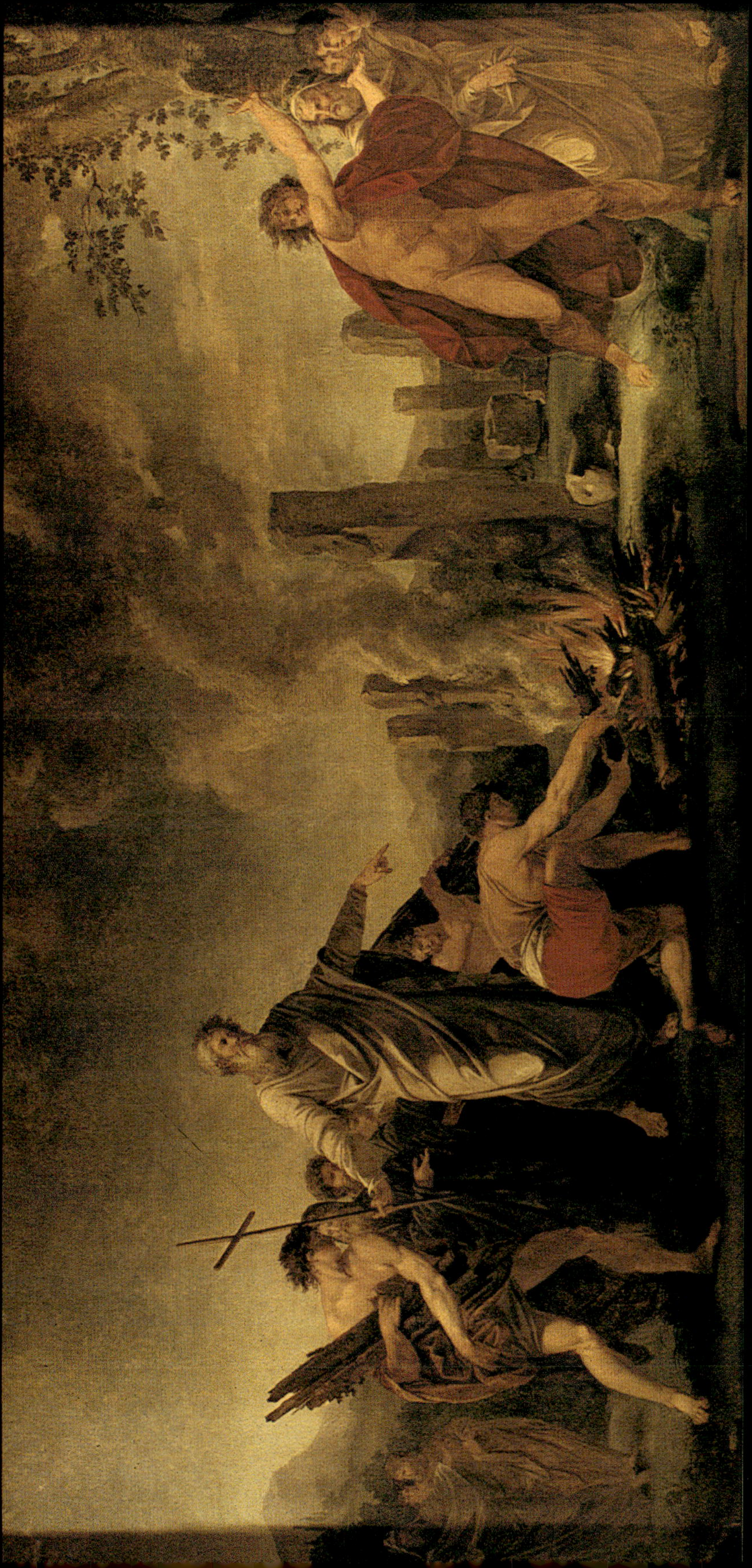

used for important state functions, most notably the inauguration of the President. The room dates originally to the middle of the 18th century, when the lord lieutenant of the time, Lord Chesterfield, embarked on a scheme of rebuilding of the Castle. Since then, it has undergone many changes in decoration: the ceiling paintings were erected at the end of the 18th century, the galleries at either end were put in place in the 1840s, while the rectangular mirrors and the nameplates of the knights which line the walls belong to the late 19th-century refurbishment of the room. The banners of the knights also date from this time; earlier banners and nameplates are in the original inauguration site of the Order, St Patrick's Cathedral.

The ceiling paintings were commissioned by George Grenville, Marquis of Buckingham, in 1787, during his second term as Lord Lieutenant of Ireland. The central painting is an allegorical representation of King George III, his throne flanked by the figures of Britannia carrying a flag, and Hibernia in a green dress. Seated on the steps below Hibernia is a female figure representing Liberty. Opposite her, carrying a sword and a set of scales, is Justice. Peace kneels before the king, presenting him with an olive branch and the crowns of the two kingdoms (Britain and Ireland), and a cornucopia full of fruit. Flying in the sky above this scene of regal tranquillity is the figure of Fame blowing her trumpet. Putti carry the crown above the head of George III, while another group hold a plumed hat and a ceremonial sword, part of the costume of the Knights of St Patrick. The baroque style of this painting and its use of allegory is derived from Rubens' painting of *The Union between England and Scotland* (1634), which is in the Banqueting House at Whitehall, London.

The other two paintings are quite different in style. The figures are laid out in a linear composition, which is in keeping with the more fashionable neoclassical style. One depicts St Patrick lighting the paschal fire at Slane – a key moment in the bringing of Christianity to Ireland. The tall imposing figure of the saint points to the fire, while the heathen Irish react with gestures of horror and surprise. The group nearest Patrick have already become Christian, and are shown gathering firewood and placing it on the bonfire. The outmoded form of religion is represented by the stone circle which is prominent in the background. Symbolically it is offset by St Patrick's cross.

The other painting shows a later event in Irish history: the paying of homage to King Henry II who came to Ireland in 1171, two years after the arrival of the Normans. Standing in his tent, clad in armour, he receives the submission of the Irish chieftains. The walls of Dublin and a round tower, believed to be based on that at Clondalkin, can be seen in the background. Henry, surrounded by knights and a bishop in full regalia, is portrayed as wealthy, powerful and sophisticated compared with the more simply clad Irish. Like St Patrick's, the left arm of the king is extended and points to a heraldic shield and rolls of parchment, which

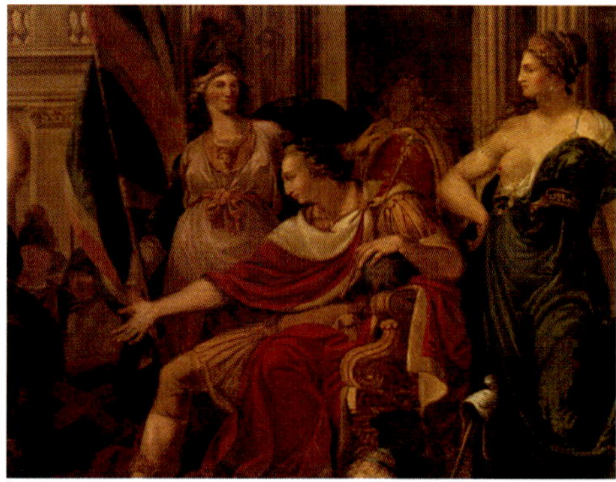

Vincenzo Waldré
Henry II receiving the submission of the Irish chieftains (detail)

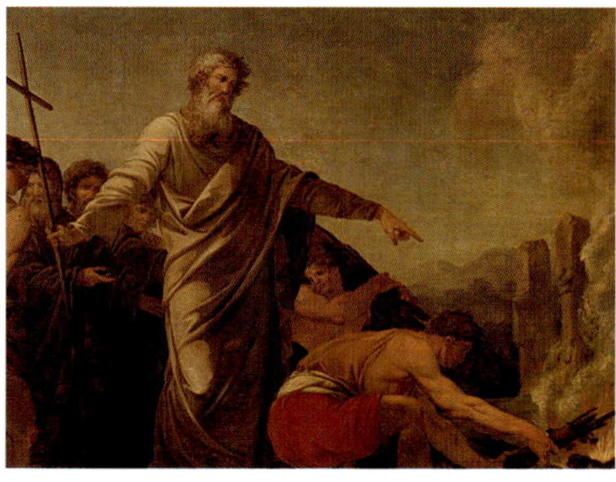

Vincenzo Waldré
George III, supported by Justice and Liberty (detail)

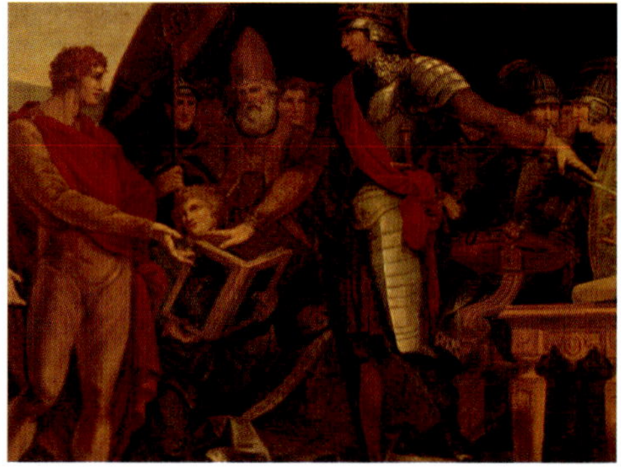

Vincenzo Waldré
St Patrick converting the Irish to Christianity (detail)

opposite
St Patrick's Hall
Lawrence Collection photograph showing Waldré's original scheme

indicate the arrival of a new chivalric and civic order in Ireland. A young Irish chieftain is shown swearing allegiance over an open book. Behind him another chief is presenting the king with a key – a symbol of fidelity – and a cloak of blue cloth carried by a child on a large tray.

The Marquis of Buckingham, who commissioned the work, was concerned with the increasing unrest in Ireland, particularly among the Ascendancy and upper classes who had formed themselves into a civilian army – the Volunteers – headed by the Duke of Leinster, Ireland's most prominent peer. In order to create an alternative focus to aristocratic life, he came up with the idea of creating a new order, an Irish equivalent to the Scottish Order of the Thistle and the English Order of the Garter, which George III was then revamping. In 1783 the Order of St Patrick held its first chapter of knights in St Patrick's Hall, formerly known as the ballroom. The Marquis of Buckingham, as Lord Lieutenant, was made the first Grand Master of the Order. During his second lord lieutenancy in 1787-88, he embarked on the ambitious redecoration of the hall, with the three easel paintings forming the nucleus of the work. It is likely that Buckingham supervised the design and subject matter of the scheme very closely.

Although the ceiling was begun and planned some twenty years before the Act of Union, it extols the benefits of a link between the two nations. The monarch dominates the central panel, which depicts the kingdom of a united Ireland and Britain as one of peace and prosperity. The two other panels also relate to the benefits brought to Ireland by its connection with Britain – St Patrick and Henry II are presented as civilising influences on the native population. One brings Christianity and stamps out superstition; the other introduces a new civic order into Irish life. The subject matter of these paintings can be linked to the aims behind the establishment of the Order of St Patrick, which brought together Irish noblemen of differing political beliefs into a single order, with the lord lieutenant – or the monarch, when he or she was in Ireland – at its head.

Although the paintings appear to have been in position by the 1790s, there has been much confusion as to when Waldré completed the decoration of the ceiling. In a memo from his wife to the lord lieutenant, written shortly after the artist's death in 1814, Mrs Waldré complains of how the constant 'duties attending' the office of Chief Architect had 'obliged him to postpone the completion of his great work', i.e. the St Patrick's Hall paintings. Waldré's designs for the ceiling were more ambitious than the three ceiling paintings suggest. The extent of the planned decoration is revealed by the modelletto (oil sketch) for the ceiling, which is now in the Royal Dublin Society. In this, the cornices of the ceiling were painted in grisaille, with friezes of figures. A 19th-century photograph of the hall shows additional paintings along the cornice of the ceiling, similar to those in the modelletto. These were removed or overpainted when the hall was renovated in the 1880s. An early 19th-century account of the Castle gives some idea of the full scheme of paintings: 'Around the ceiling to the cornice of the room, is a deep cove richly painted by the same artists, in it are some devices, wherein great judgement is displayed in managing the perspective effect from below, where the appearance is fine and perfect.'* All that remains of this scheme are the two sets of figures on either end of the ceiling who hold the Star of St Patrick aloft.

PROVENANCE – Commissioned by George Grenville, Marquis of Buckingham, Lord Lieutenant, 1787.

LITERATURE

Memorial of Mary Waldré (1814), copy in OPW A6/1/21
J. Warburton, J. Whitelaw and R. Walsh, *History of the City of Dublin* (London, 1818) i, 471-72*
W.G. Strickland, *A Dictionary of Irish Artists*, 2 vols (Dublin, 1913) ii, 494-97
Edward Croft-Murray, *Decorative Painting in England 1537-1837* (Country Life Books, London, 1970) ii, 288-89
John Gilmartin, 'Vincent Waldré's ceiling paintings in Dublin Castle', *Apollo*, xcv, January 1972, 42-47
Edward McParland, 'A note on Vincent Waldré', *Apollo*, xcv, November 1972, 467
Frederick O'Dwyer 'The Ballroom at Dublin Castle: The Origins of St Patrick's Hall' in A. Bernelle (ed.), *Decantations – A Tribute to Maurice Craig* (Lilliput Press, Dublin 1992) 149-67
Frederick O'Dwyer, 'Dublin Castle and its State Apartments 1660-1922', *The Court Historian: Newsletter of Society for Court Studies*, ii, 1 February 1997
Fintan Cullen, *Visual Politics: The Representation of Ireland 1750-1930* (Cork University Press,1997)

EXHIBITED

St Patrick converting the Irish to Christianity, Society of Artists of Ireland, 1801 (42)
Henry II receiving the submission of the Irish chieftains, Society of Artists of Ireland, 1802 (62)

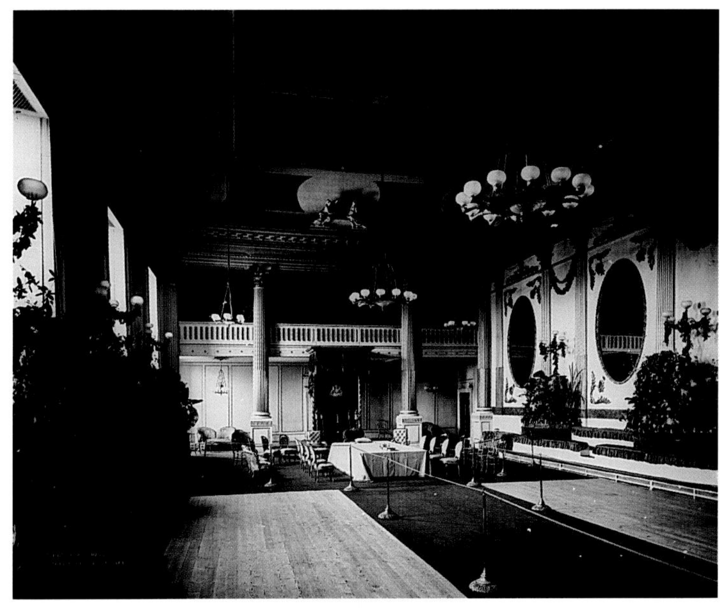

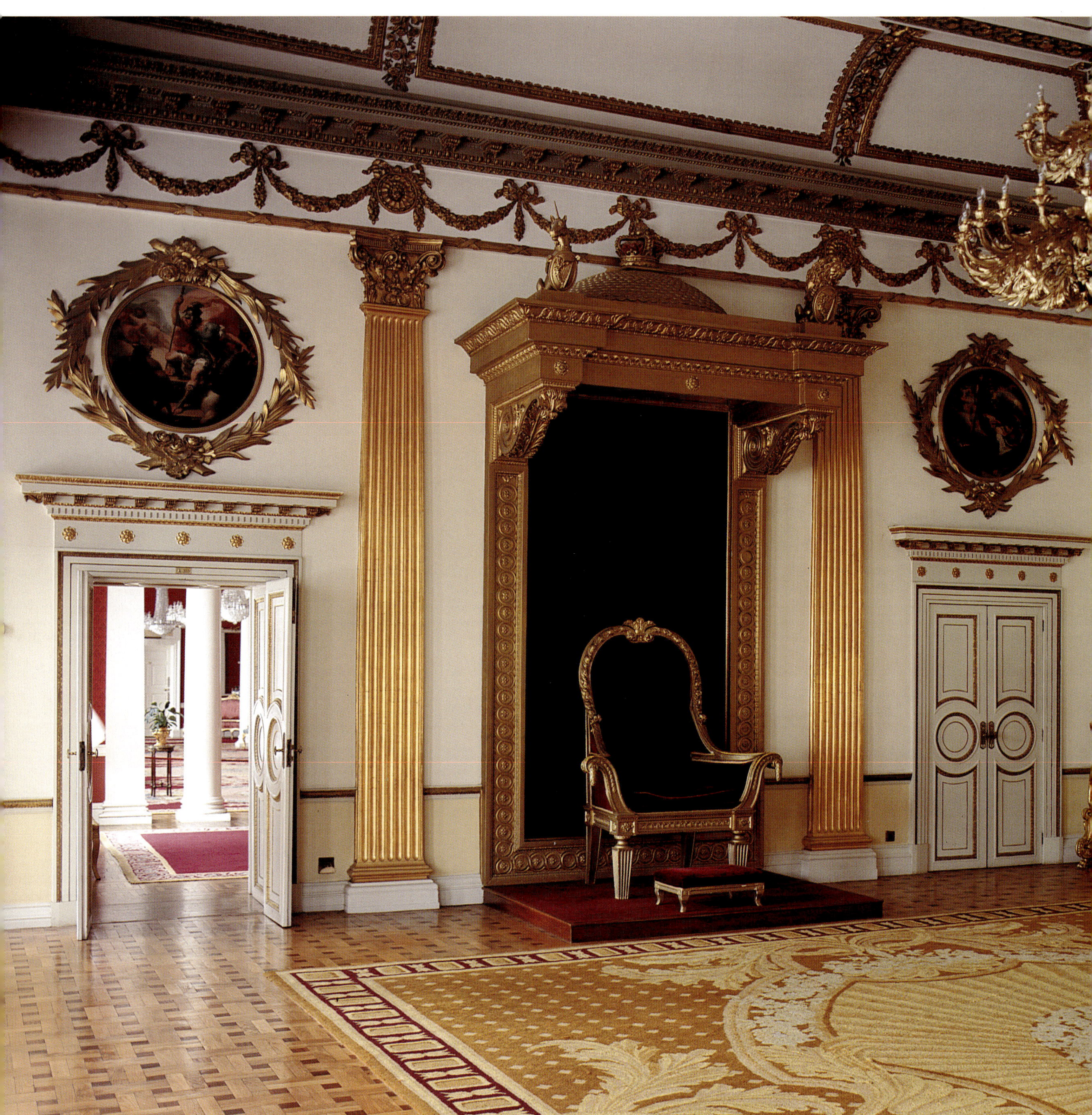

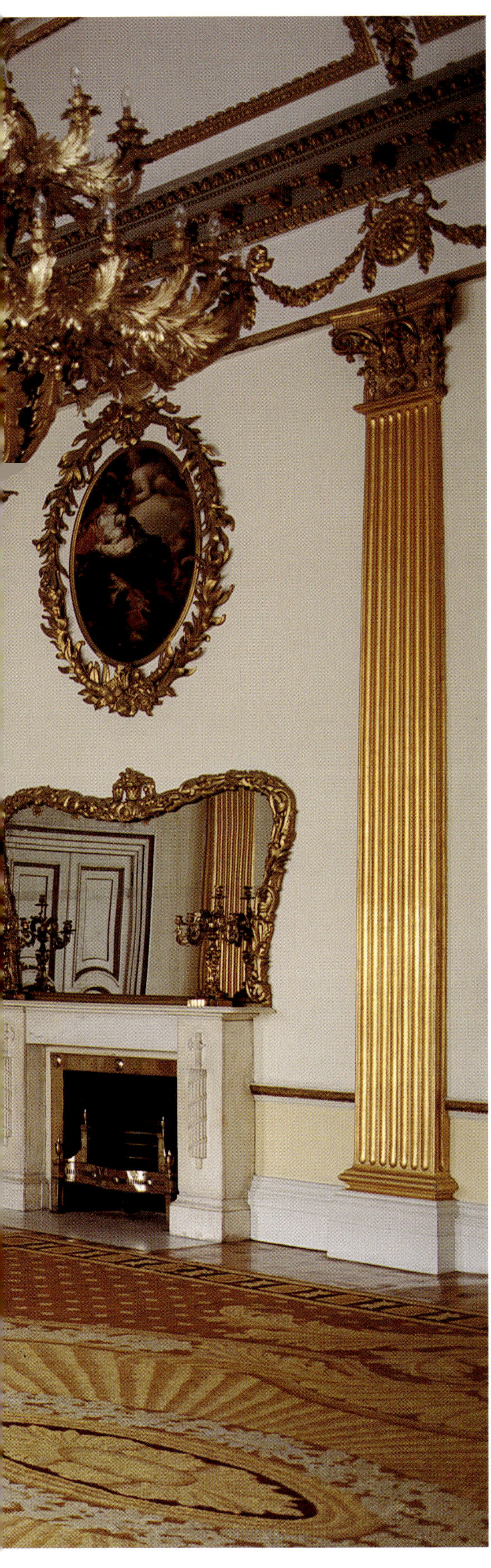

The Throne Room

Gaetano Gandolfi (1734-1802)

Born at San Matteo della Decima in the Po valley, Gaetano Gandolfi was educated at Bologna and attended the famous Accademia Clementina from c.1751 to 1756. In 1760 he spent a year in Venice, which had a profound effect on his style. After his return to Bologna, Gaetano painted a large number of religious and mythological paintings, and, particularly during the period 1770 to 1782, was in constant demand for cycles of oil and fresco paintings for the palazzi of the city. His most famous work is the cupola fresco of Sta. Maria della Vita in Bologna (1776-79).

Later, Gaetano was influenced by French rococo and English neoclassical painting which he knew through engravings. In 1787 he travelled to London, and the influence of neoclassicism was very pronounced in his work after this visit. He died in Bologna in 1802, one of the city's most famous and popular artists. His career coincided with the economic decline of that city and with the very end of the Bolognese tradition of academic painting. His brother, Ubaldo, and his son, Mauro, were also important and successful painters.

Jupiter abducting Ganymede

oil on canvas, circular painting, 101cm, signed: Cajetanus (Gandolfi) [almost lost] f:1767

This painting shows Jupiter in his chariot. With one arm he grasps the wrist of Ganymede, while his other fist holds a bright red bolt of lightning. A massive eagle with his wings outspread is perched on the front of the chariot.

Odysseus and the winds

oil on canvas, 131 x 98.5 cm, signed bottom centre: Cajet: ty? [or Ceijet: ty?] Gandolfi

There is a preparatory drawing for the composition in the Victoria and Albert Museum in London (cat. no. 1014). Pen and ink and wash within oval border. (A letter on the back is dated 12 November 1766.) (Inv. no. D2153A-1885.)

The subject comes from Homer's *Odyssey* and depicts Odysseus and a companion receiving the leather bag in which Aeolus, who was Warden of the Gales, had put the adverse winds so that Odysseus could continue safely on his journey back to Penelope. Aeolus lived on the floating island of Aeolia, which is shown as a cloud in Gandolfi's painting. Odysseus' ship can be seen in the background.

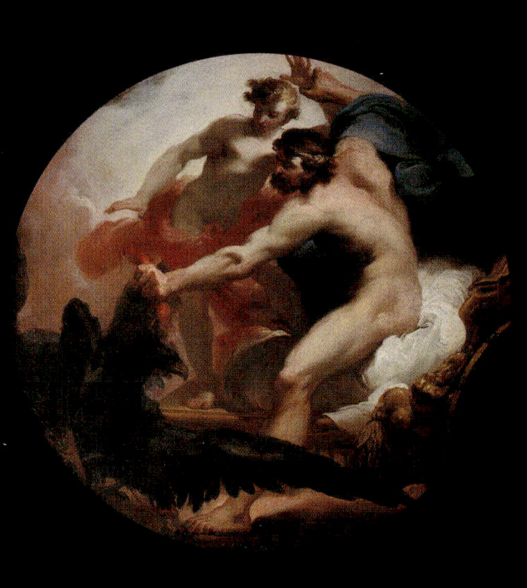

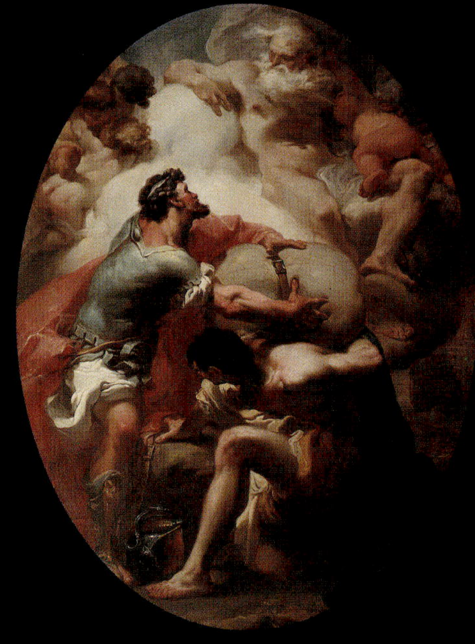

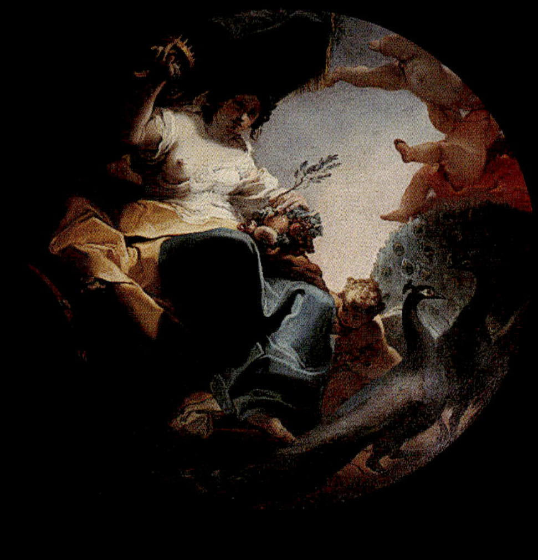

Gaetano Gandolfi

Jupiter abducting Ganymede

Odysseus and the winds

Juno and the Peacocks

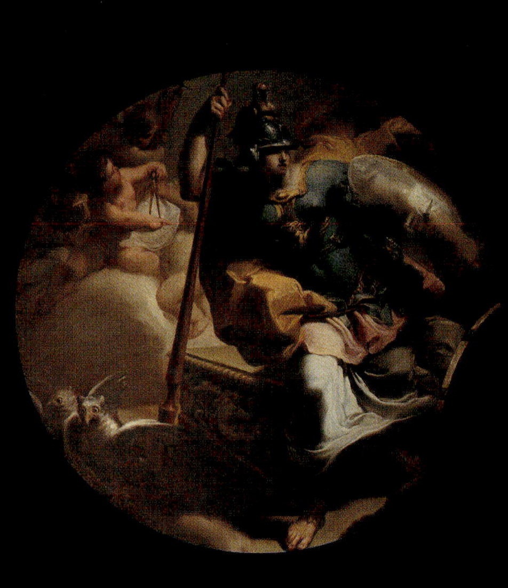

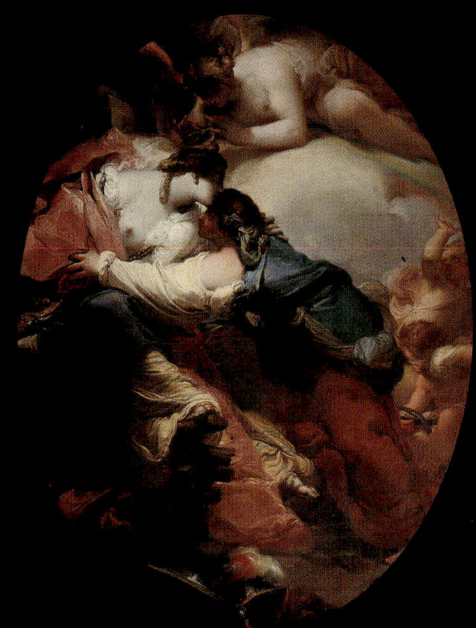

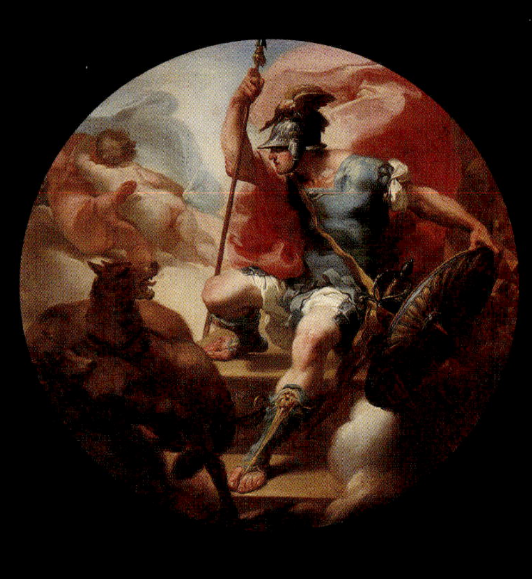

Gaetano Gandolfi

Minerva with her Sacred Bird, the Owl

Iris at the Death of Dido

Mars with his Sacred Animals, the Wolf and the Woodpecker

Juno and the Peacocks
oil on canvas, circular painting, 101cm, signed bottom centre: Cajet: ty/ [or Ceijet: ty?] Gandolfi 1767

There is a preparatory drawing for the composition in the Victoria and Albert Museum (cat. no. 1017): pen and ink and wash, heightened with white over black chalk, on pale brown paper, 190 x 196 mm.

Juno sits in her chariot under a blue canopy, surrounded by peacocks and putti. With one hand she holds aloft a crown – she is the Queen of Heaven. A large cornucopia filled with fruit rests on her lap.

Iris at the Death of Dido
oil on canvas, 131 x 98.5 cm, signed upper left-hand side: Gandolfi

Taken from Virgil's *Aeneid*, the subject of this painting is the tragic death of Dido, Queen of Carthage, who burnt herself to death after Aeneas left her. She had been tricked by Venus into falling in love with the Trojan hero, and paid for her love with a terrible death. Dido sits astride the funeral pyre while her sister embraces her for the last time. Iris, the messenger of the goddess Juno, cuts a lock from her hair.

Minerva with her Sacred Bird, the Owl
oil on canvas, circular painting, 101 cm

Minerva, goddess of wisdom and war, sits on a sarcophagus dressed partly in armour, with a lance in one hand and a glass shield in the other. Beside are two owls, symbols of her wisdom. Putti in the sky behind her carry symbols of Minerva's interest in the arts – a book, an easel and a compass.

Mars with his Sacred Animals, the Wolf and the Woodpecker
oil on canvas, circular painting, 101cm

Mars, god of war, is seated in full armour on a sarcophagus. He is accompanied by wolves who match the ferociousness of the god.

Vulcan at his Forge
1767, oil on canvas, 101 x 101 cm, signed lower right: g.g. ty [?] 1767

There is a preparatory drawing for the composition in the Victoria and Albert Museum (cat. no. 1016): pen and ink and wash, heightened with white over black chalk, on pale brown paper, 190 x 196 mm.

Vulcan, the god of fire and maker of weapons for his fellow gods, is shown at his forge. This painting, *Vulcan at his Forge*, was separated from the others at the time of their purchase by the Board of Works in 1839. The connection between it and the six in the Throne Room was forgotten, and has only been rediscovered recently. The painting was housed in the Under Secretary's Lodge, which became the Papal Nunciature in the 20th century. Dr Michael Wynne of the National Gallery of Ireland was the first to notice its similarity to the Throne Room paintings. The discovery of a preparatory drawing for the work in the Victoria and Albert Museum by the author confirmed that it is part of the group of paintings. An eighth painting, depicting Venus and the Three Graces, was hanging in the Chief Secretary's Lodge in the 1920s, but is now missing.

The identity of the artist of this group of paintings only came to light in 1995 when the works were restored and the signature of Gaetano Gandolfi was detected on a number of canvases. Their origin is unknown. They were painted in Italy in the 1760s, probably for the decoration of an unidentified palazzo. At some stage they fell into the hands of an Irish or English collector. The group of paintings, originally a set of eight, was purchased by the Board of Works in 1839 from a Dublin art dealer called Gernon for the sum of £89, 5 shillings. They had been selected by the Under Secretary, Thomas Drummond, as suitable works for the decora-

Gaetano Gandolfi
Vulcan at his Forge (photographed while undergoing restoration, 1999)

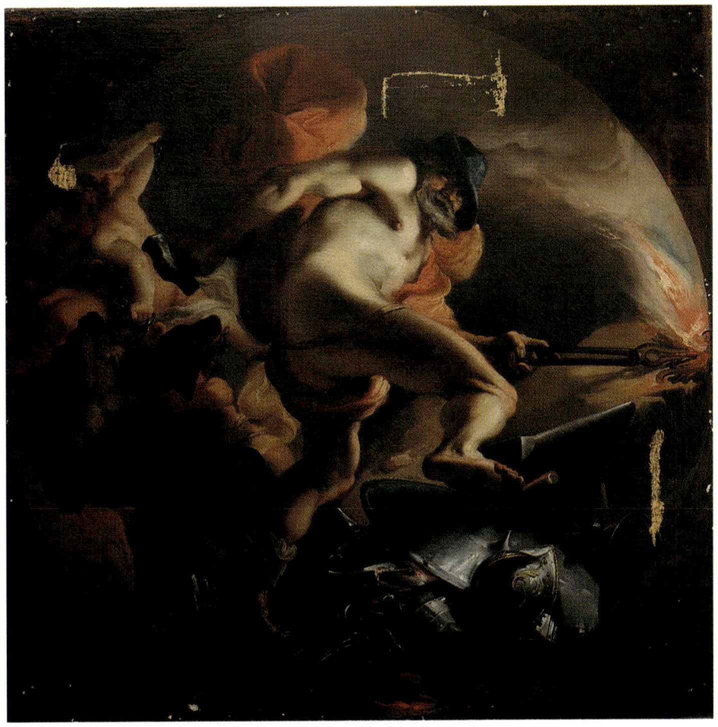

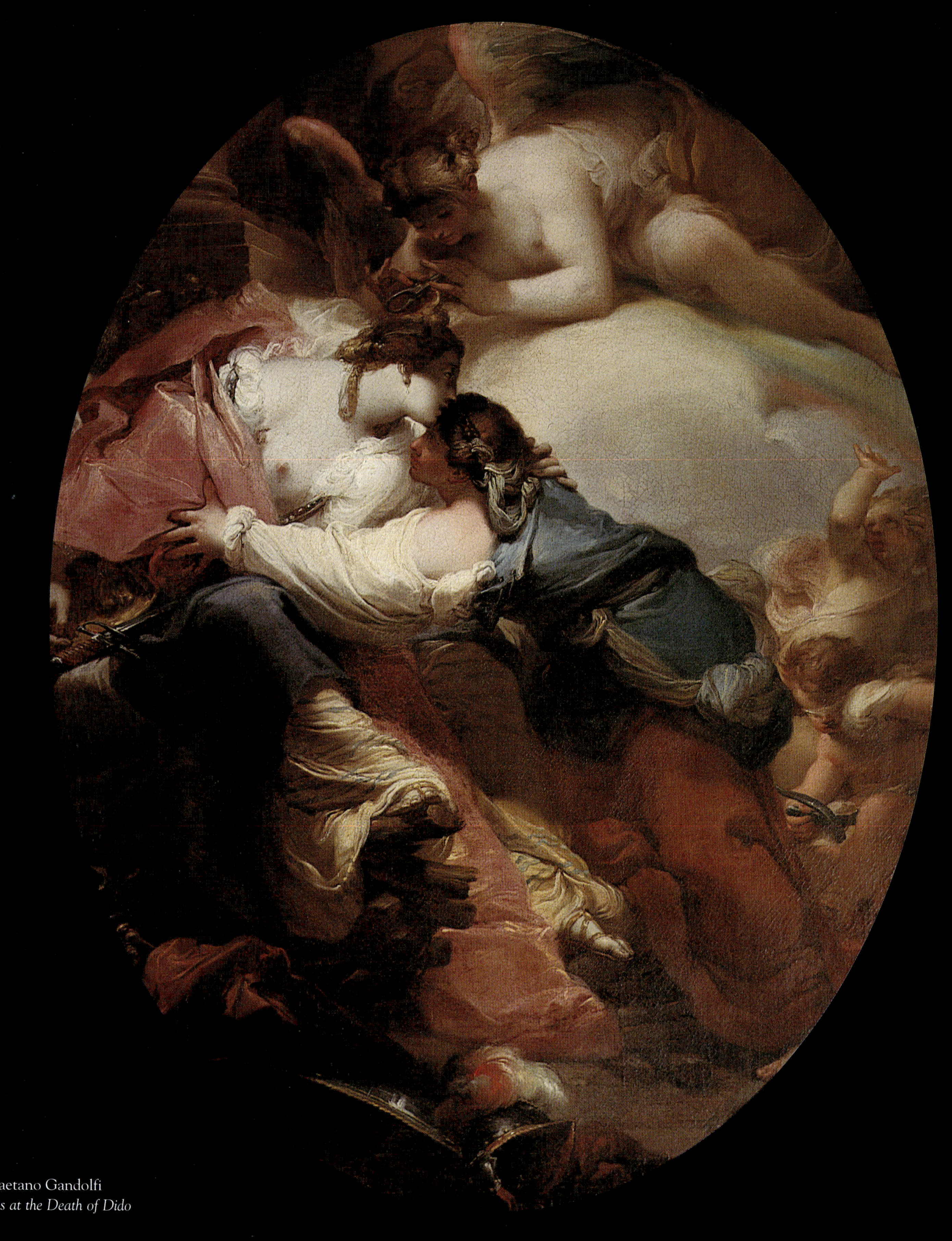

Gaetano Gandolfi
Iris at the Death of Dido

tion of the Throne Room, which was undergoing major alterations at this time. Only six of the paintings were used in the decoration of the room. The two extra paintings were probably used in other buildings belonging to the lord lieutenant and his retinue. The canvases were originally square or rectangular, with fictive spandrels painted on the corners. These were folded back when the works were hung in Dublin Castle to form oval or round paintings. The elaborate frames were commissioned especially for the paintings, and were made, along with two large mirrors, by Cornelius Callaghan of Clare Street in Dublin. The proportion of this room was altered in the 1950s by the insertion of a doorway in the south wall, situated between the two chimney pieces, and leading onto the Battleaxe landing. Prior to this, the throne was situated in the centre of the south wall, so that the two oval paintings, and the chimney pieces and mirrors, were on either side of it.

The subject matter of Gandolfi's paintings deals with the power of the gods. The circular works show the most important gods of the Roman pantheon with their attributes. The two larger oval scenes have subjects depicting the gods helping or punishing mortal men and women – represented by Odysseus and Dido.

The almost baroque quality of the paintings seems at odds with the very classical decor of the Throne Room, and indeed the style of the paintings appears to have been unfashionable in the 1830s, as the paintings were surprisingly cheap. The name of the artist was unknown even at this point, and more expense went into other decorations in the room. The paintings introduce vitality and drama into the very formal architecture of the space. They demonstrate Gandolfi's subtle use of colour – warm blues and red predominate – and also his understanding of anatomy, which was a legacy from his training at the academy in Bologna.

The Throne Room was one of the most important rooms of State in the Castle. During the season, it was used by the lord lieutenant and his court for levées. The new lord lieutenant was inaugurated here. The throne and canopy in the room were rumoured to have belonged to William III. This is unlikely: an engraving of the room published in a Dublin journal in 1795 shows the present canopy without the throne. It is probable that the throne dates to the early 19th century, possibly to the visit of George IV who spent several weeks in Dublin after his coronation in 1821. A reference in a guide book to Dublin published in 1825 states that the throne had been installed for George IV.

Another feature of the Throne Room is the spectacular gilt chandelier which hangs from the centre of the ceiling.* This is part of the 1839 decoration of the room, and has the motif of shamrock, thistle and rose entwined, which also occurs on the frames of the paintings. It replaced an earlier Waterford Crystal chandelier which had been presented to the Castle by the Duke of Rutland. The present chandelier was made, along with four smaller chandeliers, by the firm of Higginbotham, Thomas & Co of Dublin, and was originally to have been fitted with candles. The price of the five chandeliers was £316 – more than three times that of the paintings. A note in the Board of Works letterbook of 1839 requests the manufacturer to change the design to be suitable for gas. The four smaller chandeliers now hang in other rooms in the State Apartments and at Áras an Uachtaráin. At some point in the past they were removed from the Throne Room, and were accidentally rediscovered in the 1950s by an architect engaged in restoration work at the Castle.

PROVENANCE – Purchased by the Board of Works for the Throne Room from the Dublin art dealer Gernon in 1839.

LITERATURE

Letterbooks of the Board of Works, 2D-57-39, CSORP 1839 64/8732
Michael Wynne, 'Six Gaetano Gandolfi's in Dublin Castle', *Burlington Magazine*, cxli, no. 1155, June 1999, 252-54

* G.N. Wright, *A Historical Guide to the City of Dublin* (London, 1825)

The author acknowledges her gratitude to Dr Michael Wynne, who allowed her read his article prior to its publication in *Burlington Magazine*, and who has been generous with his information and advice; also to Joseph McDonnell for drawing attention to an illustration of the Throne Room in Walker's *Hibernian Magazine* (1795), part 1.

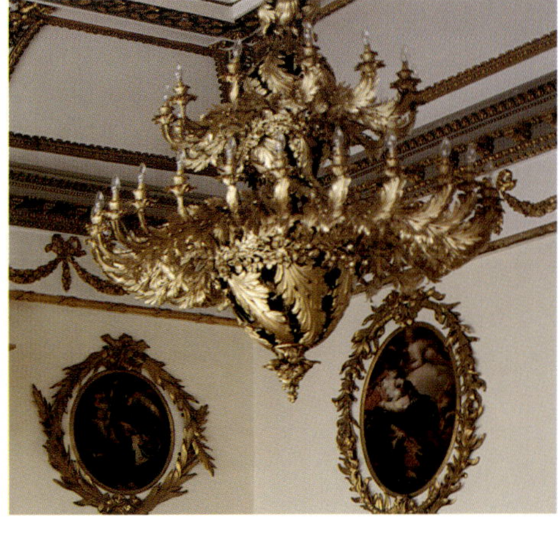

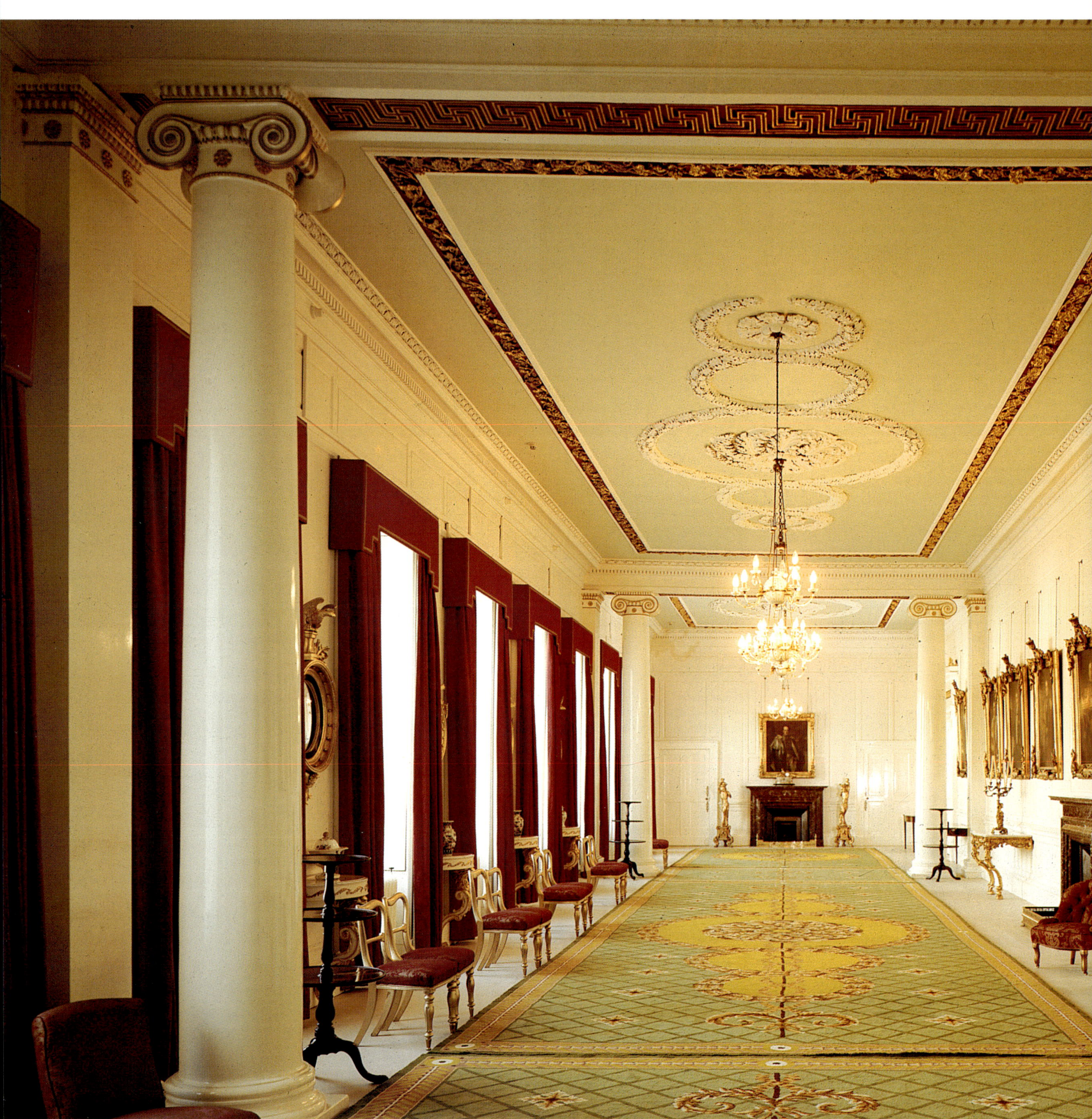

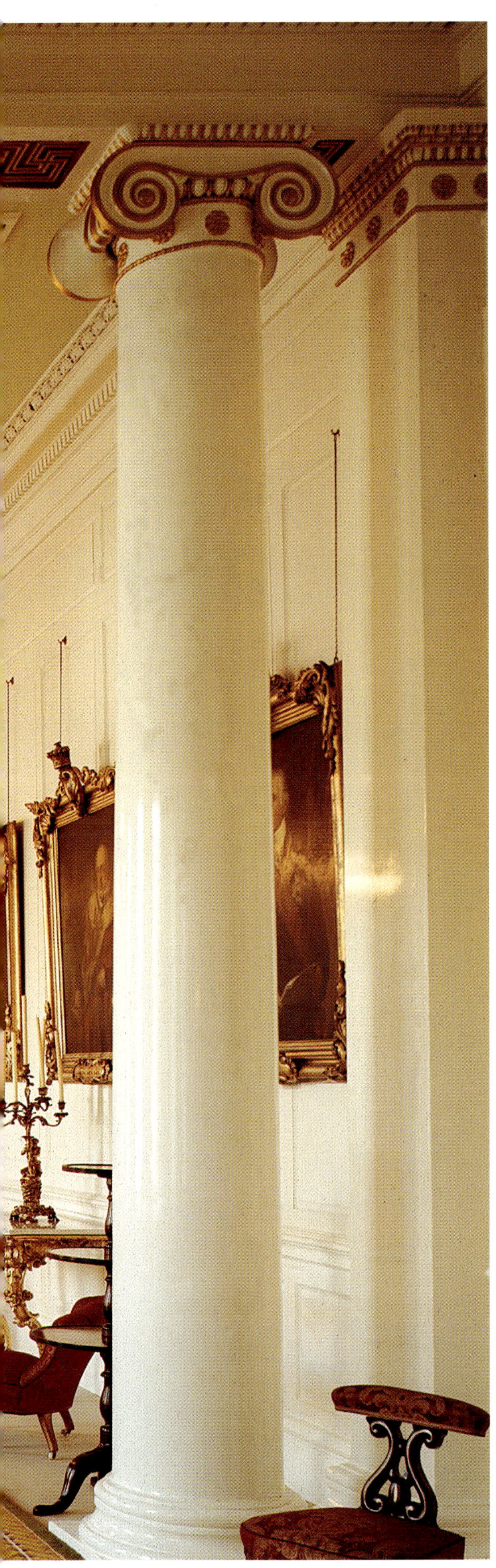

Portraits of the Lords Lieutenant – The Picture Gallery

From the Act of Union until 1902, every Lord Lieutenant of Ireland, except one, was represented by a portrait which was hung in the dining room of the State Apartments, or the Picture Gallery, as it came to be called. So far, very little documentary evidence of how and when these paintings were commissioned has come to light. A tradition was established during the early years of the 19th century that each lord lieutenant would donate a formal portrait of himself to the Castle. The paintings were all of a similar size and were framed almost identically. Today, seventeen of the original twenty-eight portraits are still on display. The increasing number of portraits meant that by the late 19th century, their display spilled over to the State drawing room, where some of them were destroyed in the 1941 fire. A further five paintings were sold off by the Board of Works at various times.

Prior to the 1770s, the lords lieutenant spent very little time in Ireland, usually coming over for the few weeks of the season between early February and St Patrick's Day. However, by the 19th century they were expected to reside in Dublin all the year round, a house in the Phoenix Park having been purchased for this purpose in 1781. This became known as the Viceregal Lodge (now Áras an Uachtaráin), and successive lords lieutenant made improvements to the house and its gardens. During the court season, the Lord Lieutenant and his family moved to the State Apartments at Dublin Castle, living in the suite of rooms to the west of St Patrick's Hall and adjoining the State corridor.

The lords lieutenant were recruited from the peerage, and usually came from wealthy aristocratic backgrounds. They were political appointees, and their term of office tended to coincide with the rise and fall of successive administrations. While they had considerable power in terms of appointments and patronage in Ireland, the real political power lay in the hands of the Chief Secretary, who was a member of the cabinet and whose offices were also located in Dublin Castle. The Lord Lieutenant, as the royal representative in Ireland, had an important symbolic and ceremonial role, and this was reflected in the decor of the State Apartments, and particularly in the creation of a gallery of portraits.

As the commissioning and presentation of the portraits was a personal activity on the part of each lord lieutenant, it is difficult to establish the exact provenance of the works. Details may be contained within the private papers of the lords lieutenant, but it has not been feasible to follow this line of research for this catalogue. Occasional references in publications and the correspondence of the Board of Works has thrown light on a number of the portraits. It seems likely that the idea of a portrait gallery dates from the 1820s or 1830s. The portraits of the earliest lords lieutenant tend to be copies or versions of existing portraits. There is no direct reference to the sitter's connection with Ireland in these works. From the mid 19th century onwards, the Order of St Patrick becomes a central feature of the paintings,* and for some years there seems to have been a tradition of commissioning the president of the Royal Hibernian Academy to paint the portraits.

* The Lord Lieutenant was made Head of the Order of Knights of St Patrick as part of his inauguration ceremony.

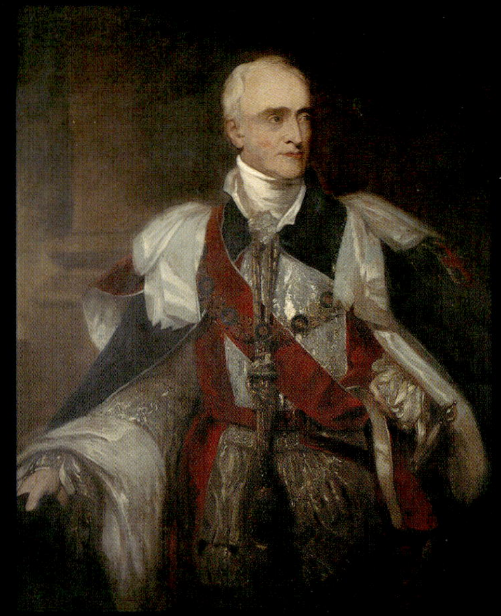

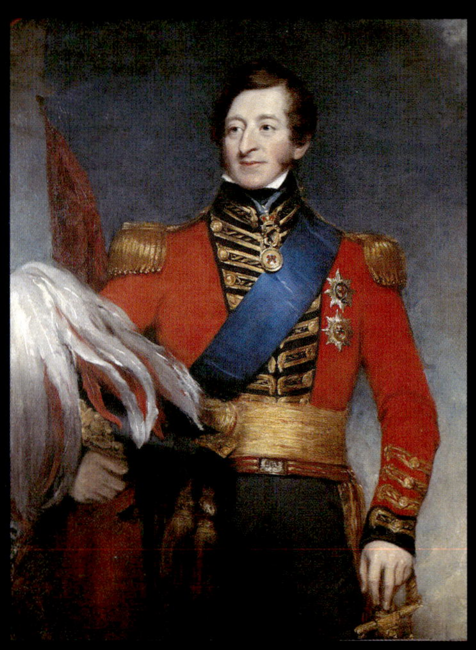

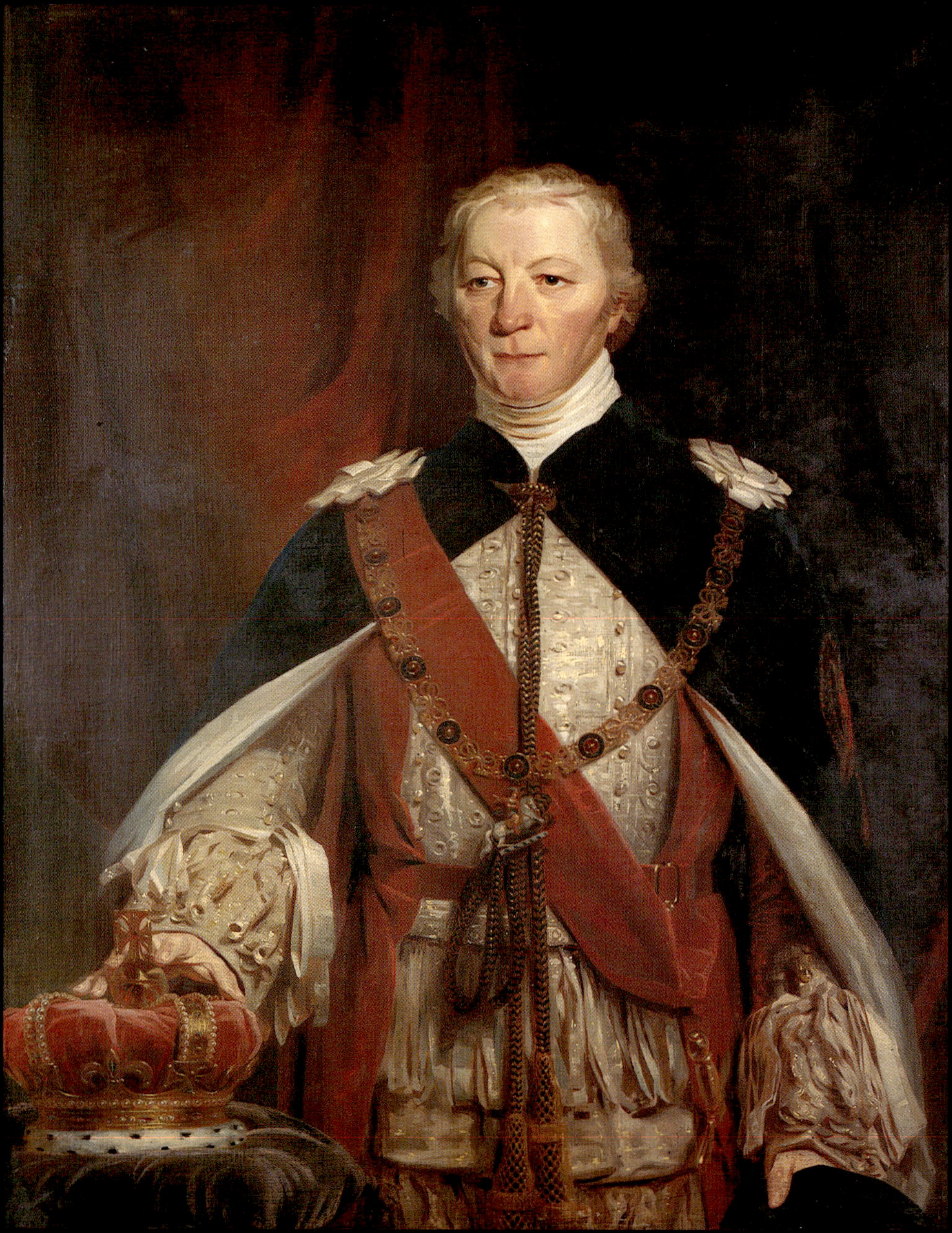

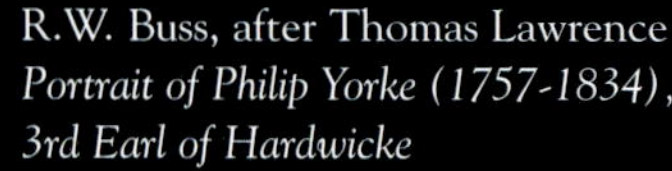

R.W. Buss, after Thomas Lawrence
Portrait of Philip Yorke (1757-1834), 3rd Earl of Hardwicke

Martin Cregan
Portrait of Hugh Percy (1785-1847), 3rd Duke of Northumberland

William Cuming
Portrait of Charles, 4th Duke of Richmond and Lennox (1764-1819)

R.W. Buss (1804-1875), after Thomas Lawrence (1769-1830)

Buss trained as an engraver with his father in London. He illustrated the works of Charles Knight and Anthony Trollope. He was also a successful portrait painter, and exhibited at the Royal Academy and the British Institution.

There are a large number of paintings after Thomas Lawrence, or studio of Lawrence, in the collection. (See below for a biography of this artist.)

Portrait of Philip Yorke (1757-1834), 3rd Earl of Hardwicke

1830, oil on canvas, 142 x 112 cm
inscribed on back of canvas: Copied by R.W. Buss from an Original Picture by Sir Thomas Lawrence at Wimploe, Cambridgeshire

Hardwicke began his career as MP for Cambridge before succeeding to the peerage in 1790. He served as Lord Lieutenant from 1801 to 1805, arriving in Ireland just after the Act of Union. Unlike his predecessor Cornwallis, Hardwicke was not made commander-in-chief, and this slight caused much resentment, with the cabinet frequently dealing directly with the Chief Secretary or other members of the establishment, rather than the Lord Lieutenant himself. According to the DNB, he did much to allay irritation caused by the Act of Union.

His work in Ireland was rewarded by his being made a Knight of the Garter in 1803, an event which took place by proxy in Dublin. While in office he made important alterations to the Viceregal Lodge; two wings were added at his behest. He became a supporter of Catholic Emancipation, and voted for the Reform Bill of 1831.

The painting is a version of a painting by Sir Thomas Lawrence (*c.*1829), which is in a private collection, a mezzotint of which was published in 1836 (engraved by W. Giller). It shows the earl in the mantle and full regalia of the Order of the Garter, and is very similar in mood to William Cuming's portrait of the Duke of Richmond. This painting has long been presumed to be by the Irish artist William Cuming, but an inscription on the back of the canvas states that it is a copy by R.W. Buss. It may have been attributed to Cuming because he painted a portrait of the earl for Dublin Corporation.

LITERATURE
W.G. Strickland, *A Dictionary of Irish Artists*, 2 vols (Dublin, 1913) i, 245 (lists portrait as by William Cuming)

COMPARATIVE LITERATURE
Kenneth Garlick, *Sir Thomas Lawrence – A Complete Catalogue of Oil Paintings* (Oxford, 1989) 204-05

Martin Cregan (1788-1870)

Cregan was a prizewinning student at the Dublin Society Schools in 1806 and 1807. His education was paid for by the Stewart family of Killymoon, Co Tyrone, in whose house Cregan was a servant. He subsequently worked in the studio of Martin Archer-Shee in London, where he lived from 1812 to 1822. Upon his return to Dublin, he became one of the founding members of the RHA, where he exhibited until 1859. He was extremely prolific, regularly exhibiting his work at the RHA, of which he was president from 1832 until his resignation in 1856. Cregan worked mainly as a portrait painter and held, in fact, the position of Portrait Painter to the Lord Lieutenant.

Portrait of Hugh Percy (1785-1847), 3rd Duke of Northumberland

1830-31, oil on canvas, 146 x 115.5.cm, signed (monogram): C 1831

Described by the diarist Charles Greville as 'an eternal talker and a prodigious bore', and by Sir Robert Peel as the best viceroy of the era, the Duke of Northumberland embodied many talents. He served as Lord Lieutenant from 1829 to 1830. His brief period of office was marked by the suppression of the Catholic Association, which began to push for repeal of the Act of Union, and his refusal to allow public money to be spent on the relief of distress. He replaced the much liked Marquis of Anglesey, who has been dismissed in 1829 for his open support of Catholic Emancipation.

Northumberland was one of the wealthiest peers of the day. During his period as Ambassador-extraordinary to Paris in 1825, he had maintained himself at his own expense, and Greville attributed his acceptance of the post in Ireland to his desire to show off his wealth. After 1830, he retired to the family seat at Alnwick Castle, and died there in 1847.

This is a half-length portrait showing the duke in full military uniform, holding a plumed helmet in one hand. He wears a blue sash, and the ribbon and badge of the Order of St Patrick hang from his neck. The star of the Order, and that of the Order of the Garter, are visible on his lapel. Cregan also painted a portrait of Charlotte, Duchess of Northumberland, which is now in the possession of the present Duke of Northumberland at Lynn House, Middlesex.

PROVENANCE – Unknown, probably commissioned by Duke of Northumberland *c.*1830.

LITERATURE
W.G. Strickland, *A Dictionary of Irish Artists*, 2 vols (Dublin, 1913) i, 230

EXHIBITED
RHA 1830 (38)

William Cuming (1769-1852)

William Cuming was president of the Royal Hibernian Academy from 1829 to 1832. He studied at the Dublin Society Schools from 1785 to 1790, winning a medal for his figure drawing. In 1793 he was commissioned to paint the Lord Mayor of Dublin, and afterwards received a number of other important portrait commissions, including some from the viceregal court. He exhibited portraits at the Society of Artists from 1800, becoming president of that society in 1811. His early style was influenced by that of George Chinnery, who was in Dublin in the early 1800s.

Portrait of Charles,
4th Duke of Richmond and Lennox (1764-1819)
c.1826, oil on canvas, 130 x 104 cm [page 32]

Having narrowly missed shooting the Duke of York in a duel as a young man, Richmond served as MP for Sussex in the 1790s. In 1806 he succeeded to the Dukedom of Richmond, and became Lord Lieutenant of Ireland the following year. During his six years in Ireland, he got into debt, spending some £50,000 of his own money on expenses incurred in his position. He was responsible for the addition of the north portico to the Viceregal Lodge, as well as a number of gate lodges at the entrances to the Phoenix Park. The duke was a notorious flirt, and his behaviour occupied the gossips of Dublin society. After leaving Ireland he settled in Brussels, and was resident there at the time of the Battle of Waterloo. In 1818 he was appointed Governor-General of British North America, and he died in Richmond, Canada, in 1819.

The painting is a version of a full-length portrait of the duke by Cuming which hangs in the Mansion House, Dublin. This painting was commissioned by the Lord Mayor, Abraham Bradley King, in 1813, and paid for by the city of Dublin. It was exhibited at the RHA in 1826 (137). In both works, the duke is shown standing with one hand outstretched and touching the crown. He wears a mantle, and is in the full regalia of the Order of the Garter. Some sense of the monumentality of the full-length portrait is retained in the Dublin Castle version. Warm rich tones are used throughout. The face is built up using square brushstrokes in the style of Henry Raeburn, one of the leading portrait painters of the period. The reference to the Order of St George rather than to St Patrick is notable in the early lord lieutenant portraits.

PROVENANCE – Unknown. This appears to have been commissioned, or at least completed, by Cuming many years after Richmond had ceased to be Lord Lieutenant.

LITERATURE
Anne Crookshank and the Knight of Glin, *The Painters of Ireland* (London, 1978) 174

Charles Wellington Furse (1868-1904)

Furse studied at the Slade under Legros around 1884, in Paris at the Académie Julian, and finally at the Westminster School of Art under Frederick Brown. He gained a reputation as a portrait painter in London, exhibiting at the Royal Academy from 1888 and at the New English Art Club from 1891. His early work is influenced by Whistler and Sargent. By the mid 1890s, his style became more academic and monumental.

In 1899 he received the commission to decorate the dome over the staircase of Liverpool Town Hall. He was assisted in this project by his cousin, the Irish artist Dermod O'Brien, who painted a portrait of the Earl of Aberdeen, which also belongs to Dublin Castle. Furse suffered from ill health throughout his short life. He was encouraged by his doctors to spend the winter months abroad, and lived in South Africa in 1895-96, as well as travelling in Italy a number of times. He died of tuberculosis in 1904, a year after his election as Associate Member of the Royal Academy.

Portrait of John Gordon Campbell (1847-1934),
7th Earl of Aberdeen
c.1889-90, oil on canvas, 128 x 102 cm, signed lower right: Charles W. Furse

The future Earl of Aberdeen was born in Edinburgh in 1847. After the deaths of his two elder brothers, he unexpectedly became Earl in 1872. In 1886, shortly after the Phoenix Park murders, Aberdeen became Lord Lieutenant of Ireland for the first time. The earl later wrote of this time: 'We found the routine of life at the Castle very irksome at first, never allowed to be alone, followed by two detectives wherever we went.' His first period of tenure lasted only a few months, but despite the highly charged political climate, the Earl and Lady Aberdeen travelled through the south of the country, and made a positive impression.

In 1906 Aberdeen was appointed Lord Lieutenant for the second time, having been Governor-General of Canada in the meantime. His second term of office, which lasted until 1915, was the longest of any lord lieutenant of Ireland. Aberdeen's liberal views did not go down well with the unionists; he openly supported the Home Rule Bill, which was passed in 1914. Lady Aberdeen took an active interest in Irish affairs, and encouraged the development of home industry and crafts. She was responsible for the use of the State Apartments as a hospital by the Red Cross during the First World War. The diplomatic skill of the earl, and his wife's enthusiasm for Irish life, were reflected in his advancement to the title of Marquis of Aberdeen and Tamair (Tara) in 1916.

This is an early work by Furse, who was apparently recommended to Aberdeen by William Gladstone. Although commis-

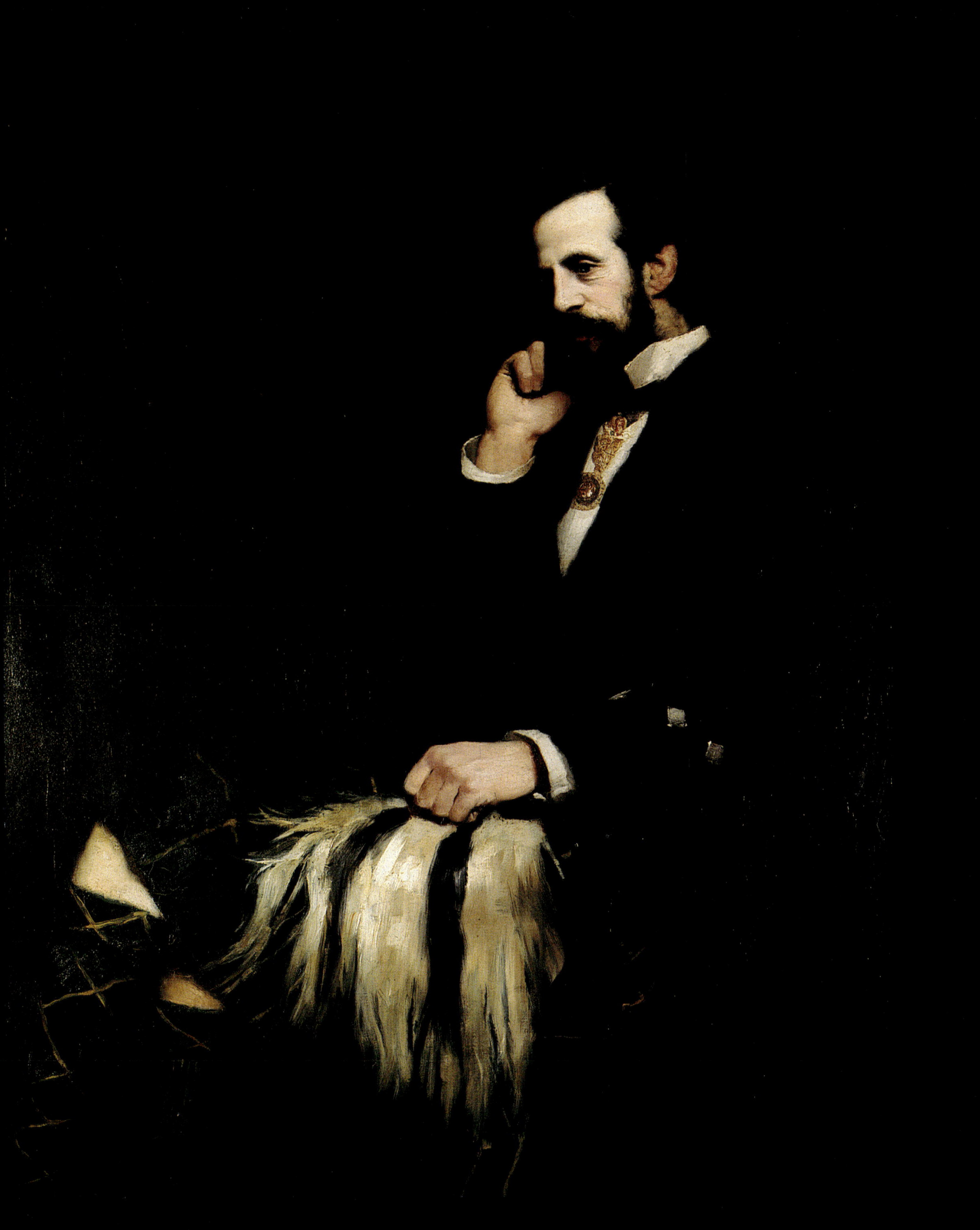

Charles Wellington Furse, *Portrait of John Gordon Campbell (1847-1934), 7th Earl of Aberdeen*

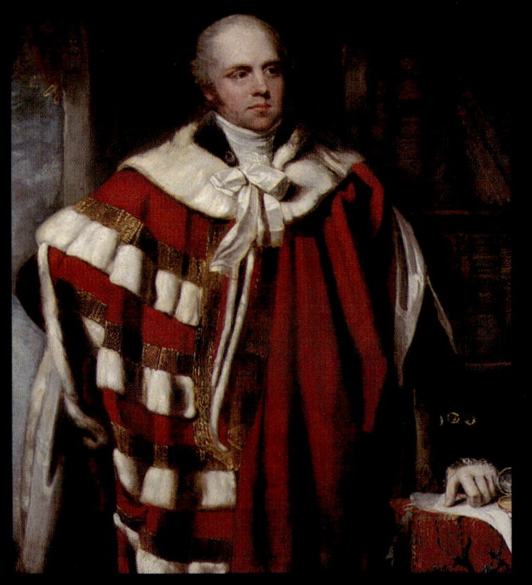

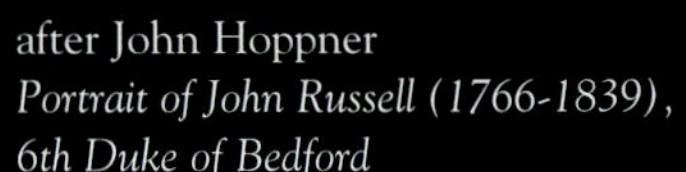

after John Hoppner
Portrait of John Russell (1766-1839), 6th Duke of Bedford

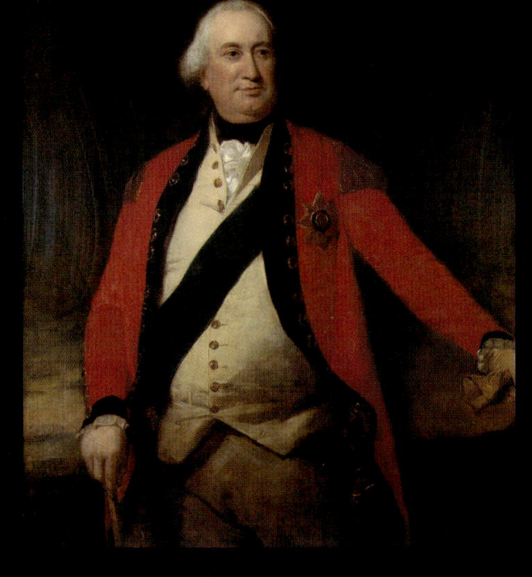

John Singleton Copley
Portrait of Charles, 1st Marquis Cornwallis (1738-1805)

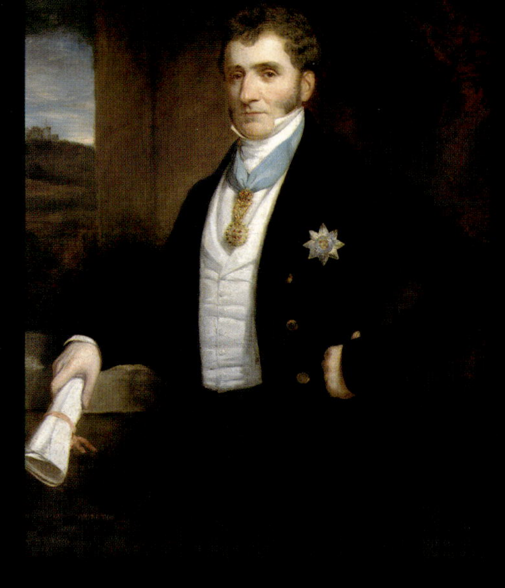

T.W. Jones
(copy of unidentified original)
Portrait of Hugh, 2nd Earl Fortescue (1783-1861)

sioned in 1886, the portrait was not painted until 1888-89 when Furse was invited to Haddo House in Scotland, where a temporary studio was erected. Aberdeen later commented on what a pleasant addition to the household Furse was; he had a fine singing voice and could give 'delightful humorous recitations'. The earl is shown in profile, seated and in highland dress, with the ribbon and badge of the Order of St Patrick around his neck. The influence of Whistler and contemporary French painting is evident in the work, which relies on a stark composition and the striking contrast of the black and dark green costume and the white of the earl's skin. It is also notable for the intense realism of the portrait, which depicts the earl in a thoughtful, self-absorbed pose. It is the most modern and original of the lord lieutenant portraits.

PROVENANCE – Commissioned by the Earl of Aberdeen in 1886.

LITERATURE
Illustrated Memoir of Charles Wellington Furse (Burlington Fine Arts Club, London, 1908) 97
Lord and Lady Aberdeen, *We Two – Reminiscences of Lord and Lady Aberdeen* (London, 1925) i, 243
R. Ormond and M. Rogers (eds) *Dictionary of British Portraiture* (National Portrait Gallery, London, n.d.) iii, 1

EXHIBITED
Royal Academy, 1890 (207)
Art of the State, 1993

after John Hoppner (1757/8-1810)

Hoppner was one of the most fashionable portrait painters in England in the last days of the 18th century. He began exhibiting at the RA in 1780, and in 1789 he was appointed Portrait Painter to the Prince of Wales. His early works were suited to what the art historian Ellis Waterhouse has described as the 'flashy taste' of the prince. He was later superseded by Thomas Lawrence. Many of his portraits took compositions or backgrounds directly from the works of Reynolds and Gainsborough.

Portrait of John Russell (1766-1839), 6th Duke of Bedford

after 1806, oil on canvas, 130 x 105.5 cm

Upon the early death of his brother in 1802, John Russell succeeded to the title of Duke of Bedford. Like the rest of the Russell family, Bedford was committed to reform and was a prominent supporter of the Liberal party. He served as Lord Lieutenant of Ireland from February 1806 to April 1807. (The duke's third son, Lord John Russell, became prime minister in 1846 in the first days of the Famine. He had spent a few months in Dublin as a child.)

After his time in Ireland, the duke retired from public life, and devoted himself to his estates in England and to other pursuits, such as his interest in agriculture and art. He lived in Italy from 1813 to 1815, and commissioned a number of important artworks from the leading artists of the time, including Canova and Thorwaldsen. These added to the splendour of the family seat at Woburn Abbey, where the duke spent the rest of his life.

This painting is a copy or version of a portrait of the duke by Hoppner which was exhibited at the Royal Academy in 1819 (47), and which was hanging in Woburn Abbey in the 19th century (present location unknown). It shows the duke in peer's robes, standing in the library, and gives some sense of the different aspects of his personality. His right hand is leaning on a table on which can be seen some of his papers and two agricultural medals – a silver one and a gold one. Hoppner also painted a portrait of the 5th Duke, which is still at Woburn Abbey.

PROVENANCE – Unknown. Located in Viceregal Lodge in 1936 (A77/7/1/39).

COMPARATIVE LITERATURE
George Scharf, *A Descriptive and Historical Catalogue of the Collection of Pictures at Woburn Abbey* (London, 1877) no. 275, gives a full description of the Woburn Abbey painting

I am grateful to Lavinia Wellicome, Curator of Woburn Abbey, for her assistance with this attribution.

T.W. Jones (fl.1832-1845), copy after John Singleton Copley

Little is known of T.W. Jones. He lived in London and exhibited biblical subjects and portraits at the Royal Academy and the British Institution from 1832 to 1845.

John Singleton Copley (1738-1815)

Copley was a American portrait and history painter who settled in London in 1775. He was renowned for his ambitious and increasingly enormous history paintings, which he began to exhibit at the Royal Academy in 1778.

Portrait of Charles, 1st Marquis Cornwallis (1738-1805)
c.1839, oil on canvas, 125 x 100 cm
signed bottom right: Charles / Marquis Cornwallis / Copied by T.W. Jones

Cornwallis had a very distinguished military and diplomatic career before his appointment as Lord Lieutenant in 1798. In the 1760s and 1770s he fought in the American War of Independence. His endeavours were rewarded by his appointment as Governor-General of Bengal in 1786, where he was involved in the Siege of Seringapatam in 1792, a crucial incident in the British colonisation of the subcontinent. In 1798 Cornwallis came to Ireland as both Commander-in-Chief of His Majesty's forces and as Lord Lieutenant, and immediately concerned himself with the suppression of the 1798 rebellion. Two years later, he presided over the Act of Union. He had pushed for Catholic Emancipation in the bill, and when this was refused by George III, Cornwallis resigned as Lord Lieutenant. He later returned to India as Governor-General and Commander-in-Chief in 1805.

The painting shows Cornwallis standing in full military dress, his left hand outstretched. He wears the star of the Order of the Garter. The work is based on the celebrated American painter Singleton Copley's portrait of Cornwallis as Lieutenant General of India, painted c.1792. The original hangs in the Guildhall, London, and is part of the City of London's collection. A number of versions are in existence including two engravings by S.W. Holl (1832) and S. Freeman (1833), published about the time the Dublin Castle version was painted. In these engravings, and in the original painting, the Indian context of the portrait is much more explicit. To Cornwallis's left can be seen the walls of the city of Seringapatam, with the British flag flying above it. In the middle distance a group of cavalry can be seen; these are depicted as an exotic train of camels and elephants in the Holl engraving. In the Dublin Castle version, the background of the painting is generalised to represent the idea of Cornwallis as a military leader, rather than referring specifically to his Indian sojourn.

The fact that this work post-dates Cornwallis's period as Lord Lieutenant by nearly forty years suggests that the idea of a picture gallery of commemorative portraits of the viceroys dates to the 1820s and 1830s, rather than the beginning of the century.

PROVENANCE – Unknown. Possibly commissioned by Earl Fortescue c.1839.

LITERATURE
W.G. Strickland, *A Dictionary of Irish Artists*, 2 vols (Dublin, 1913) ii, 563 (incorrectly attributed to Thomas Alfred Jones)

T.W. Jones (copy of unidentified original)

Portrait of Hugh, 2nd Earl Fortescue (1783-1861)
1839, oil on canvas, 129 x 103 cm
signed bottom left: Hugh, Viscount Ebrington 1839 / Copied T.W. Jones 1839

Earl Fortescue was Lord Lieutenant from April 1839 to September 1841. His mother was Hester Grenville, sister of the 1st Marquis of Buckingham, the 18th century Lord Lieutenant and founder of the Order of St Patrick. Fortescue became Viscount Ebrington at the age of six, and served as MP for Tavistock and North Devon from 1804. He was an ardent supporter of the Whig Party. In 1839 he entered the House of Lords, and two years later succeeded his father as Earl Fortescue while he was Lord Lieutenant of Ireland. It was during his time in Dublin that major alterations were made to the Throne Room and that the Gandolfi paintings were acquired. The earl may also have commissioned Jones to copy the portrait of Cornwallis. After his time in Ireland he served at court as Lord High Steward of Her Majesty's household (1846-50), and was made a Knight of the Garter in 1856.

The viscount is shown standing against a stone ledge, his right arm resting on it, and holding a scroll of paper in his right hand. He is in formal dress, with the ribbon, badge and star of the Order of St Patrick on his left lapel. Through the opening in the left-hand side of the composition, a hill with a castle perched on the top of it can be seen. This is probably the folly which resembled a ruined castle, situated in the park land of Castle Hill at Filleigh in Devon, one of the earl's seats in England. The painting may be based on a work by William Walker (1791-1867), which was engraved by S.W. Reynolds in 1833. The pose of the figure is very similar in both works. This rather wooden portrait does little justice to the earl, who is known from other portraits to have been quite dashing and fashionably romantic in appearance.

PROVENANCE – Probably commissioned by Earl Fortescue *c.*1839.

LITERATURE
W.G. Strickland, *A Dictionary of Irish Artists*, 2 vols (Dublin, 1913) ii, 563 (incorrectly attributed to Thomas Alfred Jones)

Thomas Alfred Jones (1823-1893)

Thomas Jones was an orphan who was brought up by the Archdale family in Dublin. He attended the Royal Dublin Society schools from 1833, and began exhibiting at the Royal Hibernian Academy in 1841. From 1846 to 1849 he travelled on the continent. He concentrated on portraiture, and after the death of Catterson Smith, he was one of the foremost portrait painters in the country. He succeeded the former as president of the RHA in 1869. He is known to have painted several portraits of the lords lieutenant, of which this is the only one still in situ. Jones was knighted in 1880 by the Duke of Marlborough, the Lord Lieutenant of the day, and was the first president of the RHA to receive such an honour.*

Portrait of Charles Vane-Temple-Stewart (1852-1915), 6th Marquis of Londonderry

c.1889, oil on canvas, 142 x 112.5 cm
signed bottom left (entwined monogram): TAJ; inscribed on back:
The Marquess of Londonderry. Painted by Sir Thos.A. Jones PRHA. 1889

Londonderry was elected MP for Down in 1878, and took his seat in the House of Lords in 1884 – the year he succeeded to the title. He was extremely wealthy and owned vast estates in Durham, as well as his Irish seat, Mount Stewart in Co Down. His town house, Londonderry House, became one of the most fashionable meeting places in London during the marquis's lifetime. Lady Londonderry was a celebrated hostess, and Edward VII was a frequent guest at the house.

He served as Lord Lieutenant of Ireland from 1886 to 1889. While in Dublin, Londonderry is said to have handled affairs of state with 'tact and courage'. His Chief Secretary was Arthur Balfour. Londonderry was a staunch unionist who opposed the Home Rule Bill of 1893 after his return to London, and later lead the Ulster Unionist Council's opposition to Asquith's 1906 Home Rule Bill. In 1912 he was the second signatory to the Ulster Covenant, after Sir Edward Carson. He died of pneumonia in April 1915.

This is an extraordinarily formal portrait of the marquis as Grand Master of the Order of St Patrick. He is wearing the pale blue mantle of the Order, and the chain, badge and star are prominently displayed. The star of the Order of the Garter and the Order of Victoria are also worn; the former was awarded to Londonderry in 1888.

PROVENANCE – Probably commissioned by Lord Londonderry *c.*1889.

LITERATURE
W.G. Strickland, *A Dictionary of Irish Artists*, 2 vols (Dublin, 1913) ii, 564

EXHIBITED
Art of the State, 1993

* Two other paintings listed by T.A. Jones may have been destroyed in the 1941 fire: portraits of John, 7th Duke of Marlborough, and John Poyntz, Earl Spencer.

after Thomas Lawrence (1769-1830)

Thomas Lawrence was the most successful and widely known portrait painter in England in the early 19th century. Having had a remarkable talent for drawing people as a young child, he quickly advanced through the art world. He entered the Royal Academy Schools in London in 1787, and five years later was chosen by George III as Painter in Ordinary to the King, the successor to Joshua Reynolds. He remained the favourite portraitist to royalty and the aristocracy throughout his life. In 1814 the Prince Regent commissioned Lawrence to paint all the military leaders and heads of state who had sided with the allies against Napoleon during the Napoleonic wars. He was elected president of the Royal Academy in 1820.

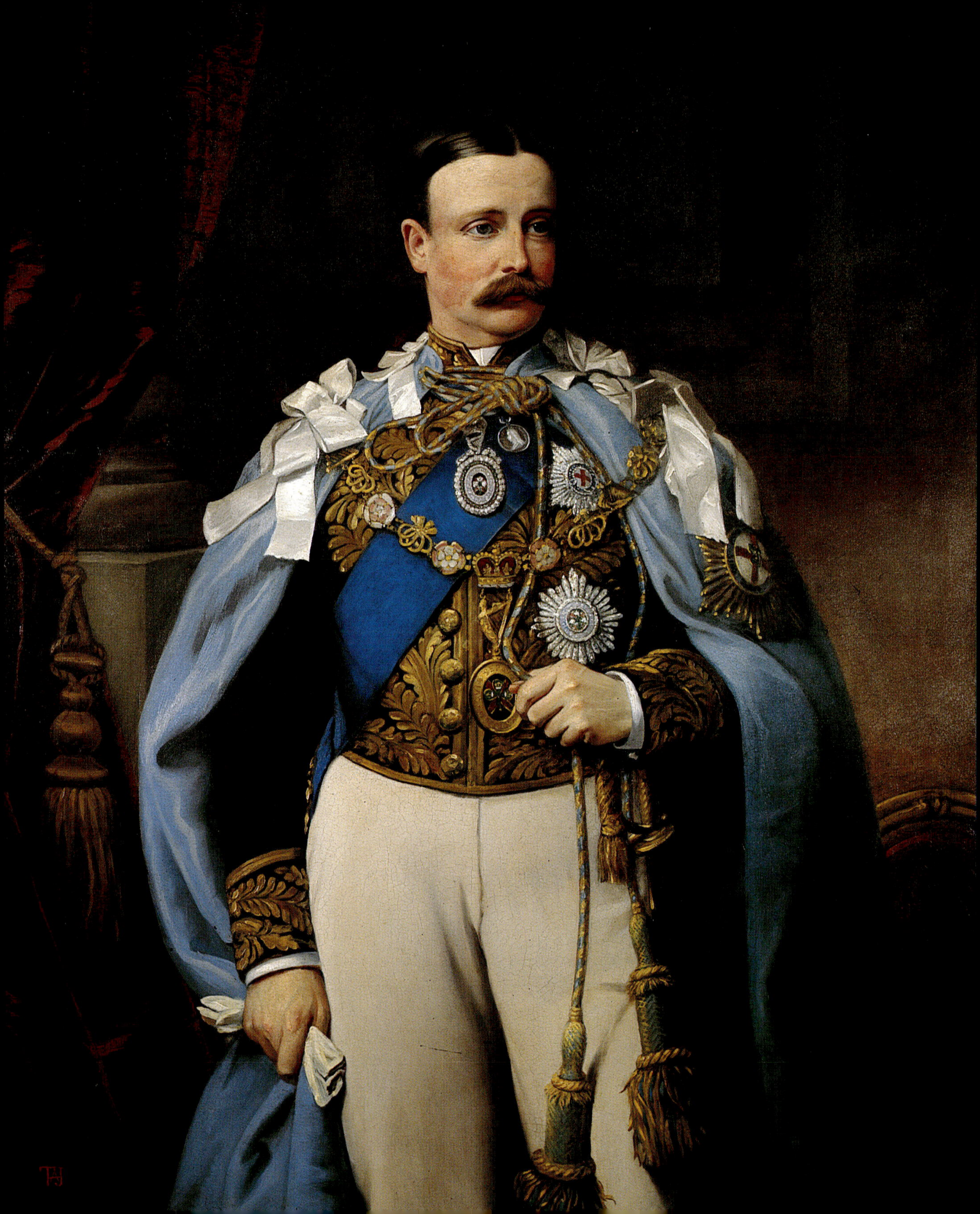

Thomas Alfred Jones, *Portrait of Charles Vane-Temple-Stewart (1852-1915)*, 6th Marquis of Londonderry

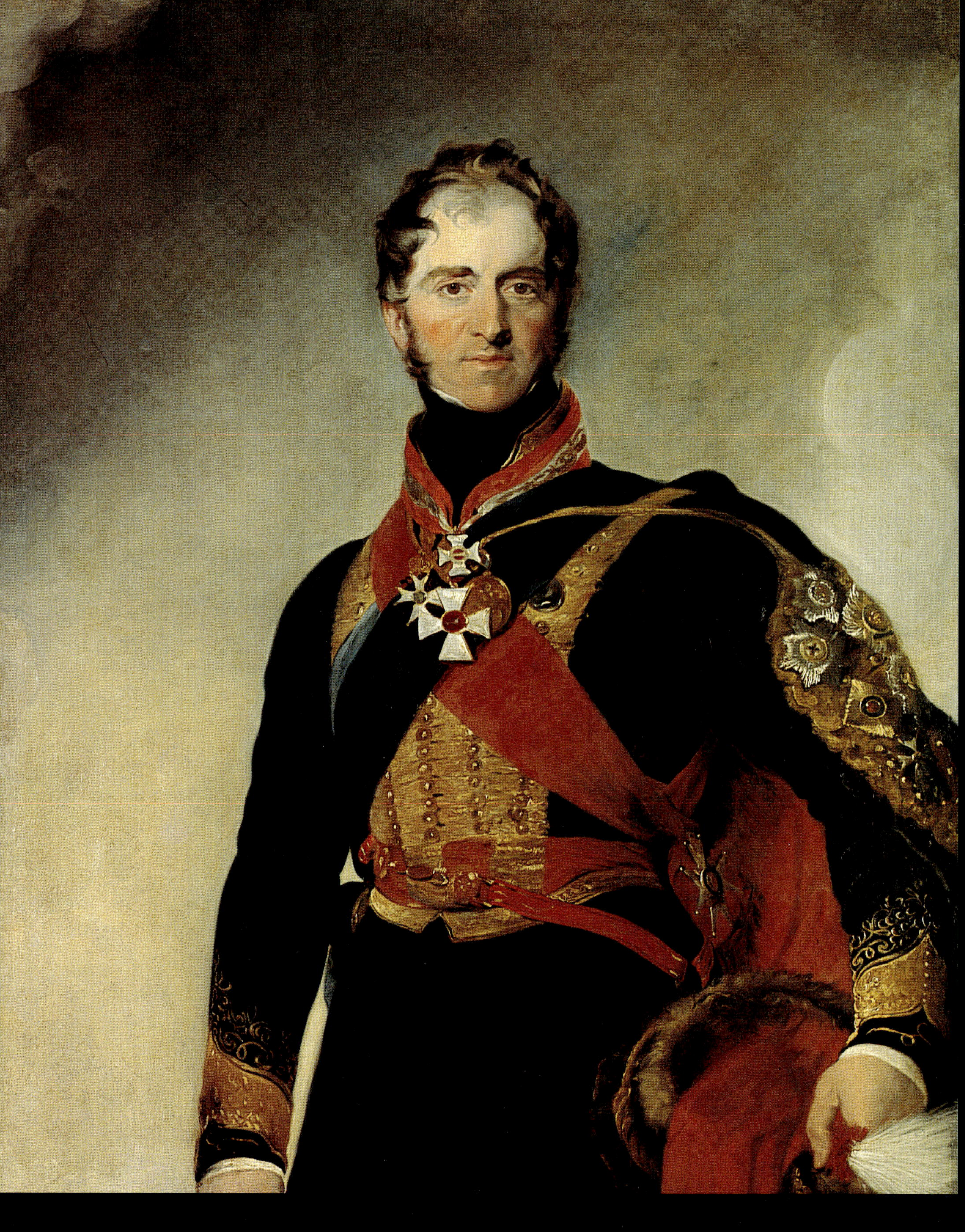

Lawrence frequently presented his sitters in a theatrical way, lighting them from above rather than in the more natural manner of Reynolds or Gainsborough. His approach was more suited to the romantic taste of the Regency period. Indeed, the painter B.R. Haydon wrote, 'Lawrence was suited to the age, and the age to Lawrence. He flattered its vanities, pampered its weaknesses, and met its meretricious tastes.' As to his ability to capture the sitter's features, his contemporary, David Wilkie, stated that 'those who knew and could compare the heads he painted with the originals must have been struck with the liberties he would take in changing and refining the features before him.' However, Wilkie also made the point that Lawrence was concerned with catching the expression rather than copying the features.

Lawrence was extremely disorganised. He kept no business records, which, considering the amount of commissions he took on, is surprising. He was frequently in debt, and many of his paintings were finished years after he had begun them. He employed assistants and apprentices throughout his career, and it is likely that some of the Dublin Castle paintings were painted by these using Lawrence's drawings or original paintings. At the time of his death in 1830, there were 150 unfinished portraits in his studio.*

Portrait of Henry William Paget (1768-1854), 1st Marquis of Anglesey

oil on canvas, 124 x 99 cm

Anglesey was born in London in 1768 and educated at Oxford. He was MP for Caernarvon from 1790 to 1796. At the same time, he became active in the Staffordshire Volunteers, a regiment which he raised himself. He turned to a military career, was active in the Peninsular Wars, and was one of the heroes of Waterloo, where he was in command of the cavalry and artillery. He lost a leg as a result of a wound sustained at the battle. An anecdote of the time recalls that Anglesey was said to have exclaimed 'By God, sir, I've lost my leg,' to which his commanding officer, the Duke of Wellington, responded 'By God, sir, so you have,' before continuing on with the battle. A few weeks after Waterloo, in July 1815, he was created Marquis of Anglesey by the Prince Regent in recognition of his bravery and military skill.

He succeeded Wellesley as Lord Lieutenant in February 1828, and, despite his association with the Tories, he was impartial in his dealings in Ireland. In November 1828, he was reprimanded for his sympathy towards the Catholic Association, and subsequently recalled to London. After Anglesey's second appointment as Lord Lieutenant in 1830, he was less popular with the Irish, as the Catholic Association was now seeking a repeal of the Act of Union, something which the Marquess could not support. He was replaced by Wellesley in September 1833.

Anglesey was married twice. He was divorced in 1810 from his first wife, the mother of his eight children. In the same year he married Charlotte Wellesley, and the couple had a further ten children. He was active in political life until the 1840s, when he eventually retired at the age of eighty-four. A monument to him was erected near the family seat at Plas Newydd in North Wales.

The original version of this painting by Lawrence is full length. It dates to c.1816-17, and is in the possession of the present Marquis of Anglesey at Plas Newydd. A replica of the painting which was commissioned from Lawrence is in the Duke of Wellington's collection at Apsley House. There are numerous studio copies and versions of the painting in existence. Many of these, like the Dublin Castle painting, are half-length versions. These testify to the popularity of this image of the marquis as the dashing hero of Waterloo, silhouetted against the smoke of battle. He wears the uniform of the 7th Hussars, and has the sashes of the Royal Hanoverian Guelphic Order and the Bath across his chest. Around his neck he wears the crosses of the Orders of Theresa of Austria, St George of Russia, and Wilhelm of Holland. His medals from the Peninsular Wars and the Battle of Waterloo are also displayed. It should be remembered that by the time he came to Ireland, Anglesey was quite a bit older and less glamorous then he appears in this portrait.

PROVENANCE – Unknown. Located in the Viceregal Lodge in 1936 (A77/7/1/39).

LITERATURE
Catalogue of the Dublin Exhibition of Arts, Industries and Manufactures, 1872, 175, no. 213

COMPARATIVE LITERATURE
Kenneth Garlick, *Sir Thomas Lawrence – A Complete Catalogue of Oil Paintings* (Oxford, 1989) 138, no. 33
S. and R. Redgrave, *A Century of British Artists* (London, 1949)

EXHIBITED
Dublin Exhibition of Arts, Industries and Manufactures, 1872 (213)
Art of the State, 1993

* This copy may have been painted by Thomas Cooley (1795-1872), who was appointed Portrait Painter to the Lord Lieutenant in 1828 (W.G. Strickland, *A Dictionary of Irish Artists*, 2 vols (Dublin, 1913) i, 206).

Portrait of Richard, 1st Marquis of Wellesley (1760-1842)

oil on canvas, 128 x 103 cm

Born in Dublin in 1760, Wellesley was the elder brother of the Duke of Wellington and son of the Earl of Mornington. He entered the Irish House of Lords at the age of twenty-one, having succeeded to his father's title. Three years later, he became an MP in the English House of Commons and began a distinguished political career. In 1798 he was made Governor-General of

Bengal, and was in office when the Battle of Seringapatam took place in 1799. He was made Marquis of Wellesley the same year, and returned to England in 1805 where he was Foreign Secretary from 1809 to 1812. Having failed in a bid to become Prime Minister in 1812, he temporarily withdrew from active politics.

In 1821 he returned to public life when he was made Lord Lieutenant of Ireland for the first time. He was involved in a number of reforms, including the establishment of the police force, the repeal of Union Duties, and the suppression of secret societies such as the Whiteboys. Wellesley was in favour of Catholic Emancipation and supported the Catholic Emancipation bill, which became law shortly after his first term of office ended in 1828. In 1825 he married an American Roman Catholic, Marianne Caton of Baltimore, at the Viceregal Lodge, where the Anglican wedding ceremony was solemnised by Dr Murray, the Roman Catholic Archbishop of Dublin. His second term of office from 1833 to 1835 was characterised by increased agrarian agitation, which had been aggravated by the Reform Bill.

The Dublin Castle painting is a copy of a Thomas Lawrence portrait of Wellesley, the original of which was commissioned by the sitter in 1811, and later presented to Queen Victoria. It is now at Windsor Castle (exhibited at the RA in 1813). The marquis is shown seated, wearing the garter, ribbon and star of the Order of the Garter. The choice of this Lawrence painting as a source for the Dublin Castle painting is rather odd, given the fact that Wellesley was painted in the more appropriate costume of the Master of the Order of St Patrick on at least two occasions. Details of how it came to the Castle are not known. It may have been selected by the marquis or his family because it is one of the best known images of Wellesley. Several copies and replicas are in existence.

PROVENANCE – Unknown

LITERATURE

Catalogue of the Dublin Exhibition of Arts, Industries and Manufactures, 1872, no. 221

Walter Armstrong, *Sir Thomas Lawrence* (London, 1913) 189

Kenneth Garlick, *Sir Thomas Lawrence – A Complete Catalogue of Oil Paintings* (Oxford, 1989) 178

EXHIBITED

Dublin Exhibition of Arts, Industries and Manufactures, 1872 (221)

Portrait of Charles, 1st Earl Whitworth (1752-1825)

oil on canvas, 128 x 102 cm

Viscount Whitworth, later Earl (1815), was Lord Lieutenant from 1813 to 1817. A distinguished diplomat, Whitworth served in Warsaw and St Petersburg in the 1780s and 1790s. He served as ambassador to Paris from 1802 to 1803, where he had to deal with the ambitions and tirades of Napoleon. After a number of years of relative retirement, he succeeded the Duke of Richmond as Lord Lieutenant of Ireland in 1813. His return to public life may have been helped by his mother-in-law, Lady Catherine Cope, who had married the Prime Minister, Lord Liverpool. Whitworth was famous in Dublin for laying the foundation stone of the General Post Office. He was the first lord lieutenant to use the Chapel Royal at Dublin Castle, and the stained glass chancel window in that building was acquired by the earl in France, and donated to the Chapel. Whitworth continued the building and renovation work of his predecessors, adding an Ionic portico to the Viceregal Lodge. The Wellington Monument, designed by Robert Smirke, was begun during his time in Dublin. In 1820 he retired from public life and settled at Knole Park.

This painting is a copy or version of a painting by Sir Thomas Lawrence (c.1806-07), now in the Louvre. The original was probably commissioned to commemorate the earl's time as ambassador to Paris. His statesmanlike qualities are emphasised in the erect pose and in the device of the letter, which the earl holds. The sitter is shown wearing the star and ribbon of the Order of the Bath. An engraving of the Lawrence painting was commissioned from Charles Turner by Whitworth from Dublin Castle in 1813. A number of copies of the Lawrence painting are in existence; one half-length exactly like the Dublin Castle one was in the collection of the Countess De La Warr, a direct descendant of the earl's wife, the Duchess of Dorset.

PROVENANCE – Unknown

LITERATURE

Catalogue of the Dublin Exhibition of Arts, Industries and Manufactures, 1872, no. 217

Kenneth Garlick, *Sir Thomas Lawrence – A Complete Catalogue of Oil Paintings* (Oxford, 1989) 282

Richard Walker, *Regency Portraits* (NPG, London, 1985) i, 553

EXHIBITED

Dublin Exhibition of Arts, Industries and Manufactures, 1872 (217)

Robert McInnes (1801-1886)

Robert McInnes was a Scottish artist who exhibited at the Royal Academy from 1846 to 1866. He spent a number of years in Italy in the 1840s, and his most famous works are genre scenes based on his experiences there.

Portrait of Thomas Hamilton (1780-1858), 9th Earl of Haddington

c.1837, oil on canvas, 128 x 101.5 cm

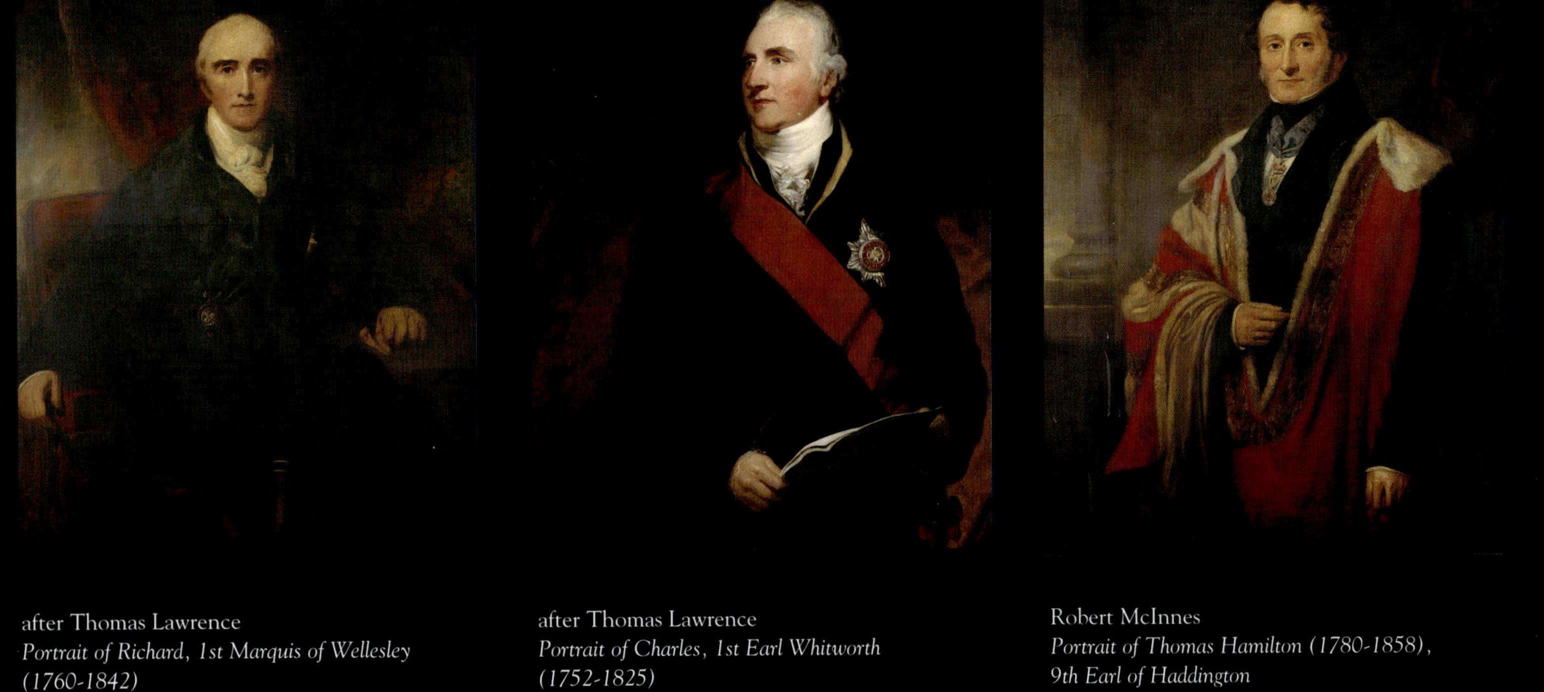

after Thomas Lawrence
Portrait of Richard, 1st Marquis of Wellesley (1760-1842)

after Thomas Lawrence
Portrait of Charles, 1st Earl Whitworth (1752-1825)

Robert McInnes
Portrait of Thomas Hamilton (1780-1858), 9th Earl of Haddington

Part of a Scottish noble family, Haddington succeeded his father as Earl of Haddington in 1828, and was appointed Lord Lieutenant of Ireland by Sir Robert Peel in 1834. He resigned when the administration fell the following year. His period in office was too brief to make any lasting impact. He served as First Lord of the Admiralty from 1841 to 1846. He confounded the diarist Greville, who wrote of Haddington's refusal of the position of Governor-General of India in 1841, 'It is a curious circumstance that a man so unimportant, so destitute not only of shining but of plausible qualities, without interest or influence, should by a mere combination of accidental circumstances have had at his disposal three of the greatest and most important offices under the crown...'

This is a version of a painting which was recorded as being in the collection of the Earl of Haddington at Tyninghame in the 1960s. This rather formal portrait shows the earl dressed in peer's robes, with the ribbon and badge of the Order of St Patrick around his neck. The Tyninghame version was engraved in mezzotint by W. Walker in 1839. A stipple engraving after the painting by J. Brown (published 1846) is in the National Gallery of Ireland.* The latter was used to illustrate H. Ryall's *Portraits of Eminent Conservatives and Statesmen* (1846).

Comparative literature
Adrian le Harivel (ed.), *National Gallery of Ireland – Illustrated Summary Catalogue of Prints and Sculpture* (Dublin, 1988) 359, cat. no. 10,887*

attributed to Frederick Richard Say (1805-1860)

Frederick Richard Say, the son of a famous engraver, William Say, was born in London. He exhibited at the Royal Academy from 1825 to 1854, and was based in London. He built up a very successful portrait practice; his sitters included Prince Albert and the Prime Minister, Earl Grey. He also painted a number of figures with Irish connections. In 1837 he painted the 3rd Earl of Roden wearing the sash, star and badge of the Order of St Patrick. A portrait of Lord Powerscourt by Say was included in the 1984 Powerscourt sale. A number of his portraits were engraved – a testament to their popularity. His work is sometimes confused with that of the young Thomas Lawrence.

Portrait of Thomas Philip de Grey (1781-1859), 2nd Earl de Grey
oil on canvas, 127 x 102.5 cm

Born in Whitehall, de Grey succeeded as Baron of Grantham in 1786. He became 2nd Earl de Grey and took on the surname de Grey in 1833. He was First Lord of the Admiralty from 1834 to 1835. In September 1841 he was appointed Lord Lieutenant of Ireland, a post he held until the summer of 1844. His period in office proved to be one of disappointment in which de Grey failed

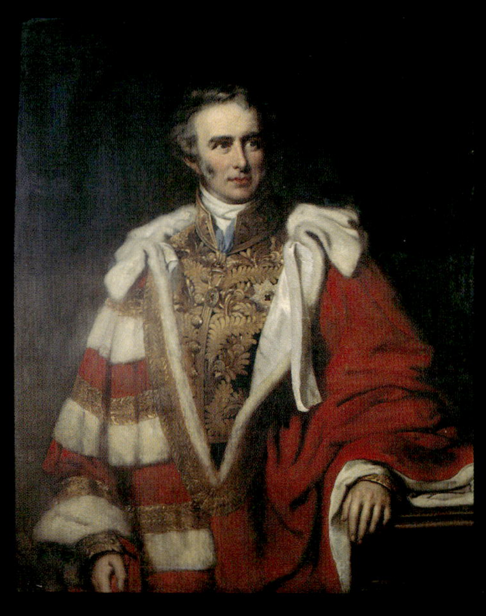

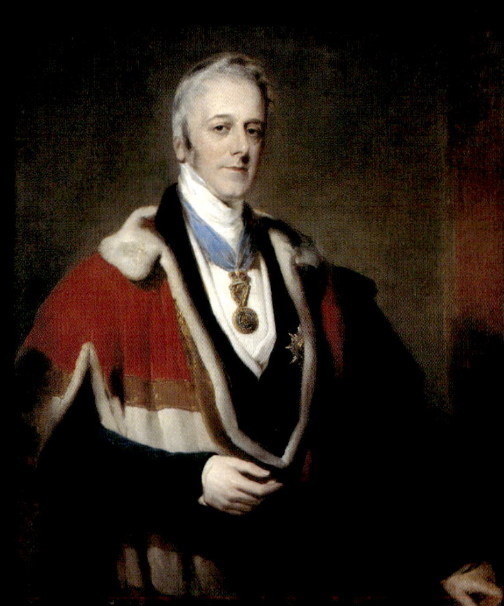

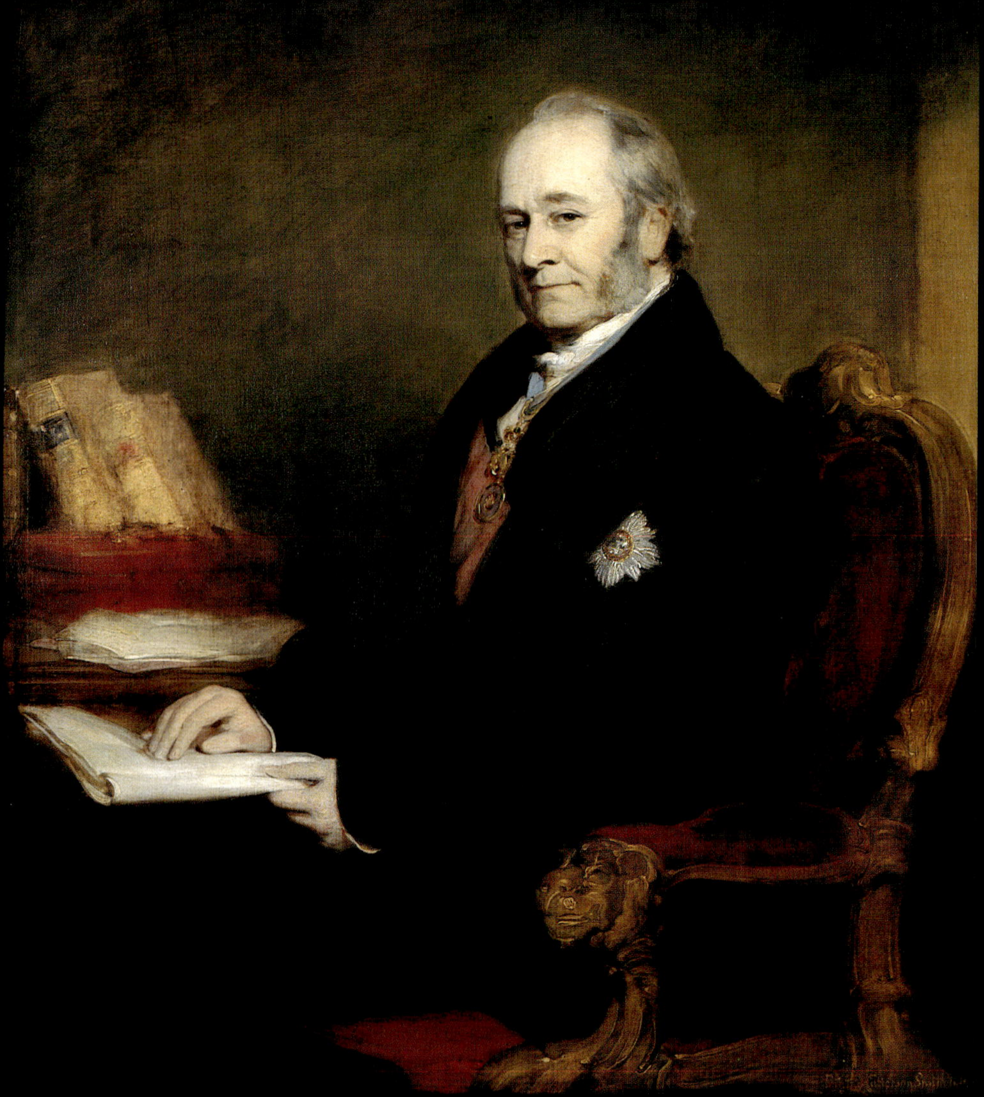

attributed to Frederick Richard Say
Portrait of Thomas Philip de Grey (1781-1859),
2nd Earl de Grey

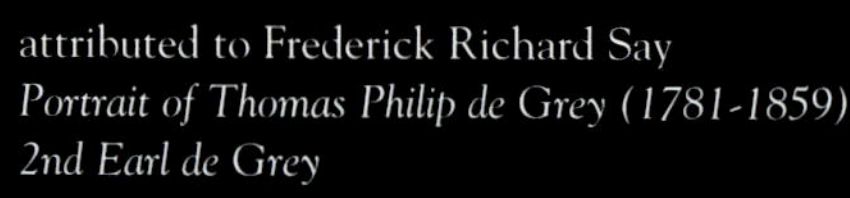

Stephen Catterson Smith
Portrait of John William Ponsonby (1781-1847),
4th Earl of Bessborough

Stephen Catterson Smith
Portrait of William A'Court (1779-1860),
Baron Heytesbury

to instigate Sir Robert Peel's policy of placating the growing Catholic middle classes. He refused to win over their favour through patronage or other measures, and was replaced by Lord Heytesbury. He is perhaps best known as the first president of the Royal Institute of British Architects, which was founded in 1834.

De Grey is shown wearing the red and white peer's robes over a gold uniform. The star of St Patrick is visible on the right-hand side, pinned onto the gold. The pose and appearance of the sitter is very similar to that of a portrait by F.R. Say, dated 1845 (photograph in the Heinz Archive, National Portrait Gallery, London).

PROVENANCE – Unknown

Stephen Catterson Smith (1806-1872)

Catterson Smith, an Englishman by birth, trained at the Royal Academy Schools in London before moving to Ireland in 1839, working initially in the Derry area. He settled in Dublin in 1845, and was a regular exhibitor at the RHA, of which he became president in 1859. He was painter to the lords lieutenant for many years, having established himself as a portrait painter early in his career.

Portrait of William A'Court (1779-1860), Baron Heytesbury

c.1846, oil on canvas, 129 x 109 cm
signed bottom right: Pinxt Catterson Smith RHA

Heytesbury was a distinguished diplomat who had served as Envoy-Extraordinary to Spain in 1822, ambassador to Portugal in 1824, and ambassador to Russia from 1828 to 1832. In 1828 he was created Baron Heytesbury of Heytesbury in Wiltshire. In 1835 Peel nominated him as Governor-General of India, but the administration fell before Heytesbury could accept. His lord lieutenancy of Ireland (1844-46) coincided with the early days of the Famine. He was already warning Sir Robert Peel of the potential disaster in his correspondence of 1845, when the first signs of a serious potato blight were becoming apparent. Heytesbury was active in raising subscriptions on behalf of victims of the Famine, but his days as Lord Lieutenant ended with the fall of Peel's government in June 1846.

Heytesbury is shown seated at his writing desk. Catterson Smith has attempted to give a sense of the informality of the sitter by showing him consulting his papers and seated in profile with his head turned to the viewer. The star and badge of the Order of St Patrick are clearly but subtly displayed. Despite the pose of the figure and the warm tonality of the red, gold and green in the background, the overall effect of the portrait is rather forced and stiff.

LITERATURE
Anne Crookshank and the Knight of Glin, *Painters of Ireland* (London, 1978) 134

EXHIBITED
RHA, 1846 (89)

Portrait of John William Ponsonby (1781-1847), 4th Earl of Bessborough

c.1846, oil on canvas, 127 x 102 cm
signed bottom right: Catterson Smith RHA

Bessborough was a member of the Ponsonby family who owned lands in Carlow, Kilkenny and Tipperary. The family seat was Bessborough House, Co Kilkenny (now demolished). Bessborough was MP for Kilkenny in the 1820s and early 1830s, but was opposed by Catholic Association sympathisers, supported by Daniel O'Connell, and narrowly missed losing his seat on a couple of occasions. He moved to a constituency in England in the 1830s. Despite this, Bessborough was a supporter of Catholic Emancipation and reform, and became a friend of Daniel O'Connell. His appointment as Lord Lieutenant in July 1846, the first resident Irishman to be appointed for a generation, was greeted with approval. Bessborough did all in his power to curtail the effects of the potato famine, but his efforts were inhibited by the existing administration and the scale of the disaster. He died less than a year after taking office on 16th May 1847, the day after Daniel O'Connell died in Italy. The death of a lord lieutenant in office was a rare event, and Bessborough was given a State funeral by the Castle authorities.

This portrait shows the earl in peer's robes, wearing the star and badge of the Order of St Patrick. There is a similar portrait of the earl, in oval form, in the collection of the National Gallery of Ireland, and this may have formed the basis of the Dublin Castle painting.

COMPARATIVE LITERATURE
Anne Crookshank and the Knight of Glin, *Irish Portraits 1660-1860* (Paul Mellon Foundation for British Art, London, 1969) 72

Solomon Joseph Solomon (1860-1927)

Solomon Joseph Solomon was a fashionable portrait painter in London from the late 1880s until his death in 1927. He came from a prominent Jewish family, and, in 1906, was only the second Jew to be elected a Royal Academician.

Solomon trained at the Royal Academy Schools, where he later taught, and at the Ecole des Beaux-Arts in Paris under the academic painter Cabanel. He maintained his commitment to academic painting throughout his career, although he was a founding member of the more progressive New English Art Club in 1886.

He moved from an interest in biblical and mythological subjects to a concentration on portraiture. In the latter field he received many distinguished commissions from politicians and the royal family. He also painted numerous portraits of his own family. During the First World War, Solomon was involved in the development of camouflage, which required him to work at the front in France. He worked on aeroplane camouflage, the concealment of ground targets – for which he became an expert on sciagraphy – and the improvement of Observation Post Trees, one of the successes of camouflage work during the war.

Portrait of George, 5th Earl of Cadogan (1840-1915)

c.1904, oil on canvas, 131.5 x 102.2 cm
signed bottom right (entwined monogram): SJS

Cadogan was Lord Lieutenant from June 1895 until August 1902. He was related to the Marquis of Wellesley and the Duke of Wellington through his mother, Mary Wellesley, who was a niece of the two men. In 1873 he took his seat in the House of Lords. Under Lord Salisbury, he was responsible for Irish affairs from 1886 to 1892, and in 1887 he introduced the Land Act. He was concerned with land reform in Ireland, and supported more liberal terms for tenants. As Lord Lieutenant he sponsored the 1899 Agricultural and Technical Instruction Act, which set up the new Department of Agriculture for Ireland. In 1900 he was elected the first mayor of Chelsea, where he owned a vast amount of property and built model dwellings for his tenants. He was married twice and had eight children.

He was for a time advisor to Queen Victoria on domestic affairs, and in 1891 she made him a knight of the Order of the Garter. The queen paid her final visit to Ireland in April 1900 when Cadogan was in office. At the time that Solomon was working on this portrait, he had an unfinished portrait of the queen in his studio – a work he had abandoned due to her death. Cadogan commissioned a finished version of this, which was hung in Culford Hall, Norfolk.

This portrait is a fine example of the skill of Solomon Joseph Solomon. Through a dramatic use of light and shade, he draws attention to the face of Lord Cadogan. The earl is shown wearing the cloak and insignia of the Order of St Patrick. His body is framed by the architecture of the column and the tower of the Castle in the background. Solomon uses thick impasto brushstrokes, and creates a strong feeling of movement and immediacy in what is otherwise a very formal portrait. This and the interest in light and shade reflect his admiration for the work of Velazquez.

PROVENANCE – Presented to Dublin Castle by Earl of Cadogan, 1904. It was located in the Viceregal Lodge in 1936 (A77/7/1/39).

LITERATURE
National Archives OPW 589/05: letter from Earl of Cadogan to George Holmes, 27th December 1904

COMPARATIVE LITERATURE
Olga Somech Phillips, *Solomon J. Solomon – A Memoir to Peace and War* (London, 1933)
Jenny Pery, *Solomon J. Solomon R.A.* (Ben Uri Art Gallery, London, 1990)

EXHIBITED
Royal Academy, 1904 (357)

Emily Way (fl.1886-1896)

Way resided in London and exhibited portraits at the Royal Academy from 1886 to 1896. Very little is known of her life. She did paint a number of portraits of Irish sitters, including one of Major General J.C. Dormer, which was exhibited at the RHA in 1887. There is a portrait by Way of James Wilson, a successful spirit merchant, in the Belfast Harbour Commissioners Office. She also painted a number of members of the nobility, including the Earl of Montagu (1887) and the Earl and Countess of Sandwich (1888).

Portrait of Lawrence Dundas (1844-1929), 1st Earl of Zetland

1892, oil on canvas, 138 x 95 cm, signed bottom right: E.C. Way / 1892

The Earl of Zetland was educated in Harrow and Cambridge, and was MP for Richmond from 1872 to 1873. He was Lord Lieutenant from 1889 to August 1892. His time in Ireland coincided with some of the most difficult years of the Land Wars, and Zetland was rewarded for his diplomatic handling of affairs by being made Marquis of Zetland and Earl of Ronaldsay.

Apart from his terrible short-sightedness, Zetland is remembered as a keen sportsman. He was interested in fox hunting, deer stalking and fishing, and was a member of the English Jockey Club from 1875. His trophies formed the centrepiece of the table at formal dinners during his 'reign' at the Castle.

This portrait, which is currently undergoing restoration, shows the earl in official lord lieutenant attire – the collar and badge of St Patrick are prominently displayed. Over this, the artist

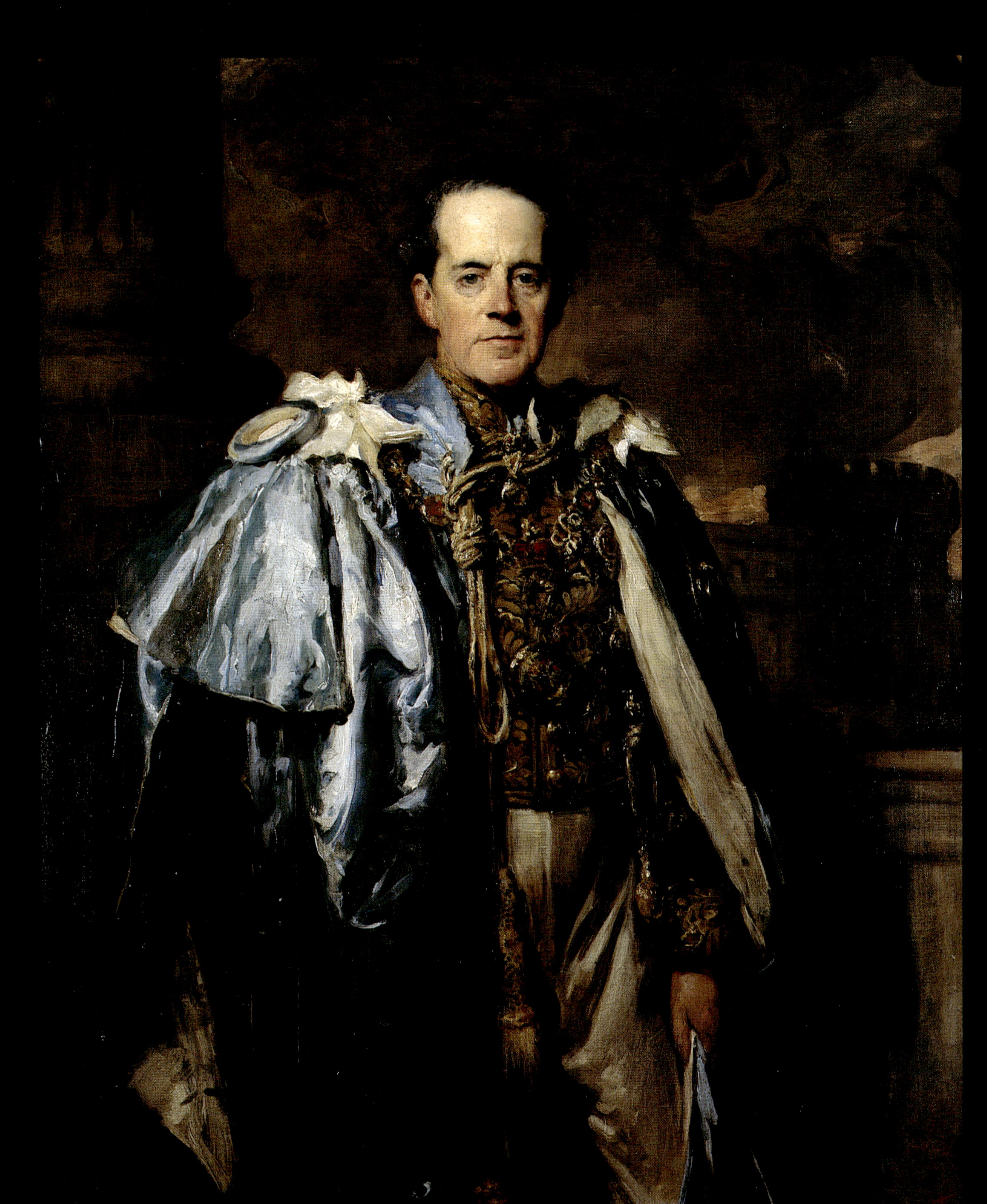

Solomon Joseph Solomon , *Portrait of George, 5th Earl of Cadogan* (1840-1915)

shows him wearing a rather flamboyant fur coat. Perhaps this is a reference to the earl's rather eccentric personality and his preference for the outdoor life. According to the earl's obituary in the *Daily Telegraph*, he once made an official tour of the west coast as Lord Lieutenant, attired in oilskins and sou'wester.

PROVENANCE – Commissioned by Zetland c.1892, and presented to Dublin Castle.

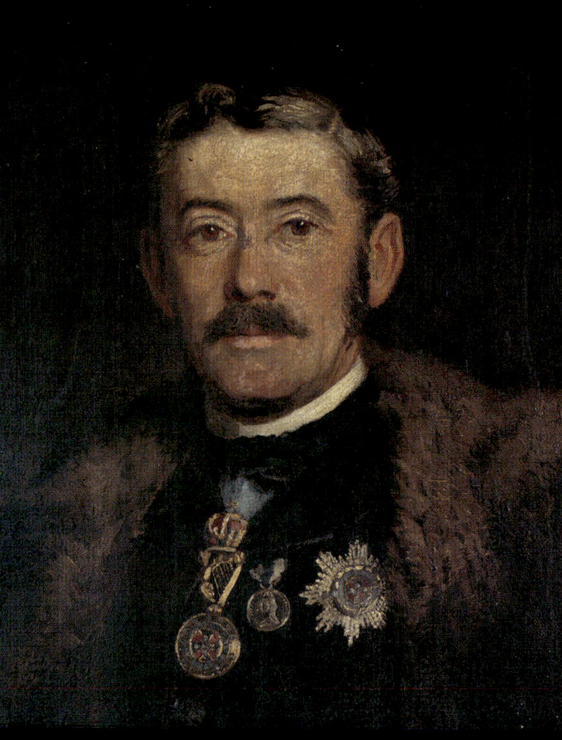

Emily Way
Portrait of Lawrence Dundas (1844-1929), 1st Earl of Zetland
(detail; awaiting restoration)

Unknown

Portrait of Charles Chetwynd (1777-1849), 2nd Earl Talbot
c.1839, oil on canvas, 127 x 102 cm

Talbot succeeded to the peerage in 1793. In the late 1790s he was voluntary attaché at the British Embassy in Russia, where Lord Whitworth was ambassador. In 1800 he returned to England, and concentrated on improving his estates in Staffordshire and pursuing his interest in farming. In the same year he married Frances Thomasine Lambert (d.1819), daughter of the owner of Beau Parc, Co Meath. During Talbot's lord lieutenancy (1817-1821), his main area of concern was in agriculture, and he was given the Freedom of the City of Drogheda in recognition of his contribution. His period in office is remembered for the glittering visit of George IV in the early autumn of 1821.

This painting shows the earl as a much older man than he was at the time of his lord lieutenancy. From his features, and from other dated portraits, it would appear to date to the 1830s or early 1840s. The pose is very like that of the earl in an engraving by J.B. Hunt, after a work by J. Bostock. The costume is exactly like a portrait of the earl by John Linnell (1839) in the collection of the Earl of Shrewsbury, in which he also appears to be about the same age as he is in the Dublin painting.

PROVENANCE – Unknown

Unknown
Portrait of Charles Chetwynd (1777-1849), 2nd Earl Talbot

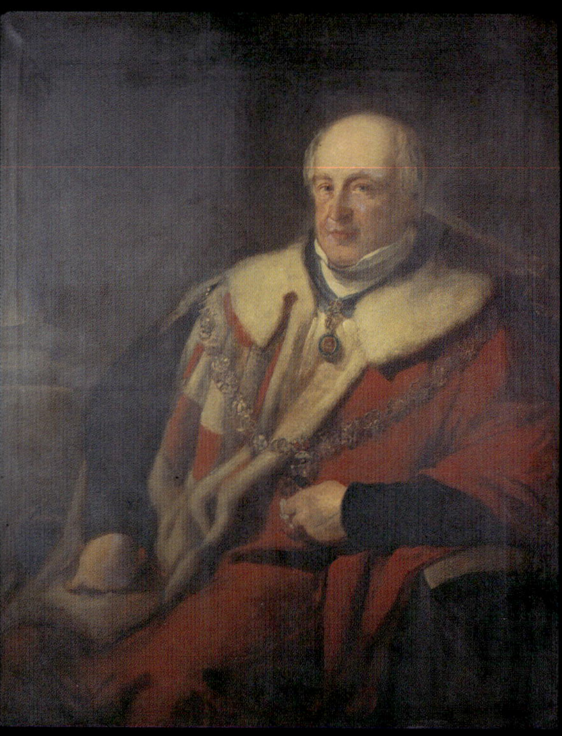

Royal Portraits

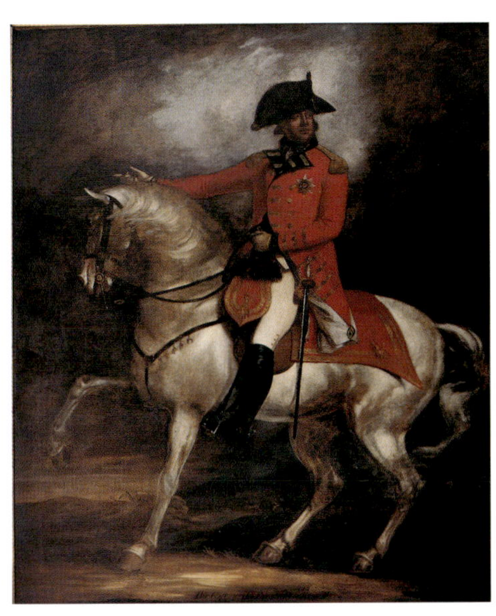

after William Beechey
Portrait of George III (1738-1820) on horseback

The Office of Public Works has portraits of all the British monarchs from George II to Queen Victoria in its collection at Dublin Castle. (There are also a number of royal portraits in the collection at the Royal Hospital, Kilmainham, including many pre-Georgian examples.) Some of these were presented to the Viceregal Lodge by lords lieutenant or by members of the royal family. Over the years, the portraits were moved between the Castle and the Viceregal Lodge; a number of them have only come to the Castle in recent years. After independence, these portraits naturally became undesirable, as the buildings of State were being transformed into use for the new establishment. Douglas Hyde had any remaining royal portraits removed from Áras an Uachtaráin (formerly the Viceregal Lodge) when he became the first President of Ireland in the 1930s. Most of the portraits spent the interim years in storage in various locations, mainly in Dublin Castle and its surrounding buildings. Since the refurbishment of the Castle in the late 1980s, the decision has been made to take these works out of storage and rehang them. They represent an important part of the history of the Castle and its former function. Many of them are in a poor state of repair and an ongoing programme of conservation is in place.

after William Beechey (1753-1839)

Beechey was born in Burford in Oxfordshire, and appears initially to have embarked on a legal career. However, in 1782 he entered the Royal Academy Schools, and specialised in portraiture. He worked in Norwich from 1782 to 1787, after which he returned to London, where he attracted the attention of George III. He was appointed Portrait Painter to Queen Charlotte in 1793. He was initially a favourite of George III, although his popularity waned slightly after 1804, when, according to Oliver Millar, he was subjected to 'an outburst at Windsor', and told that the king 'wanted no more of his pictures'.

Beechey ran a successful portrait practice, but was overtaken by Thomas Lawrence in the early years of the 19th century. His solid approach to portraiture suited the taste of the king and queen better than the more flamboyant Thomas Lawrence, who was favoured by the future George IV. Beechey, while paying careful attention to the drawing and painting of his portraits, created rather dull works which lack spontaneity. He retired from painting in 1836 at the age of eighty-three, and died at Hampstead three years later.

Portrait of George III (1738-1820) on horseback
oil on canvas, 286 x 247 cm

George III, the grandson of George II, succeeded to the throne in 1760. His father died when he was thirteen years old, and the young prince was very influenced by his mother,

Augusta, daughter of Frederick II of Saxe-Coburg. She is believed to have encouraged her son to develop a rather old-fashioned and authoritarian view of kingship. In 1761 he married Charlotte, sister of the Duke of Mecklenburg, and the couple lived a relatively frugal and quiet domestic life. They had fifteen children, including the future George IV.

While George III went through periods of great unpopularity, his personality made him a well-liked figure, especially among the middle classes. He was extremely conservative, and conscious of his position as defender of the realm. He bitterly opposed American independence, and sought full political union with Ireland. George III was frequently caricatured in the popular press for his eccentricities. His passion for farming earned him the nickname Farmer George, and he was renowned for the informality of his private life, where his curiosity into all things mechanical and agricultural led him into long chats with local tenants and peasants. His life was blighted by bouts of insanity, which eventually permanently incapacitated him in 1810, when his son, George, was made Regent until the king's death in 1820.

This portrait of George III mounted on his horse, Adonis, is taken from a larger composition which shows the king with the Prince of Wales, the Duke of York, and other courtiers, reviewing troops in Hyde Park. This original work was painted for George III in 1797-98, and was hanging at Windsor until it was destroyed in the recent fire. The painting was extremely popular; a number of copies exist, including a full-size one in the collection of the Marquis of Anglesey. Beechey was knighted, and became a member of the Royal Academy in the year the work was completed. The painting was engraved by Ward and published in 1799.

Several versions of this painting showing George III alone also exist, and this too was made into a print. (There is one on display in Westport House, Co Mayo.) The king is dressed in military uniform and wears the star of the Garter. He points to the (imagined) troops in the distance. Beechey has based this portrait on the royal equestrian portrait which can be traced in the history of art from Titian (Charles V) to Velazquez (Philip II) to the more obvious English precedent of van Dyck (Charles I). The origin of the subject belongs to the classical equestrian monument of Roman times.

PROVENANCE – Presented by Earl of Hardwicke to Viceregal Lodge; hung in dining room of that house (1909 inventory); painting was still located in Viceregal Lodge (Governor-General's Lodge) in 1936 (A77/7/1/39, p.15). Put into storage at the National Gallery in March 1969, where it remained until late 1980s. Restored in 1990s and displayed in Dublin Castle.

LITERATURE
OPW file 14882/28

COMPARATIVE LITERATURE
Oliver Millar, *The Later Georgian Pictures in the Collection of Her Majesty, The Queen*, 2 vols (London, 1969)

after Godfrey Kneller (1645-1723)

Sir Godfrey Kneller was the leading portrait painter in England from his appointment as Principal Painter in 1688 until his death in 1723. He was knighted in 1692, and in 1715 he was created a baronet – an extraordinary achievement for an artist at that time. His academy (founded 1711) was a forerunner of the Royal Academy Schools in London.

Kneller was born in Lubeck in northern Germany, and had been a pupil of Ferdinand Bol, a follower of Rembrandt. Like many other court portraitists, Kneller operated a factory system, employing assistants to produce copies for distribution, and specialist drapery artists to complete the costume of the sitters. In 1716 he painted full-length portraits of George II and Caroline, when they were Prince and Princess of Wales. These were widely copied, and prints of them were published after the accession of George II to the throne in 1727. The artist of the Dublin Castle paintings used prints or copies of these works as the basis for his portraits.

Portrait of George II (1683-1760)
oil on canvas, 122 x 95.5 cm

George II was born in Herrenhausen in 1683, and was brought up by his grandparents, the Elector of Hanover and Electress Sophia, a granddaughter of James I. In 1714 George and his father, George I, came to England, after the death of Queen Anne. Upon the death of his domineering father in 1727, George II lived a more extravagant lifestyle. His and Queen Caroline's coronation was a glittering affair.

The king took an active interest in military affairs and in foreign policy, and in 1743, at the Battle of Dettingen, he was the last English monarch to appear on the battlefield. The most famous incident in his reign was the Jacobite uprising of 1745, when the English army saw Bonnie Prince Charlie and Jacobite pretensions out of British politics once and for all. Prior to his accession, George was Chancellor of Trinity College, Dublin for a number of years.

The king's fondness for Hanover, which he visited regularly, helped add to his unpopularity with the British public, although unlike his father, he did, at least, speak English. He had a constant stream of mistresses, and yet was genuinely devastated by the death of the queen in 1737. At his own death, he left instructions that his remains were to be mixed with hers, and in accordance with his wishes, his coffin, which was open on one side, was linked with hers, and both placed in a stone sarcophagus in Westminster Abbey.

The painting shows George II in his robes as Prince of Wales, with the chain of the Order of the Garter around his shoulders. His right hand holds the pommel of his sword. While there are similarities with Sir Godfrey Kneller's famous portrait of George as Prince of Wales, the pose of the figure with his body turned slightly to the left and his left hand on his hip is quite different. The head of the figure appears to be modelled on that of the Kneller portrait which was widely known from copies and engravings. It is possible that the work is by the Irish artist, Michael Mitchell, who painted the king and his queen for the Mayor's Hall, Dublin, in 1735. He is also recorded as painting full-length portraits of the pair, which once hung in the Tholsel and were last recorded in a sorry state in the Blue Coat School at the beginning of the 19th century. The only fully documented portrait by Mitchell is in Dr Steevens' Hospital in Dublin. It is a portrait of the foundress of that institution, Miss Grizel Steevens, and was painted in 1741. There is some resemblance in the pose, and particularly in the hands, between this portrait and the one of Queen Caroline (see below). The painting of the face is not unlike that of George II.

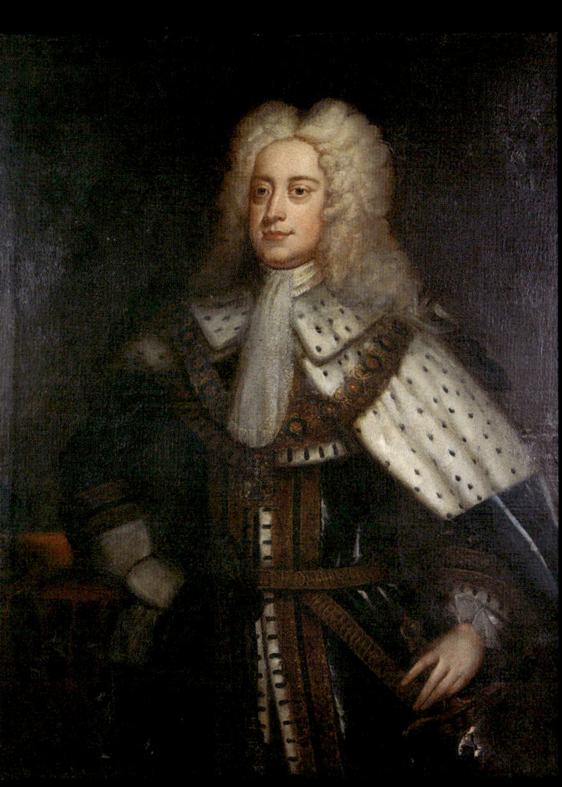

after Godfrey Kneller
Portrait of George II (1683-1760)

PROVENANCE – According to a memo in an OPW file (OPW 14882/28), this painting, and the portrait of Queen Caroline, were lent for safekeeping to the Castle in the 18th century by an unidentified owner. For many years the pair hung over the grand staircase, apparently in the hope that the true owner would recognise and claim them. In 1897 the paintings were removed to the Viceregal Lodge, where they hung in the dining room.*

LITERATURE
OPW file 14882/28

* F.E.R., *Historical Reminiscences of Dublin Castle* (Dublin, 1901) 64, mentions a portrait of George II hanging in the annex at the end of the State corridor. According to F.E.R., it is accompanied by a portrait of Queen Mary; this is probably the portrait of Queen Caroline.

after Godfrey Kneller and Charles Jervas (1675-1739)

Jervas was born in Dublin and trained with Kneller in London in the mid-1690s. He travelled to Paris and Italy before settling in London *c.*1709. He paid regular visits to Ireland after that, when he painted a number of Irish sitters. In 1723 he succeeded Kneller as Principal Painter to the king.

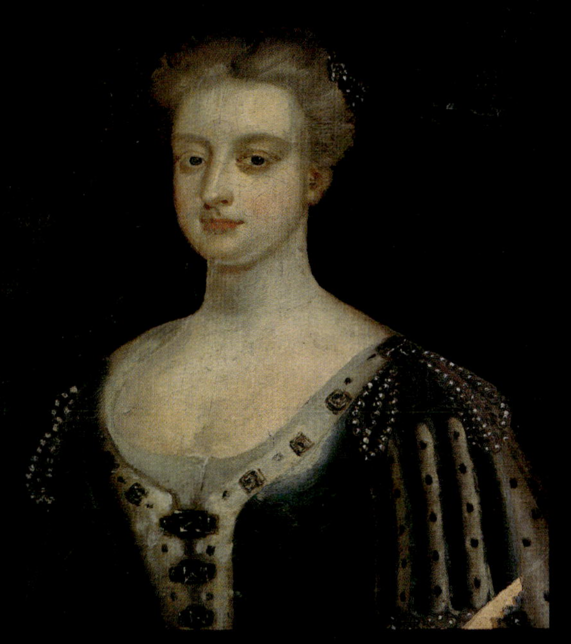

after Godfrey Kneller and Charles Jervas
Portrait of Queen Caroline (1683-1737)
(detail; awaiting restoration)

Portrait of Queen Caroline (1683-1737)

oil on canvas, 122 x 95 cm

Caroline, daughter of the Markgraf of Brandenburg-Anspach, married the future king in Herrenhausen in 1705, and followed him to England in 1714. Caroline was considered an intelligent woman, more intelligent than her husband, whose opinion she influenced. A popular chant of the day was 'You may strut, dapper George, but t'will all be in vain; We know 'tis Queen Caroline, not you that reign.' Lord Chesterfield, on the other hand, had a different opinion of her. He wrote that she 'would have been an agreeable woman in social, if she had not aimed at being a great one in public, life'.

The painting, a pendant to the portrait of George II, appears to combine the compositions of Kneller's *Portrait of Caroline as Princess of Wales*, and Jervas's *Coronation Portrait*. She stands wearing ermine trimmed robes, with her left hand resting on a table, on which sits the coronet of the Princess of Wales. Her pose with her right hand holding up her train is almost exactly like that of Kneller's portrait. The face and costume of the queen are much closer to the Jervas-type portrait. As stated in the previous entry, there is a possibility that this was painted by Michael Mitchell. This painting is currently awaiting conservation.

PROVENANCE – As for George II (see previous entry)

LITERATURE
OPW file 14882/28

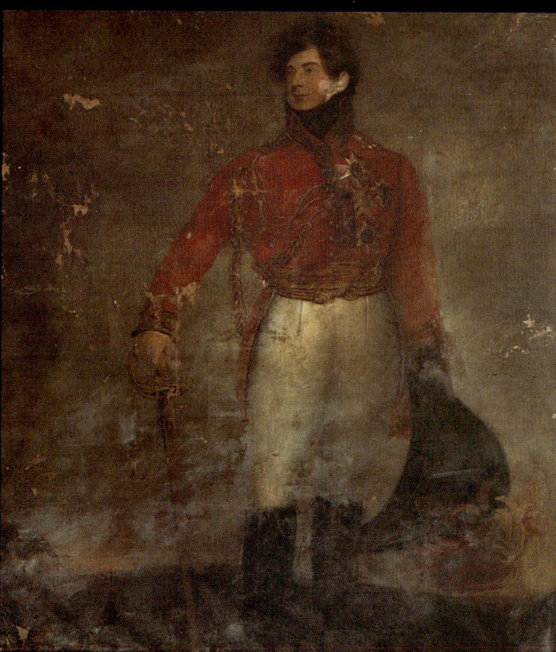

after Thomas Lawrence
Portrait of George IV (1762-1830)
(detail; photographed during restoration)

after Thomas Lawrence
Portrait of William IV (1765-1837)

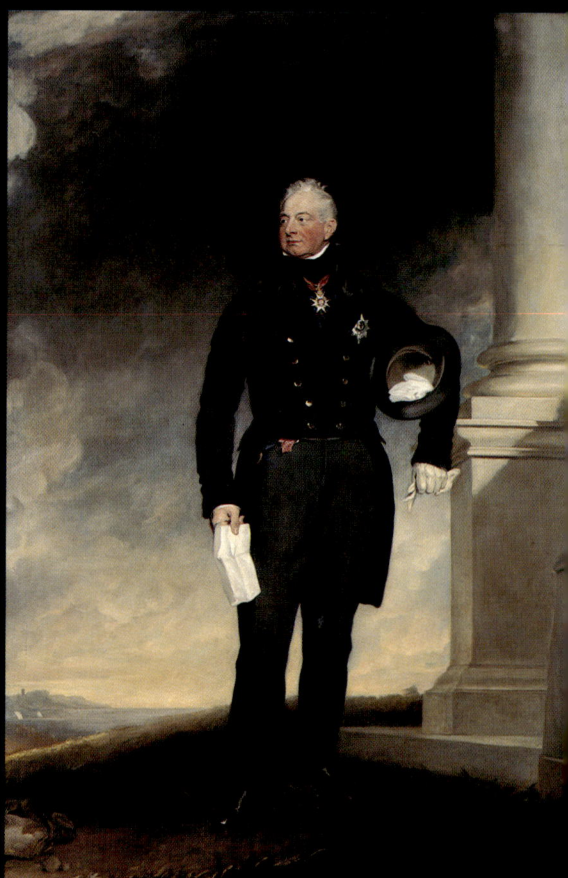

after Thomas Lawrence

(For a biography of the artist, see page 38.)

Portrait of George IV (1762-1830)
c.1816-17, oil on canvas, 272 x 179 cm

George IV was the eldest son of King George III and Queen Charlotte. During his father's final insanity in 1811, George became Regent, and eventually succeeded as King in 1820. Like his brothers, he rebelled against the strict upbringing and control of his father. He took as his companion Mrs Fitzherbert, whom he married in secret. During his years as Prince of Wales, he associated with the Whigs and appeared to support reform and Catholic Emancipation, which placed him on the opposite side of the political spectrum to his father. Upon achieving power himself, he quickly revoked his earlier opinions, but in 1829 he very reluctantly agreed to parliament's introduction of the Catholic Relief Bill. His unpopularity with the public was caused by his extravagance, vanity, and his treatment of his wife, Queen Caroline, who was prevented from attending the coronation, and who was excluded from all State functions during their marriage.

George IV took some interest in Irish affairs. In 1797, having been persuaded by Henry Grattan, he petitioned the Prime Minister, William Pitt, to make him Viceroy of Ireland. The following year he tried to get a pardon for Lord Edward Fitzgerald, who had been sentenced to death for his part in the rising. After his ostentatious coronation, he visited Dublin in August 1821, his arrival coinciding with the death of Queen Caroline. This royal visit was the first for well over one hundred years, and was the occasion of much celebration in the city. The king stayed for a number of weeks at Dublin Castle. The highlight of the visit was an installation of the Knights of St Patrick, which took place in St Patrick's Cathedral. This was the only installation at which the monarch, and head of the Order, presided.

The painting is a copy of an 1815 portrait belonging to the Marquis of Londonderry. George, then Prince Regent, is depicted in field-marshal uniform, wearing the stars of the Garter, the Bath and the St Esprit, and at his neck, the Golden Fleece, which he had been awarded in 1814. In later life George was subject to delusions about his military career. In reality, his military ambitions were always carefully curtailed by his father, who felt that active service was not appropriate for the heir to the throne. Some sense of the regent's love of costume and pose can be seen in this work. When the original painting was exhibited at the Royal Academy in 1815, the youthful appearance of the prince caused some hilarity in the press.

At the time of the original commission, there were apparently five copies of the painting made. One hangs at Knole, the home of Sir Charles Whitworth (Lord Lieutenant, 1813-17), who presented this work to the Viceregal Lodge. The Knole version differs from the original: it is without the ribbon of Hanover, as is the Dublin Castle painting. It is probable that this is a copy, commissioned by Whitworth, of the work from the studio of Lawrence, which hung at Knole. The painting remained in the dining room of the Lodge until the 1930s, when it was put into storage. It is currently being restored.

PROVENANCE – Presented to Viceregal Lodge by Charles, Earl of Whitworth; hung in dining room (1909 inventory); still hanging there in 1928 (OPW 14882/28, J.Cassidy 1928, copy in A77/7/1/39, 207). Put into storage at the National Gallery in March 1969, where it remained until the late 1980s.

LITERATURE
OPW 2947/11

COMPARATIVE LITERATURE
Kenneth Garlick, *Sir Thomas Lawrence – A Complete Catalogue of Oil Paintings* (Oxford, 1989) 193
Richard Walker, *Regency Portraits in the National Portrait Gallery*, 2 vols (London, 1989)

Portrait of William IV (1765-1837)

oil on canvas, 267 x 176 cm

William IV was the third son of King George III and Queen Charlotte. In 1779, at the behest of his father, he began a long and controversial naval career. He spent part of his early years in North America, and narrowly missed being kidnapped by an agent of George Washington in 1782. In 1789 George III recognised his son's achievements by creating him Duke of Clarence, a title by which he was known for most of his life. Destined to spend his days as the younger son of the king, and living happily with his mistress, Mrs Jordan, and their ten children, the duke's life changed dramatically when the heir to the throne, Princess Charlotte, daughter of the Prince Regent, died in childbirth in 1817. Fulfilling his family's wishes, and in an attempt to provide a legitimate heir, the duke separated from Mrs Jordan and married Adelaide, daughter of the Duke of Saxe-Coburg, in 1818. In 1827, upon the death of his brother, the Duke of York, the duke became heir to the throne and succeeded his brother George IV in 1830.

Like his brothers, William IV was an eccentric, but he was well-liked and apparently extremely convivial and informal in his habits. He was commonly referred to as the 'sailor king', in reference to his passion for all things maritime. He was succeeded by his much-loved niece, Victoria, in 1837.

This painting is a copy of a work by Thomas Lawrence which dates to 1827, a few years before William came to the throne. The original belongs to the collection of the queen at Buckingham Palace. It is a dramatic portrayal of the Duke of Clarence, as he then was. He wears the star of the Garter and the badge of the Order of the Bath. At the time the original was painted it would have been apparent that William was likely to become King, his elder brother, the Duke of York, having died, and George IV already old and infirm. The sea is given prominence in the background; this has added significance when one considers that at the time the original was painted, William was made Lord High Admiral, a post which his erratic behaviour soon forced him to relinquish.

PROVENANCE – Presented to Viceregal Lodge by Queen Adelaide; hung in dining room of Viceregal Lodge (1909 inventory). It was still at the Lodge in 1936 (A77/7/1/39). Put into storage at the National Gallery in 1969, where it remained until late 1980s.

LITERATURE
OPW file 14882/28; OPW 2947/11

COMPARATIVE LITERATURE
Kenneth Garlick, *Sir Thomas Lawrence – A Complete Catalogue of Oil Paintings* (Oxford, 1989) 193

John Lucas (1807-74)

John Lucas was apprenticed to the engraver S.W. Reynolds in 1821 but chose to become a painter. He began exhibiting at the Royal Academy in 1829, and by the 1830s he had established himself as a fashionable portrait painter based in London. He painted Queen Adelaide in 1837. In the early 1810s, he did several portraits of the royal family, including a full-length portrait of Prince Albert, his brother Ernest II, Duke of Saxe-Coburg-Gotha, and his father Ernest I. He also painted a number of portraits of the Duke of Wellington at this time. He continued to exhibit at the Royal Academy until his death in 1874. Many of his portraits are still in the private collections of the families for whom they were originally commissioned.

Portrait of Prince Albert (1819-1861)

c.1843, oil on canvas, 142.5 x 111.5 cm

Prince Albert was born near Coburg in Bavaria, the son of the Duke of Saxe-Coburg. After his marriage to Victoria in 1840, he became her closest advisor. Although the young Victoria was passionately in love with him, his position in British public life was a difficult one. He was an important supporter of the arts, and took a close interest in the commissioning of new artwork for the Houses of Parliament, which were being rebuilt in 1840s. The triumph of his career was the organisation of the Great Exhibition of 1851, which attracted thousands of visitors and revolutionised British design. He died, partly of exhaustion and overwork, in 1861.

The painting is similar to the full-length portrait of Albert which Lucas painted in 1841 and which was presented to King Louis Philippe. It is part of the collection at Versailles. In all, Lucas painted the prince four times. At his initial visit to Windsor, Prince Albert presented the artist with a sketch which he had drawn himself and which gave an idea of how he wanted the finished portrait to appear. In 1843 word from St James's was sent to Lucas informing him that the queen wanted him to forward a second portrait of the prince to Dublin. It was to hang in the same room as a portrait of Victoria. Albert is shown with the ribbon and star of the order of the Garter, with which he was invested in January 1840, prior to his marriage to Victoria. Around his neck he wears the collar of the order of the Golden Fleece.

The painting has been in storage for most of the 20th century, and has suffered quite severe damage. In 1999 the decision was taken to restore the work. (See the next entry on the portrait of Queen Victoria.)

PROVENANCE – Presented by Queen Victoria to Dublin Castle; hung in portico dining room of Viceregal Lodge (1909 inventory); still located at Viceregal Lodge, 1936 (A771711139). In storage in State Apartments, Dublin Castle (A6/1/21). Stored in National Gallery of Ireland, 1969. In storage in RHK, 1980s. Returned to Dublin Castle, 1999.

LITERATURE

Arthur Lucas, *John Lucas Portrait Painter 1828-75 – A Memoir of his Life mainly deduced from the correspondence of his sitters* (London, 1910) 41, 103
OPW file 14882/28; OPW A6/1/21; A6/1/70: A77/7/1/39

COMPARATIVE LITERATURE

Oliver Millar, *The Victorian Pictures in the Collection of Her Majesty, The Queen* (Cambridge University Press, 1992) 178

John Partridge (1790-1872)

Born in Glasgow, Partridge studied with the portrait painter Thomas Phillips, and entered the Royal Academy Schools in 1816. From 1823 to 1827 he travelled and worked in Italy, and became an associate of the RA in 1829. Unfortunately he fell from favour with the academicians, apparently because of a dispute with the painter R.R. Reinagle. Partridge had been asked by the owner of one of Reinagle's portraits to make 'improvements' to it. Unfortunately for Partridge he agreed to this, and from then on was snubbed by the Royal Academicians. He stopped exhibiting at the Academy in 1846, thus severely limiting access to his work on the part of the public, critics and potential patrons.

Prince Albert was an important supporter of Partridge in the 1840s. In 1843 he was appointed Royal Portrait Painter Extraordinary to Victoria and Albert. He probably came to their attention through his portrait of Leopold, Duke of Brabant, which the royal family acquired in 1841, and of which Victoria was very fond. His period of importance only lasted a few years, as the royal couple experimented with English portraitists. In May 1842, the artist Winterhalter arrived in London, and within a year had monopolised the portraiture of the royal family. From 1844 to 1846, Partridge embarked on an ambitious group portrait of the Fine Arts Commissioners (for the new Palace of Westminster). He was encouraged and helped by Prince Albert in this venture, but in the end the artist could find no purchaser for the work. He presented it to the National Portrait Gallery in London.

Portrait of Queen Victoria (1819-1901)

1842, oil on canvas, 142.5 x 112 cm

Queen Victoria, daughter of the Duke of York, the brother of George IV and William IV, succeeded to the throne in 1837 at the age of eighteen. In 1840 she married her German cousin, Prince Albert of Saxe-Coburg, and was closely guided by him until his early death in 1861, which left her heartbroken. She took an active interest in politics. In the earlier part of her reign, she had a significant role in mediating between factions in the House of Commons who were trying to establish coalition governments. In later years, she became associated with imperialism and with conservative rather than liberal ideas.

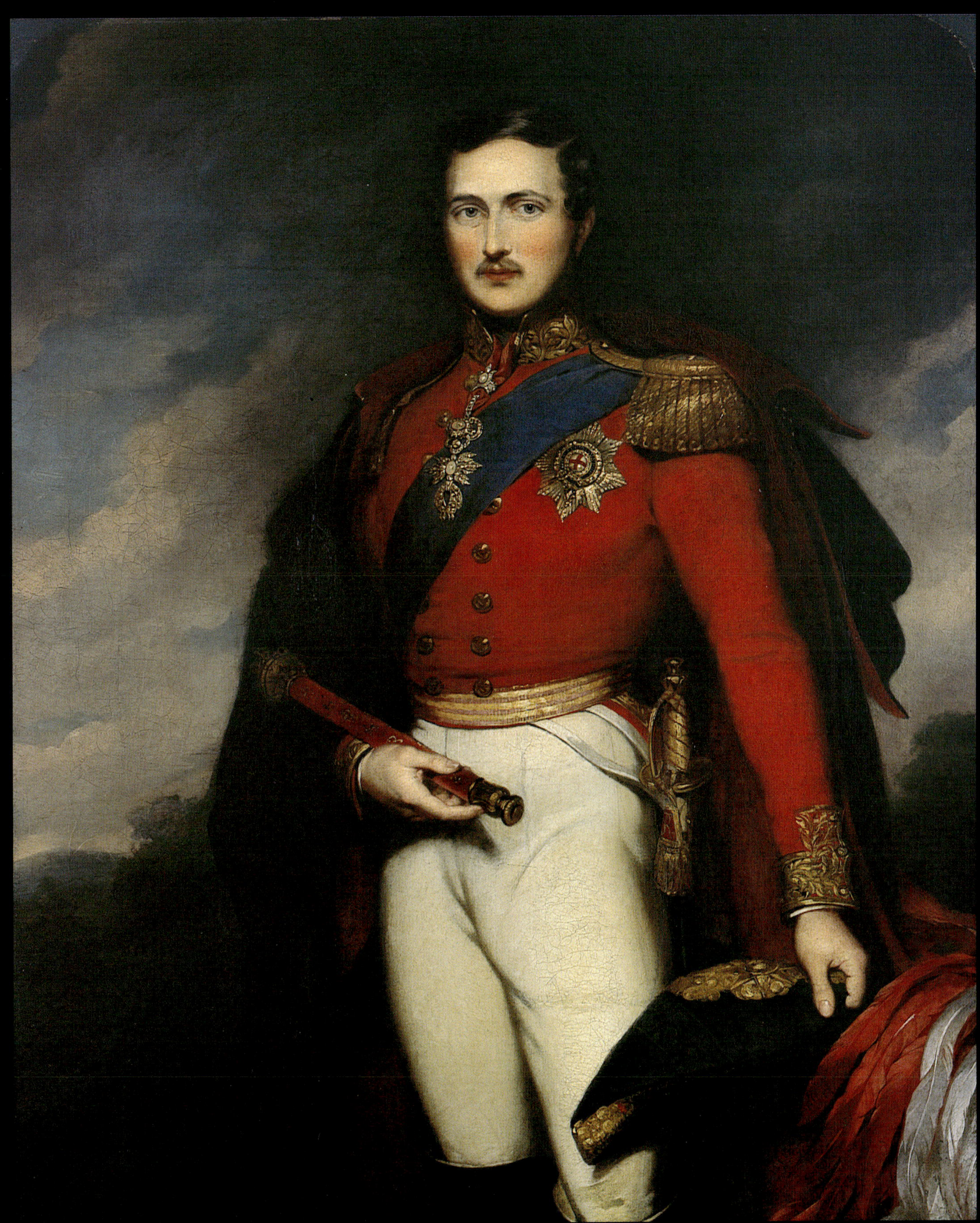

John Lucas, *Portrait of Prince Albert* (1819-1861)

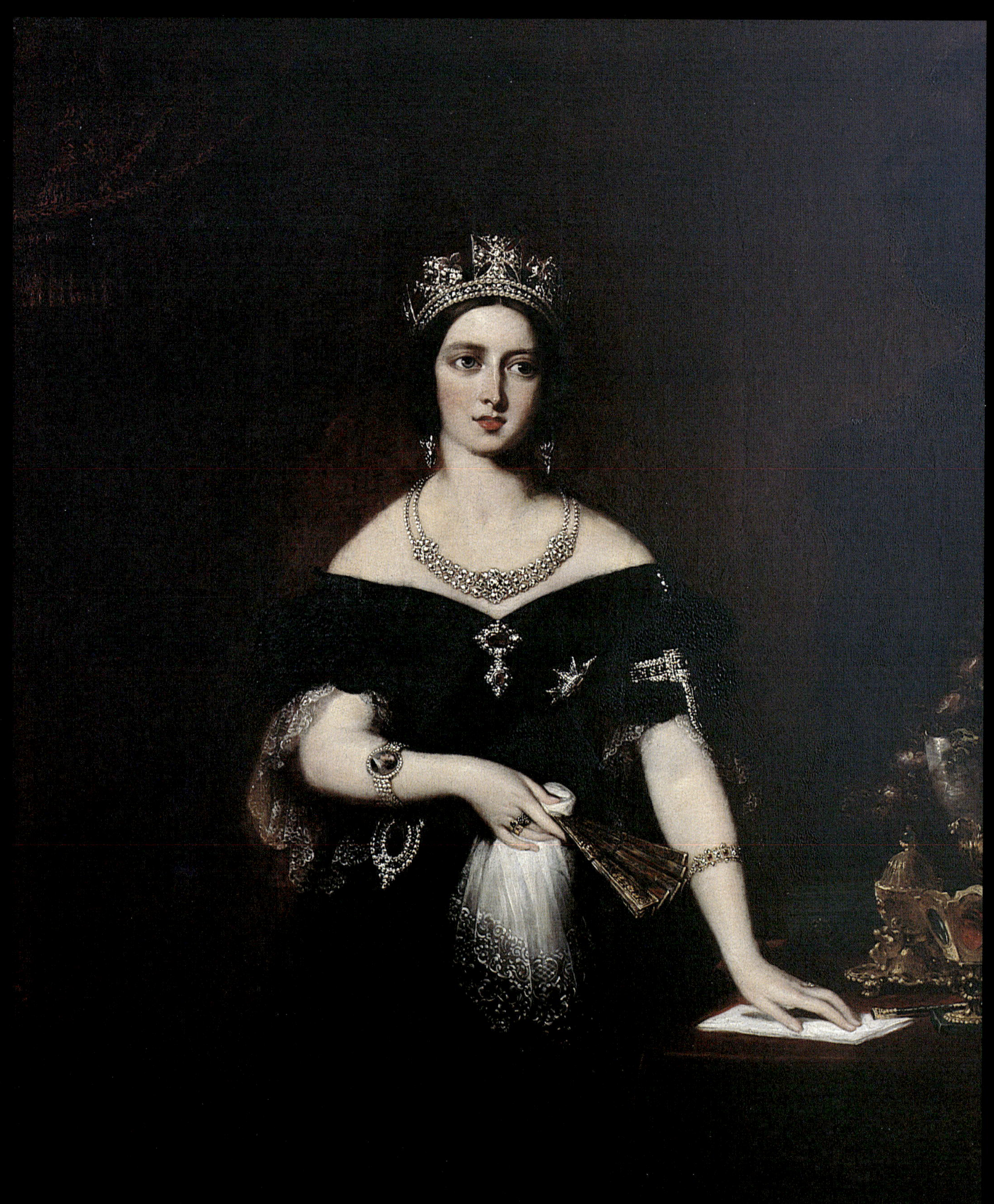

John Partridge, *Portrait of Queen Victoria* (1819-1901)

In Ireland, Victoria's reign is most closely associated with the Famine, and with the economic decline of the country. She visited Ireland on a number of occasions during her long reign, and always stayed at the Viceregal Lodge. Levées and balls were held by her in the State Apartments on these occasions.

This painting is a version of a portrait of Victoria in the Royal Collection at Buckingham Palace (dated 1840) in which she is shown wearing a rather elaborate black and silver headdress instead of a crown. Partridge painted a number of versions of the painting at her request, one of which she gave to Prince Albert as a Christmas present in 1840. The Dublin Castle painting is recorded in the artist's sitter-book of 1842, when he received £157 and 10 shillings for it. He also painted a full-length version for Mauritius at the same time. Although Partridge's records state that the work was destined for Dublin Castle, the *Dublin Evening News* of 14th August 1849 states: 'The Drawing-Room [of the Viceregal Lodge] ... is adorned with two splendid portraits – one of Her Majesty the Queen, and the other of her illustrious consort.' The painting remained in the Lodge until the 1930s.

The queen is shown wearing an evening dress with the star of the Garter. Her left hand rests on a letter on the table, while she holds a fan and a handkerchief in her other hand. On her right wrist is a miniature portrait of Albert. On the table beside her is a gilt metal inkstand mounted with semi-precious stones, which was given as a birthday present to the queen from Albert in May 1840.

The painting, and its companion piece of Albert, has had a chequered history. It was removed from the Viceregal Lodge in the 1930s, and put into storage in the Coach House in Dublin Castle. In the 1960s it was stored at the National Gallery, but later removed to the Royal Hospital, Kilmainham, where it was found in a very neglected state during the course of preparation for this catalogue. The decision was made to restore it.

PROVENANCE – Hung in portico dining room of Viceregal Lodge (1909 inventory); still located at Viceregal Lodge, 1936 (A77/7/1/39). In storage in Coach House, Dublin Castle (A6/1/21). Stored in National Gallery of Ireland,1969. In storage in RHK, 1980s. Returned to Dublin Castle 1999.

LITERATURE
OPW file 14882/28; OPW A6/1/21; OPW A6/1/70
O.Millar, *The Victorian Pictures in the Collection of Her Majesty The Queen* (Cambridge University Press, 1992) xxv, 194-95

Studio of Allan Ramsay (1713-1784)

Allan Ramsay was born in Edinburgh in 1713, and began his career as a portrait painter in that city. In 1736 he travelled to Italy and Paris, where he was influenced by the work of Pompeo Batoni. Upon his return to Britain in 1738 he settled in London. Later on in the 1740s, Ramsay's style changed when he became interested in the naturalism of French art and the work of such artists as La Tour and Nattier. He abandoned his earlier baroque style, and painted more in the light French rococo style.

Ramsay first painted George III as Prince of Wales in 1757. In 1760 he was commissioned to paint the king after his ascent to the throne. Due to a misunderstanding, Ramsay was not made court painter until the death of the artist John Shackleton in 1767. He retired from painting in 1773, after a fall from a ladder.

Portrait of George III (1738-1760)

after 1762, oil on canvas, approx. 250 x 163 cm

(For a biography of George III, see entry under William Beechey page 49)

This is a copy of the original coronation portrait of George III (Royal Collection), which was commissioned in October 1760 after George had ascended to the throne. After the king's coronation, which took place the following year, Ramsay repainted part of the work showing George in his coronation robes. For some twenty years after the coronation portrait was painted, numerous copies of it were produced in Ramsay's studio in London. Ramsay employed assistants to help with this, although he insisted on painting the head himself for a number of years.* In 1767 he moved into a new studio in Harley Street, in which he had a long gallery built specially for this purpose. There are several copies still extant in collections all over Ireland and Britain. The State owns a second copy, which is on display in the Royal Hospital, Kilmainham.

This painting, and its companion piece (see next entry), were on display in George's Hall from the 1960s until that room was refurbished for use as a conference room in the late 1980s. Both portraits are currently in storage. A newspaper account of the visit of George IV to Dublin Castle in 1821 mentions two impressive portraits of his parents hanging in the Throne Room. These may well have been this work and its pendant of Queen Charlotte.

PROVENANCE – Hung in dining room of Viceregal Lodge (1909 inventory); still located in Viceregal Lodge in 1936 (A77/7/1/39). George's Hall, Dublin Castle, in 1960s. Currently in storage

LITERATURE
OPW file 14882/28

COMPARATIVE LITERATURE
* Alastair Smart, *Allan Ramsay 1713-1784* (Scottish National Portrait Gallery, Edinburgh, 1992) 133-134

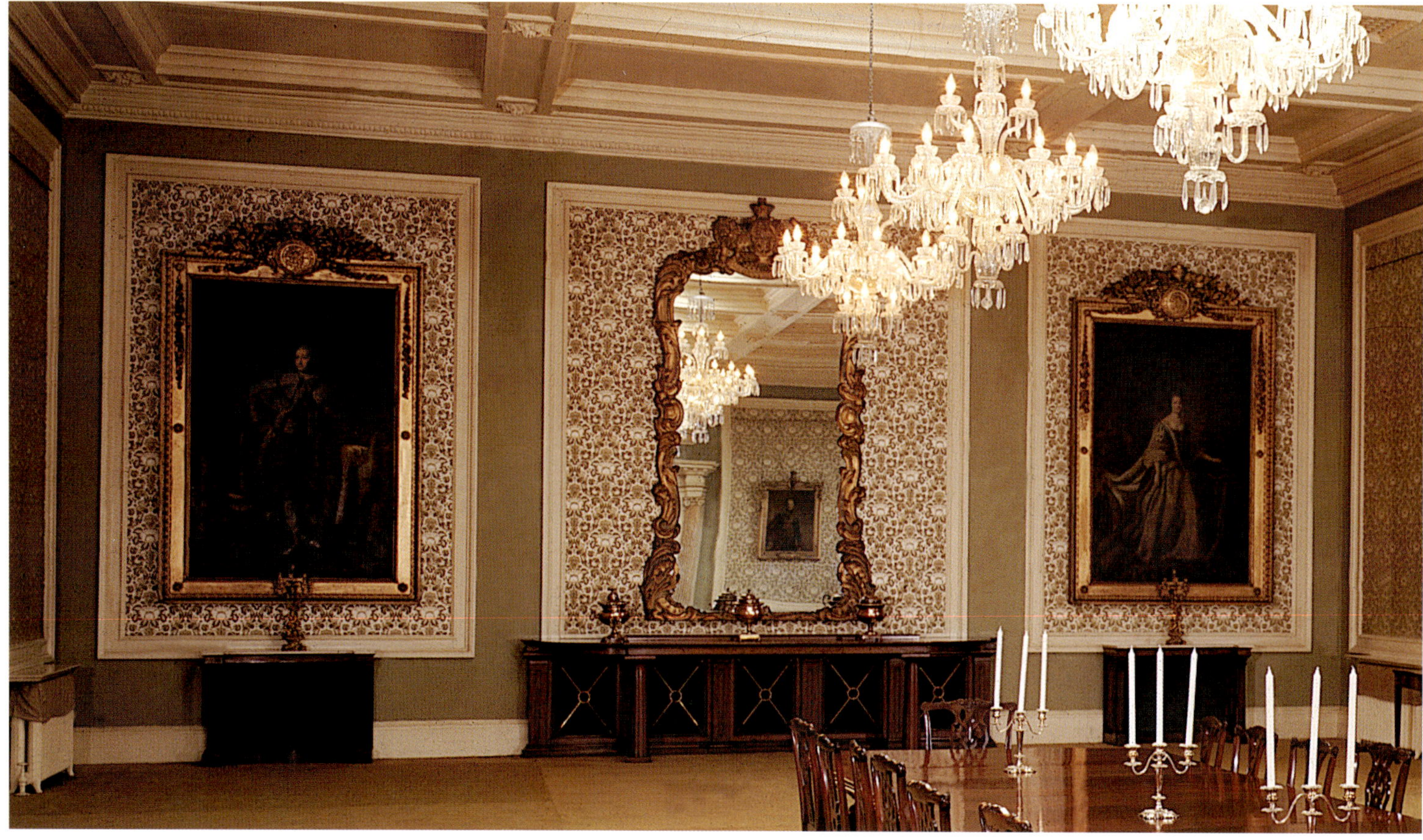

Portrait of Queen Charlotte (1744-1818)
c. 1762, oil on canvas, approx. 250 x 164 cm

Charlotte was the daughter of Karl I of Mecklenburg-Strelitz. She married George III in 1761, and was crowned with him a few weeks later on 22nd September. The couple had fifteen children.

The original painting, of which this is a copy, was commissioned as a pendant to the coronation portrait of George III. This shows the young queen in full coronation dress. On the table by her outstretched arm lie the crown jewels and regalia, which Ramsay was allowed to take away and paint in his own house.

PROVENANCE – Hung in dining room of Viceregal Lodge (1909 inventory); still located in Viceregal Lodge in 1936 (A77/7/1/39). George's Hall, Dublin Castle, in 1960s. Currently in storage.

LITERATURE
OPW file 14882/28

COMPARATIVE LITERATURE
Alastair Smart, *Allan Ramsay 1713-1784* (Scottish National Portrait Gallery, Edinburgh, 1992) 135

George's Hall, Dublin Castle
(photographed prior to refurbishment in 1980s)

left
Studio of Allan Ramsay
Portrait of George III (1738-1760)

right
Studio of Allan Ramsay
Portrait of Queen Charlotte (1744-1818)

Granard Gift

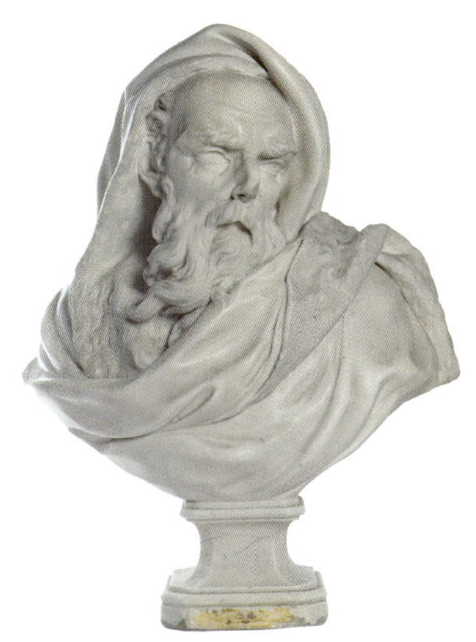

Venetian, early 18th-century sculpture
Winter

The Granard gift of paintings, sculpture and furniture was presented to the State Apartments by the 9th Earl of Granard (1915-92) in June 1973. It was given in memory of the earl's mother, the Countess of Granard, widow of the 8th Earl of Granard, who had recently died. The countess, Beatrice (née Mills), married Bernard Hastings Forbes, 8th Earl, in 1909. She was an American, daughter of Ogden Mills of Staatsburg, and is said to have met her husband at a ball in Dublin Castle. She asked that some of her artworks and furniture be donated to the Irish state after her death.

The 8th Earl of Granard (1874-1948), was a distinguished statesman both before and after independence. A Knight of St Patrick, he was Lord-in-Waiting to Edward VII from 1905 to 1907, and Deputy Speaker of the House of Lords. After independence he became a member of the Irish senate (1922-34). The earl and countess owned houses in London and Paris, as well as their Irish seat, Castleforbes in Co Longford. Their eldest son, Sir Arthur Hastings Forbes, 9th Earl of Granard, married Marie Madeleine Maurel in

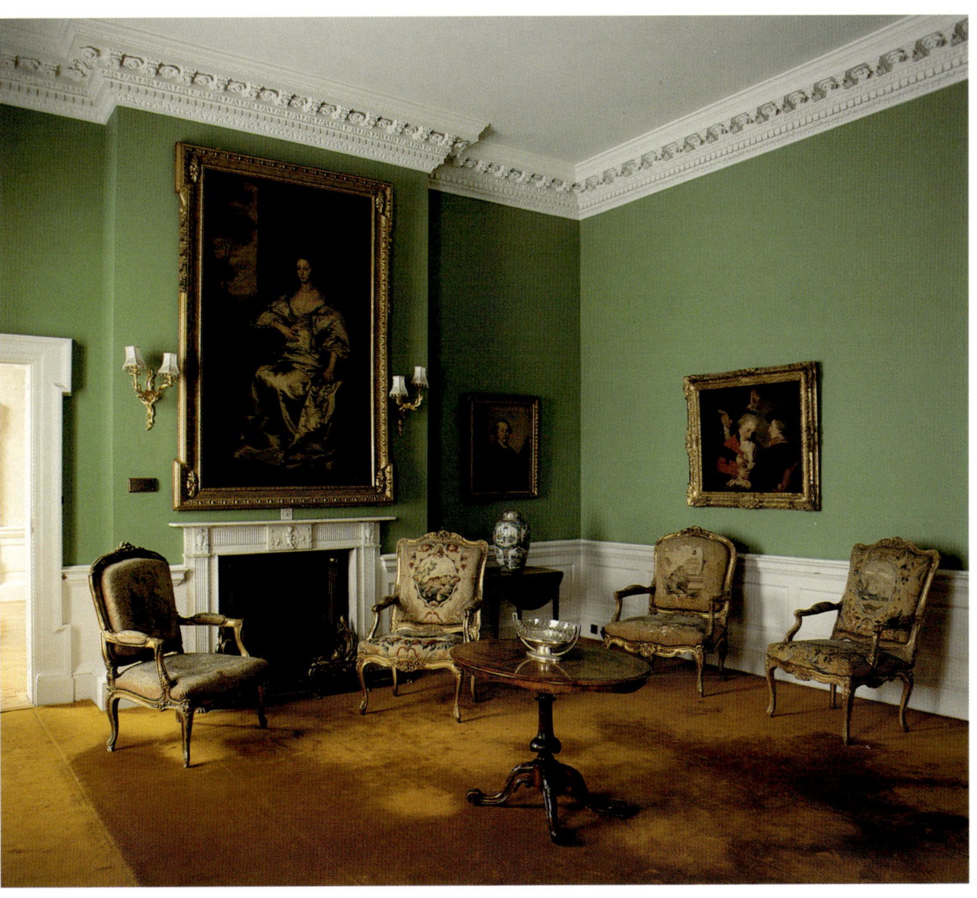

Granard Room, State Apartments, Dublin Castle

1949, and the couple lived in Paris. Due to the Parisian connections in both marriages, the Granard Gift has a distinct continental flavour. Apart from the four paintings and two pieces of sculpture, the Granard Gift includes a number of pieces of furniture, most of which are French. In the Granard Room itself is part of a suite of giltwood armchairs, upholstered in 18th-century Beauvais tapestry showing the fables of La Fontaine. Most of the delicate Louis XVI style furniture in the queen's dressing room also came from this gift. The two Flemish tapestries on the Battleaxe landing, *The Fortune Teller* and *The Smokers*, are early 18th century and signed DL (in this case denoting Delphin Layniers). The subjects are taken directly from the paintings of the Dutch 17th-century painter, Teniers. Many of the clocks, as well as other furniture in the bedroom suite of the State Apartments, come from the Granard family. The star of St Patrick which is on display in St Patrick's Hall belonged to the 8th Earl, and is on loan from the family to the Castle. After the death of the 9th Earl, further family treasures were presented to the Castle.

Anthony van Dyck (1599-1641)

Born in Antwerp, van Dyck was influenced early in his career by the work of Rubens, the dominant artist of that city. He became an accomplished painter at a young age, and entered the city's guild as a master in 1618. Two years later he visited London, where he attracted the attention of James I. From 1622 to 1627 he travelled in Italy, where his style and approach to portraiture were influenced by the work of Titian. He settled in London in 1632, and became Principal Painter to Charles I. He was one of the great court portraitists of all time, creating stunning images of the king and his family, which combined the flamboyancy of the baroque style with the directness of Titian. His portraits were almost totally confined to members of the royal family and aristocracy. He created dynamic and seductive poses and settings for his sitters, many of which were imitated by later painters who knew them through engravings. He gave particular attention to the face, which he drew with meticulous care, and it is here that a true sense of the sitter's character is found. Van Dyck died in London in 1641, an honorary member of the Court. He was one of the most influential portraitists of the 17th century.

Elizabeth Leigh, Countess of Southampton

c.1640-41, oil on canvas, 221 x 129 cm
inscribed: Elizabeth, Countess of Southampton

This is a portrait of Elizabeth Leigh, daughter of Sir Francis Leigh, afterwards the Earl of Chichester. She married Thomas Wriothesley (1607-1667), Earl of Southampton, in 1642, and had four daughters, only one of whom survived. Her husband was an important courtier to Charles I. In 1638 he had been granted the island of Mauritius by the king, and in 1642 he was admitted to the Privy Council. Later he visited Charles in prison, prior to the king's execution. Southampton managed to avoid fighting in the Civil War, and retired from public life during the Commonwealth.

This portrait was probably commissioned by Southampton on the occasion of the couple's engagement around the year 1640. This makes it one of van Dyck's last works. According to one source, Elizabeth Leigh died at the age of sixteen, but as she had four children this is unlikely. She did, however, die at a young age. The story was possibly inspired by this portrait of Elizabeth in which her delicate features and rather timid expression are emphasised. She is seated on a stone bench, with a tapestry on the wall behind her and a vista out into a garden over her right elbow. These suitably aristocratic surroundings are enhanced by the subtle colours of the sitter's white satin dress and green shawl. Her right hand touches her stomach, a reference to her forthcoming marriage and her hoped for fertility. The overall tone of the painting is one of understated elegance.

The painting was inherited by Southampton's third wife upon his death, and its provenance was well documented until the beginning of this century, when it was photographed in the collection of Lady Lucas in London. It disappeared from the records in the 1920s, and has been listed as missing in catalogues of van Dyck's work since then. It was acquired by the Countess of Granard in the interim period. This is the work's first reappearance in print for many years.

PROVENANCE – Bequeathed to Lady Frances Seymour, 1677; Lord D'Arcy, 10th Earl of Kent, 1683; Dowager Countess Cowper, 1872; Lady Lucas, 1888. Presented to the State Apartments by 9th Earl of Granard, 1973.

LITERATURE
Richard W. Goulding 'Wriothesley Portraits', *The Walpole Society*, viii (1920)
Erik Larsen, *L'Opera Completa di Van Dyck* (Rizzoli, Milan, 1980) no. 949
Erik Larsen, *The Paintings of Van Dyck*, 2 vols (Luca Verlag Freren, Dusseldorf, 1988) i, 386; ii, 389

EXHIBITED
Burlington Exhibition of Old Masters, 1873 (22)

after Giovacchino Fortini (1670-1736)

Fortini was a born at Settignano near Florence, and was one of the most important artists in that city at the turn of the 18th century. He worked as a sculptor, architect and medallist, and was in the patronage of the Medici family, who appointed him Chief Court Architect. His most important work is a series of marble

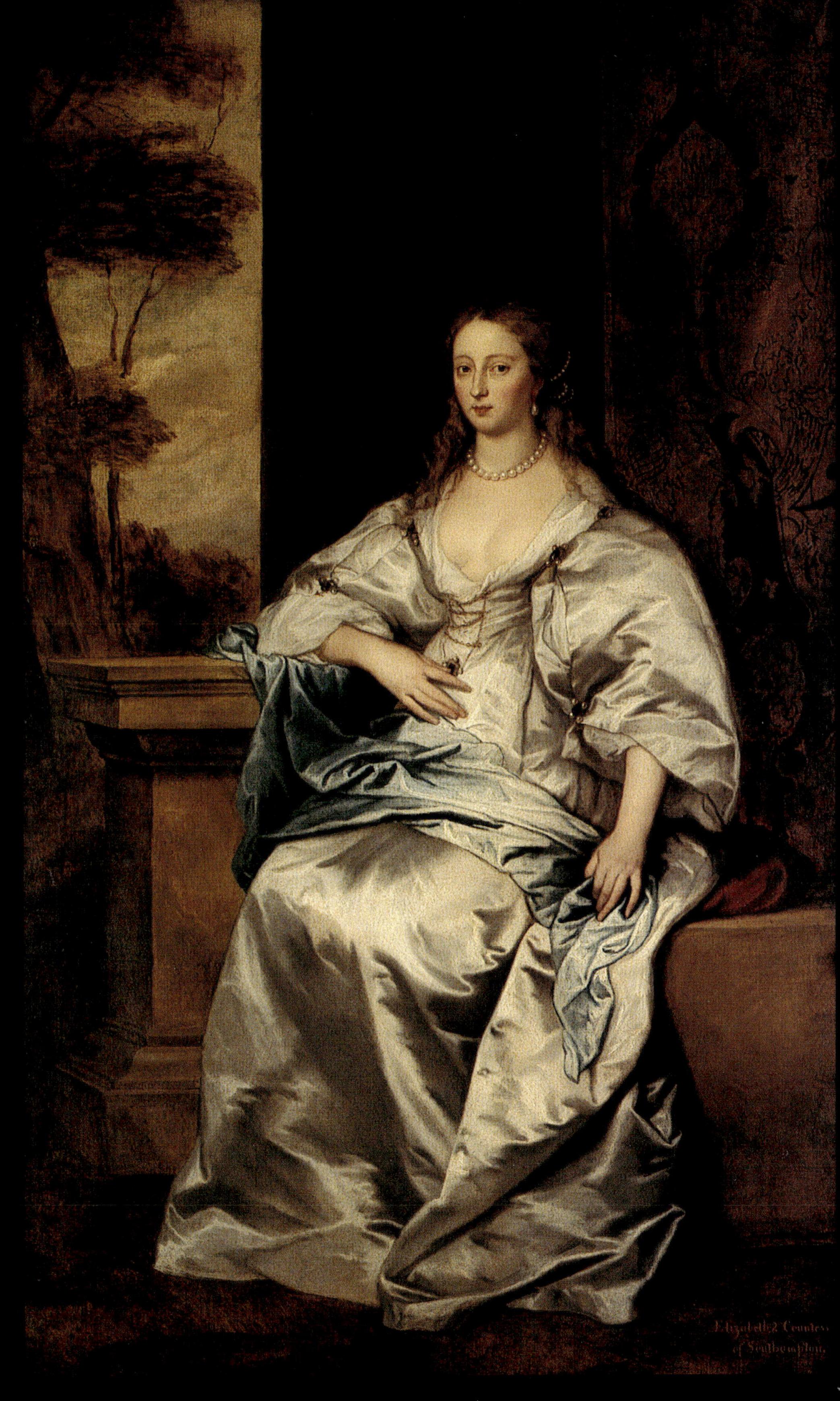

Anthony van Dyck
Elizabeth Leigh, Countess of Southampton

works for the Church of San Annunziata (1704-06). He also made a number of portrait busts and reliefs. His best documented work is a marble funerary monument to Baron von Hochkirchen in Cologne Cathedral, from which his other works have been attributed.

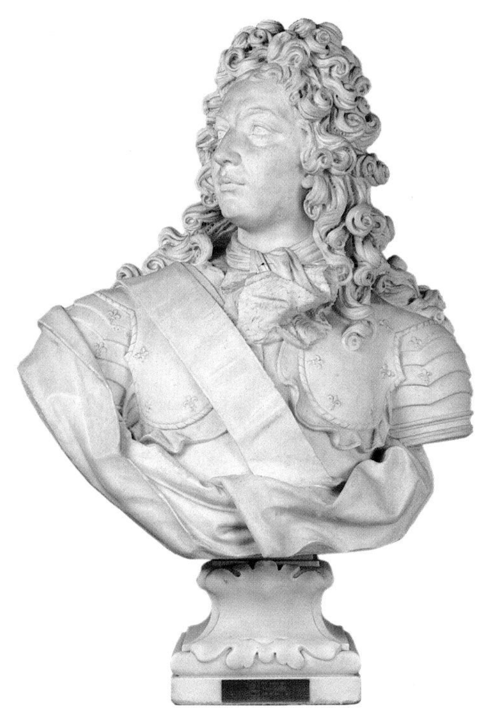

after Giovacchino Fortini
Philippe II, duc d'Orléans (1674-1723)

after Louis Pierre Legros
Marble pedestal

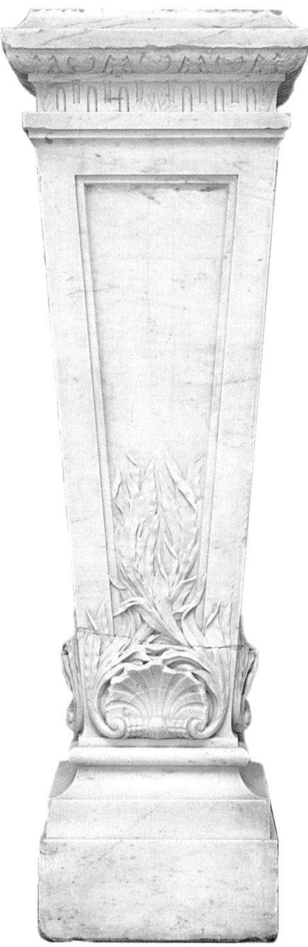

Philippe II, duc d'Orléans (1674-1723)

marble, bust: 78 cm, socle: 20cm

This work was presented to the Castle as a bust of Louis XIV. The prominent display of the fleur-de-lys indicates that this is a member of the French royal family. The features of the face and the style of the hair are like those of Philippe II, duc d'Orléans. In fact, the Dublin Castle bust has features very close to a bust of the duke which is in a private collection in Paris.* Philippe II was a nephew of Louis XIV. He served as Regent of France during the minority of Louis XV (1715-23), when the Court became notorious for its licentious behaviour. The duke distinguished himself in the military campaigns of the Grand Alliance (1688-97), and the war of the Spanish Succession (1701-04).

There appears to be important similarities between the Dublin Castle bust and a group of portrait busts of the Bourbon family attributed to Fortini. In the first case, the fleur-de-lys on all the busts attributed to this artist are Italian in style, not French. Secondly, all have a distinctive socle with a mannerist-type plaque on its front. Thirdly, the dimensions of the bust, the treatment of the armour, and the distinctive carving of the curls of the wig where the sculptor has drilled a series of small holes are all of the same character. Until more detailed research can be carried out, it appears that this work is related stylistically to the Fortini busts, but is probably a 19th-century pastiche.

PROVENANCE – Presented to the State Apartments by 9th Earl of Granard, 1973.

LITERATURE

* F. Hamilton Hazlehurst, 'Five Portrait Busts: A question of identification and authorship', *Studies in Art History*, 24 (1990) 89-107. (I am grateful to Joseph McDonnell for drawing my attention to this article.)

after Louis Pierre Legros (1629-1714)

Legros was born in Chartres, the son of a grocer, who later became a stone mason in Paris. Legros became a member of the Académie in 1666, from which time he was employed by the king on various projects. In 1669 he began working at Versailles, but. retired from his work for the Crown when he was made professor at the Académie in 1702.

Marble pedestal
marble, 136 cm

The pedestal resembles those of the Fontaines de la Victoire et de la Gloire, which Legros was commissioned to make in 1681 for the Bosquet de l'Arc de Triomphe in the gardens of Versailles. However, the Dublin Castle pedestal is 20 cm taller than the French examples and does not have the marks of the original 17th-century metal decoration.

PROVENANCE – Presented to State Apartments by 9th Earl of Granard, 1973.

COMPARATIVE LITERATURE
P. Verlet, 'Objets prestigieux retrouvés', *Revue de l'art*, 34 (1976) 61
F. Souchal, *French Sculptors – The Reign of Louis XIV* (1987) Legros, no. 26e

I am grateful to Simone Hoog for his assistance with this entry.

Rev Matthew William Peters (1741-1814)

Matthew William Peters was born on the Isle of Wight in 1741. His father was Belfast-born, but had grown up at Stowe, where he became an expert in gardening and agriculture. Around the time of Matthew's birth, the family moved to Dublin where his father ran a seed shop. Peters trained at Robert West's drawing school, and won prizes at the Dublin Society Schools in 1756 and 1758. According to Strickland, the Dublin Society paid for the young artist to travel to Italy where, in 1763, he became a member of the Florentine Academy. According to another writer, Peters studied in London under the portrait painter Thomas Hudson before going to Italy.

In 1766 he established himself chiefly as a portrait painter in London, exhibiting with the Royal Academy from 1769. In 1778, at the height of his career, he became a Royal Academician. The oil sketch for his diploma piece is in the Castle's collection. He was ordained an Anglican priest in 1783, and from 1784 to 1788 he was chaplain to the Prince of Wales, later George IV. Most of the work he produced after his ordination was portraiture, and occasional religious subjects. He had previously painted mainly 'fancy pictures' (portraits in which the sitters appear in fancy dress). Many of these were engraved; their rather sentimental quality was extremely popular. In subsequent years, Peters' reputation was eclipsed by that of his contemporaries Reynolds and Gainsborough, but in his own day he was a widely admired and respected artist.

Rev Matthew William Peters
Children with Fruit and Flowers

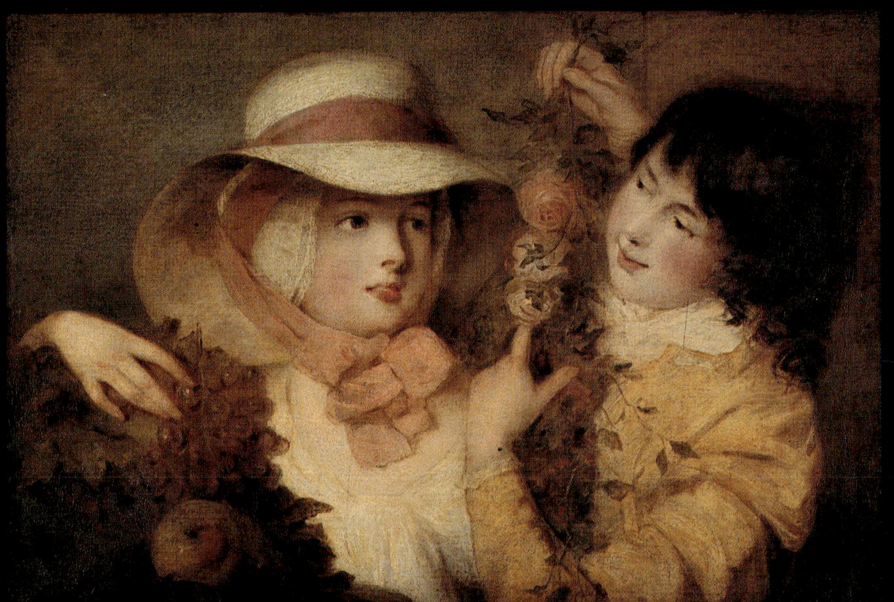

Rev Matthew William Peters
Portrait of Sir James Dashwood (1715-1779)

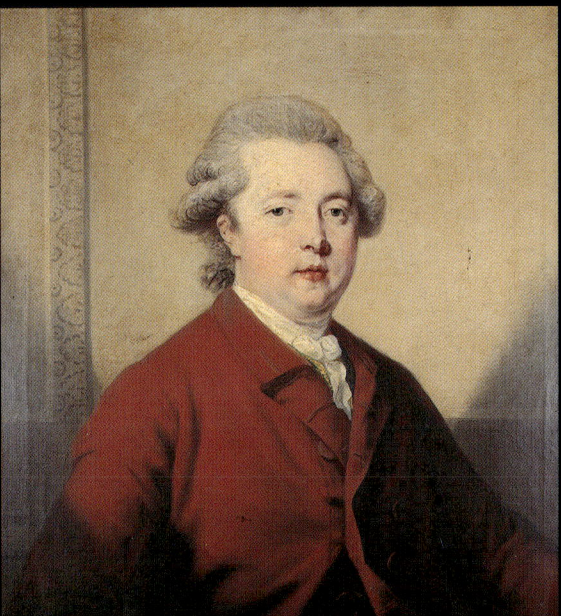

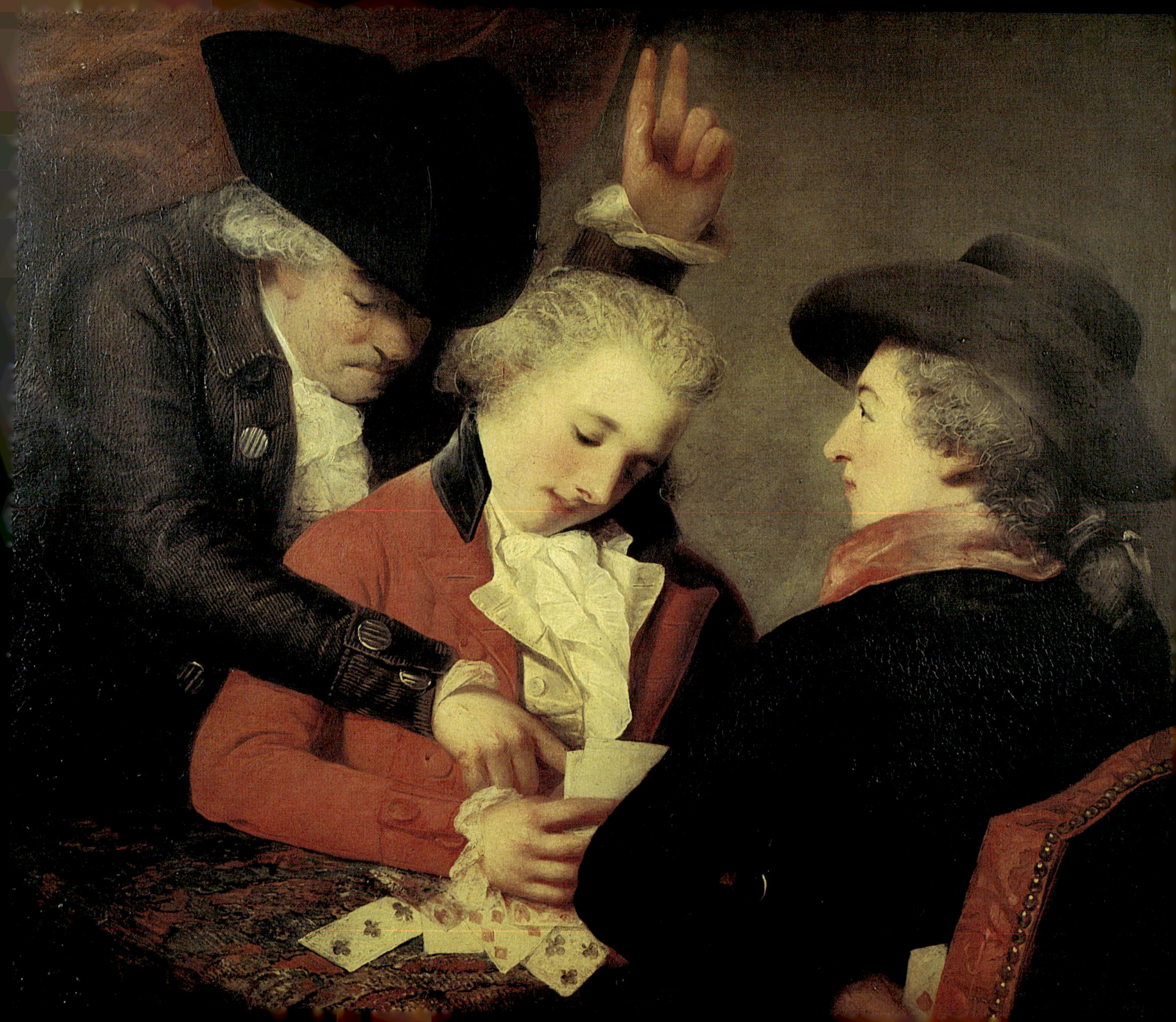

The Gamesters
c.1785, oil on canvas, 84 x 95 cm

Lady Elizabeth Manners has dated this painting to 1785, the year before a mezzotint of it was published. The painting appears very like an 18th-century version of the popular card-sharpers subject, most famously depicted by Caravaggio. A fresh-faced youth, fashionably dressed, is being advised on his hand of cards by an older acquaintance. This seemingly helpful figure signals to his associate on the other side of the table. The work is a humorous reminder of the dangers of vice. The mezzotint of the painting has the following verse printed on it: 'Vice, whatever sex or form it may assume, leadeth to destruction; woe to the unwary youth who hath been seduced into the acquaintance. To the young nobility of England this plate is most humbly inscribed.'

Two of the figures in the work have been identified, thanks to a annotated copy of the print which the art historian Lady Elizabeth Manners saw in the British Museum. The central figure of the young and gullible youth is Lord Courtenay, while the right-hand figure, seated opposite, is the cartoonist Thomas Rowlandson. Courtenay was a young English nobleman who succeeded to his title in 1788, and who spent the rest of his life abroad. Peters painted a group portrait of the Courtenay family in 1785.

PROVENANCE – Leopold Hirsch, 1902. Presented to the State Apartments by 9th Earl of Granard, 1973.

LITERATURE
Lady Elizabeth Manners, *Matthew William Peters* (London, 1913) 43-45, 53
Denys Sutton, *Aspects of Irish Art* (National Gallery of Fine Arts, Ohio, 1974) 84

EXHIBITED
English Painters of the 18th Century, Guildhall, London, 1902 (54)
Aspects of Irish Art, National Gallery of Ireland touring exhibition, 1974
Art of the State, 1993

ENGRAVED – Mezzotint 1786; engraver: William Ward

Children with Fruit and Flowers
c.1777, oil on canvas, 65 x 79 cm

A label on the back of the painting describes this work as an original finished study for Peters' diploma picture, which he presented to the Royal Academy on becoming a member in 1778. A version of it was engraved by J.B. Michel in 1786. This painting of children and fruit and flowers is the type of work for which Peters was widely admired in his own day. Like *The Gamesters*, this seemingly straightforward genre painting contains portraits of real people. The features of the girl are very similar to those of Eliza H Phelps, who occurs in a number of Peters' paintings.

PROVENANCE – Collection of Mrs Graham. Presented to the State Apartments by 9th Earl of Granard, 1973.

Portrait of Sir James Dashwood (1715-1779)
oil on canvas, 76.5 x 64 cm

Sir James Dashwood was MP for Oxford from 1740 to 1754 and 1760 to 1768. He succeeded his grandfather, Sir Robert Dashwood, to the title of baronet in 1734. In 1739 he married Elizabeth Spencer, and they had two sons. He is recorded as church warden of St George's, Hanover Square, London, in 1759. There is a portrait of James Dashwood as a young man in the Metropolitan Museum of Art, New York, by Enoch Seeman.

PROVENANCE – Collection of Mrs Graham; purchased by the Countess of Granard from Tooth & Sons, London; presented to the State Apartments by 9th Earl of Granard, 1973

Venetian, early 18th-century sculpture

Winter
marble, 49 cm

Although presented as a *Head of an Old Man*, this would appear to be an allegorical figure representing winter. The age of the figure, his flowing beard, and his fur-lined cloak are usual features for this subject. These representations of the seasons usually occur in groups of four, or sometimes just as winter and summer, the latter usually shown in the form of a young girl. The style of the work is Venetian 18th century, rather like the work of Orazio Marinali (1643-1720) who made a set of the seasons, which is in the Giardino Barnabo in Venice.

PROVENANCE – Presented to the State Apartments by 9th Earl of Granard, 1973.

The author acknowledges the assistance of Philip Ward-Jackson in the attribution of this work.

Miscellaneous paintings

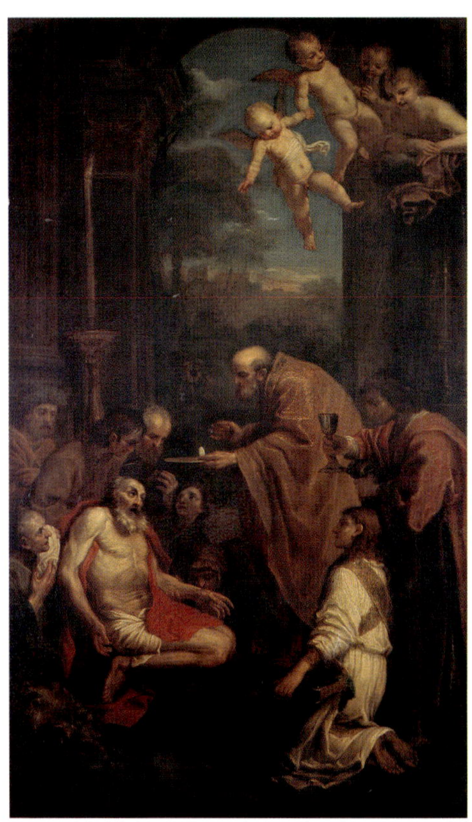

after Domenichino
The Last Communion of St Jerome

after Domenichino (1581-1641)

Domenichino was one of the major Bolognese artists working in Rome in the early 17th century. In 1631 he moved to Naples to decorate a chapel in the cathedral of that city. His style is restrained and classical.

The Last Communion of St Jerome
oil on canvas, 172.5x 101 cm

This is a copy of one of Domenichino's best known works, which is now in the Pinacoteca in the Vatican. The original work was painted for the church of San Girolamo della Carita in Rome in 1614. It depicts St Jerome, one of the four Fathers of the Church, at the altar in the act of receiving the Eucharist. The large lion, which is curled up on the floor beside him, is one of the standard symbols of the saint.

This painting was enormously influential in the 17th, 18th and 19th centuries. Its admirers included Rubens, Poussin, the Irish artist James Barry, and, rather surprisingly, the English painter John Constable, who commented on the placid landscape in the background. Numerous copies of this work dating from the 18th and 19th centuries exist. It is rather an unlikely painting to find in the collection of Dublin Castle.

PROVENANCE – Unknown

COMPARATIVE LITERATURE
Richard E. Spear, *Domenichino* (Yale University Press, 1982) i, 175-78

Continental school, early 18th century

The Sacrifice of Iphigenia
oil on canvas, 95 x 151 cm

Although rather crude in quality, this painting tells the story of Iphigenia quite effectively, and is very ambitious in terms of its composition. Iphigenia was the daughter of Agamemnon, the Greek king who led the attack on Troy. In order to appease Diana, one of whose deer he had killed, he was told that he must sacrifice Iphigenia to the goddess. The princess complied out of duty to her father and her country. She is shown kneeling before an altar, with the priest behind her about to cut her throat. A Greek warrior holds out the platter for the knife. Diana watches from the sky, while Agamemnon is shown weeping in the left-hand corner. Below the goddess, the Greek ships are shown ready to

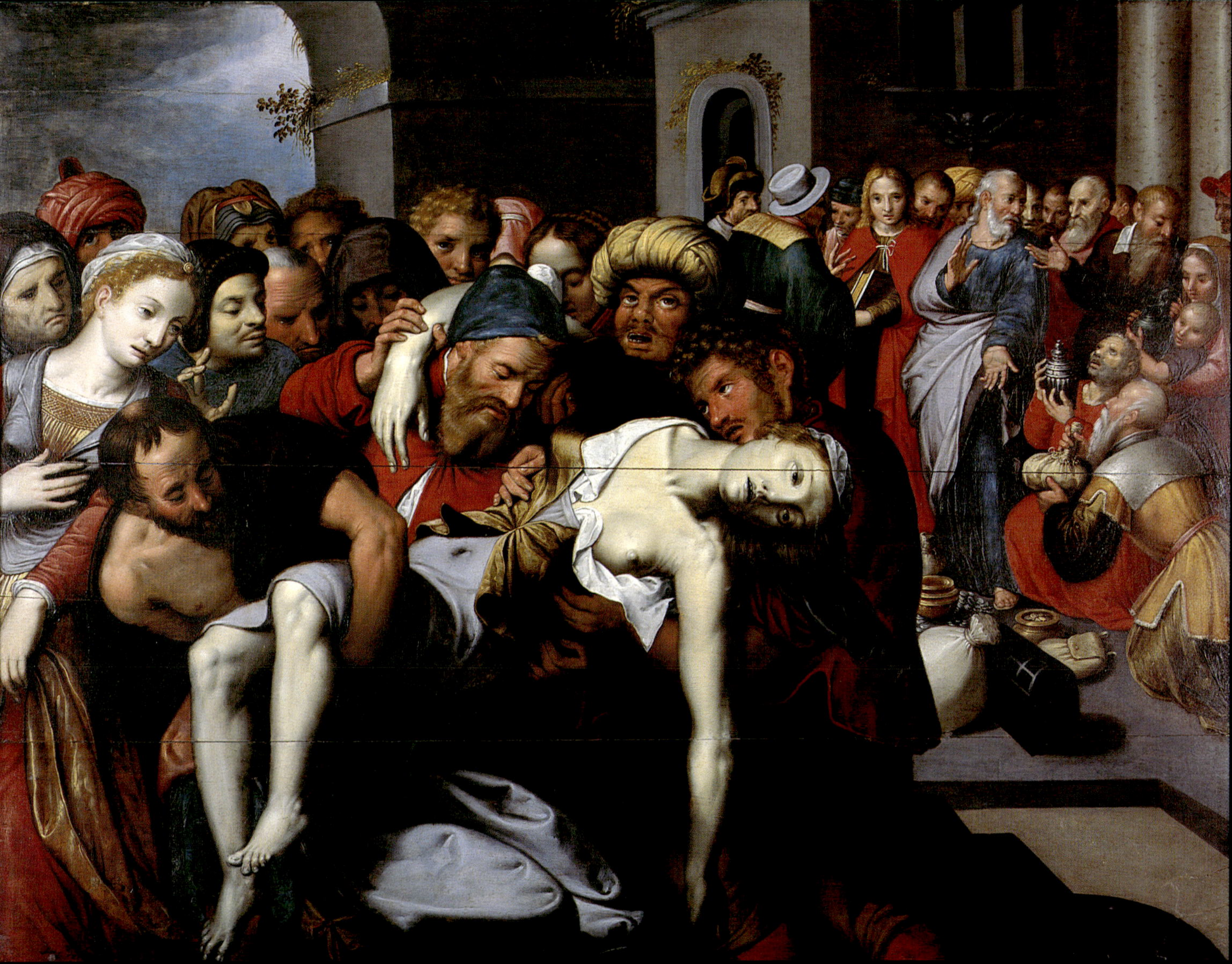

ollower of Ambrosius Francken I
he Death of Sapphira

Continental school, early 18th century
he Sacrifice of Iphigenia
detail)

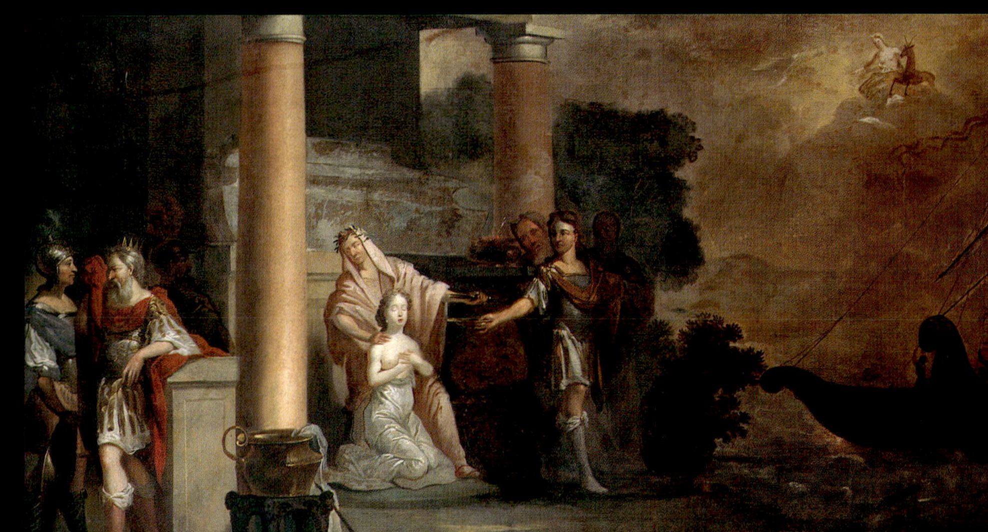

sail for war as soon as she has been appeased. The artist has gone to some trouble to dress the figures in suitable costume, and has used a number of interesting props, including the carved stool in the foreground. The work may originally have been intended as an overdoor, or acquired to serve this purpose, in George's Hall.

PROVENANCE – Purchased by the OPW from Dooley, Dublin antique dealer, 1950s.

English or Irish school, early 18th century

Portrait of Lady Alice Hume (c.1679-1750)
oil on canvas, 125 x 100 cm

Lady Alice Hume was the elder daughter of the 3rd Earl of Drogheda, who fought with William at the Battle of the Boyne. She married Sir Gustavus Hume of Castlehume, Co Fermanagh, in 1697, and had three daughters and three sons. Her husband died in 1731, having outlived their sons, and his title became extinct. Lady Alice died in 1750. Her daughter Mary married Nicholas Loftus, the future Earl of Ely, in 1736.*

The portrait is in the style of Sir Peter Lely and Sir Godfrey Kneller. The pose of the sitter was probably influenced by engravings of their work. It is still in its early 18th-century frame. Lady Alice is seated in a classical interior, with a lamb and a garland of flowers in her lap. The lamb is a symbol of St Agnes, the patron saint of women about to be married, and thus it is likely that this was painted to commemorate her forthcoming wedding.

PROVENANCE – Purchased by the OPW from Naylor's, Liffey Street, Dublin, c.1954/5.

I am grateful to Dr Jane Fenlon for assistance in the dating and attribution of this work, and to Ann Stewart for information about the Ely sale.

* A Portrait of Lady Alicia Hume attributed to Lely was sold at the Marquis of Ely's sale, removed from Loftus Hall, Co Wexford, 25th July 1891, Christie's, London (lot 165).

follower of Ambrosius Francken I (1544/45-1618)

Ambrosius Francken was born in Herentals and died at Antwerp in 1618, where he painted a number of important altarpieces which are now in the Royal Museum of Fine Art in that city. They are the *Miracle of the Loaves and Fishes* (1598) for the cathedral, the *Martyrdom of St Jacob* (1608), and *The Last Supper*. These

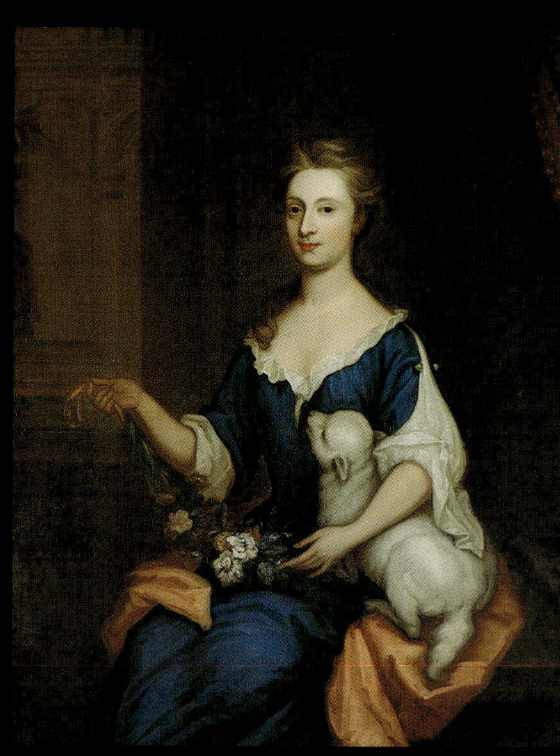

English or Irish school, early 18th century
Portrait of Lady Alice Hume (c.1679-1750)

Michelangelo Hayes
St Patrick's Day, Military Parade at Dublin Castle

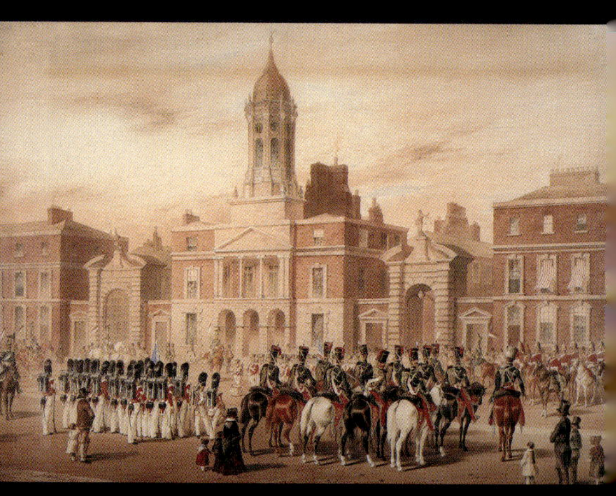

works, which were enormously influential, required the help of assistants, and helped to spread Francken's style of classical prototypes and opulent costumes and colours. Earlier in his career he is recorded at Fontainebleau, where he would have seen the mannerist decoration and paintings of Rosso Fiorentino and Francesco Primaticcio.

The Death of Sapphira

oil on wood, 93 x 121 cm

This painting, or an identical one, was sold in New York in 1943 when it was attributed to Willem Key. This is an unlikely attribution, as is the former attribution to Simon de Vos.* Edwin Buijsen, curator of early Netherlandish painting at the Netherlands Institute for Art History, believes this painting to be by a follower of the late 15th century artist, Ambrosius Francken.

The unusual subject is the *Death of Sapphira*, which comes from the Acts of the Apostles (5, 1-11). Sapphira was the wife of Ananias, who sold a possession but kept some of the proceeds for himself, only offering part of the money to the church. He was struck down by God for his dishonesty. His wife Sapphira suffered the same fate, as she too lied to the apostles about her husband's gift. In the background of the painting are the figures of Peter and the Christ-like John, who are accepting gifts for the church from the assembled crowd. In the foreground, another group of figures are gathered around the dead body of Sapphira. Three men lift it up, as in an entombment or lamentation scene while the others look on in surprise and horror. According to the Acts of the Apostles, after Sapphira's death, 'great fear came upon all the church and upon all who heard these things'.

The work is typical early-16th century, northern mannerist in style. It combines northern realism with a familiarity with current Italian art and with classicism in general. The elongated figures of Peter and the woman in the left foreground corner are stock mannerist figures – elegant and self-conscious.They are set-pieces showing off the artist's sense of style and knowledge of classical art. The costumes are a strange combination of contemporary and classical dress, with an emphasis on sumptuous fabrics and colours. Another feature of this style is the claustrophobic sense of space which the figures occupy. This adds to the deliberate artificiality of the painting.

PROVENANCE – Purchased by the OPW from Naylor's, Liffey Street, Dublin, 1950s.

I am grateful to Dr John Loughman for identifying the subject matter of this painting and for carrying out research into its attribution.

* The attribution to Simon de Vos is puzzling. Francken was influenced by an artist called Marten de Vos; perhaps the confusion began because of this.

Michelangelo Hayes (1820-1877)

Michelangelo Hayes was the son of the artist, Edward Hayes. His four paintings of *Car-Travelling in Ireland* were engraved and published by Ackermann in 1836, and can still be seen in hotels and houses all over the country. He began exhibiting at the RHA in 1837, the beginning of a long and stormy relationship with this establishment. Having been secretary of the Academy, he was expelled in 1857, reinstated in 1860, and re-elected secretary in 1861.

He specialised in military subjects and in equestrian painting, and was appointed Military Painter-in-Ordinary to the Lord Lieutenant in 1842. He spent the following years in London, exhibiting at the Society of Watercolour Painters. He returned to Dublin, where he became embroiled in the affairs of the RHA. In 1876 he read a paper on the depiction of horses in motion to the Royal Dublin Society. He was married to a sister of Peter Paul McSwiney, Lord Mayor of Dublin, who appointed him his secretary when in office. Strickland recounts Hayes's unusual death: while examining a water tank in the roof of his house, he fell in and drowned.

St Patrick's Day, Military Parade at Dublin Castle

1844, watercolour heightened with white on paper, 74 x 104 cm
signed bottom left: M Angelo Hayes 1844

This painting depicts a military parade in the Upper Yard of Dublin Castle. A number of different regiments are shown, with the 11th Hussars in the foreground. The others include the trumpeters from the 3rd Dragoon Guards, and the infantry of the 16th Regiment. St Patrick's Day, the last day of the Court season, was a highlight in the social calendar of the Castle. On that day, a ball was held in the evening, and during the day there were military parades in the Upper Castle Yard. These were described by one writer as 'a trooping of the colour'. The Lord Lieutenant and his family watched the parade from the windows of the Throne Room, above the entrance to the State Apartments.

The artist has depicted the scene from the south-east side of the upper yard. The two entrance gates and Bedford Hall form the backdrop to the event. At this time, Bedford Hall had a third storey, which had only been added a few years earlier, and which was removed during the 1980s refurbishment of this building. Striped awnings can be seen on the windows of the north range of buildings, which were the Chief Secretary's offices. The date 1844 adds a note of irony to this scene of gentility for the modern viewer; the participants appear unconscious of the burgeoning chaos and suffering outside the Castle walls.

This is one of a number of depictions of 'official' events connected with the Castle by Hayes. A later *St Patrick's Day*

Parade (1864) by him was presented to the Lord Lieutenant, the Earl of Carlisle. His most ambitious work was a six-by-eight-foot painting of *The Inauguration of the Prince of Wales as Knight of St Patrick in St Patrick's Cathedral in 1868* (1872).

PROVENANCE – Commissioned by Earl de Grey, Lord Lieutenant of Ireland. Lady Lucas of Wrest Park, Ampthill, Bedfordshire (sold 1917). Purchased by OPW at Phillips, London, 11th November 1997 (lot 54).

LITERATURE
Watercolours and Miniatures (Phillips, London, 1997)

Thomas Hudson (1701-1779) or studio of same

Son-in-law of the portrait painter Jonathan Richardson, Hudson was a successful portraitist based in London from the 1730s. Sir Joshua Reynolds was his pupil from 1740 to 1743. The art historian Ellis Waterhouse has summarised his talents rather unkindly: 'Hudson may fairly be described as the last of the conscienceless artists ... who turned out to standard patterns and executed comparatively little of the work themselves.' It is the distinct nature of Hudson's portraits that have led to the attribution of the Dublin Castle painting to him. He uses combinations of strong colours, his sitters are usually seated in elaborately carved chairs or thrones, and a great deal of attention is paid to drapery. Hudson employed other artists to paint the latter, in particular the van Aken brothers, who also worked for Allan Ramsay. He largely retired from painting in the 1760s when Reynolds was at the height of his career.

Portrait of Philip Dormer Stanhope (1694-1773), 4th Earl of Chesterfield

c.1745-46, oil on canvas, 125.5 x 100 cm

Philip Stanhope was born in London in 1794 and educated at Cambridge. In 1715 he was appointed Gentleman of the Bedchamber to the Prince of Wales, the future George II. He travelled widely, living in Paris from 1715 to 1717. In 1726 he succeeded to his father's title and took his seat in the House of Lords. His dislike of the Prime Minister, Horace Walpole, and his correspondence with Henrietta Howard, the king's mistress, hampered his career until the death of Queen Caroline in 1737. In spite of this, he was made ambassador to the Netherlands in 1728, and a Knight of the Garter in 1730.

In 1745 Chesterfield was made Lord Lieutenant of Ireland. During his eight months in office he made a positive impression. On his arrival in Dublin, he found his apartments in the Castle 'not only in the most ruinous condition but in immediate danger of falling to the Ground although continually propped'. He was responsible for the initial building of the State Apartments, and he, in particular, instigated the building of the ballroom (later to become St Patrick's Hall) and the State dining room or Picture Gallery. He allowed the public access to the Phoenix Park, and erected the Phoenix Column at his own expense. He also allowed Roman Catholic chapels to be built in the city of Dublin.

Chesterfield was a man of letters. He was a friend of Alexander Pope and an admirer of Jonathan Swift. He is chiefly remembered for his *Letters to his Son*, which were published by his son's widow shortly after Chesterfield's death in 1774. An important edition of the work was published in Dublin in 1776. In his letters, Chesterfield imparted worldly advice and showed a shrewd understanding of society and its behaviour.

The earl is shown seated in an elaborately carved chair, with a scroll of parchment in his left hand. He wears the badge and garter of the Order of the Garter. The rather awkward appearance of the sitter may have as much to do with Lord Chesterfield's appearance as with the artist's skill. Chesterfield was not known for his good looks – he was very short with a disproportionately large head. The style of the painting – the carved chair, the attention to the drapery, and the strong combination of colour – is very like the work of Thomas Hudson. Although no documentary evidence has yet come to light, the work matches a description of a painting of the earl which Hudson painted while he was Lord Lieutenant. This portrait was at Duff House, in the collection of the Duke of Fife, and was sold at Christie's, London, in 1907 (present whereabouts unknown). According to the sale catalogue, it showed Chesterfield 'in red dress, with powdered wig: wearing the Riband and Star of the Garter (25½ x 19"). Painted for Solomon Dayrolles, Master of the Revels to George II and Gentleman Usher to Lord Chesterfield when Lord Lieutenant of Ireland, 1745. Exhibited at the Hanoverian Exhibition, New Gallery, 1890-91.' It seems feasible that a second copy of the painting was painted by Hudson, or possibly an assistant, at the same time, and that this is the Dublin Castle work.

According to an OPW file (14882/28), the painting once had an inscription on the back of it which gave its history: 'This picture was presented by the Earl of Chesterfield, on his departure from Ireland, to a Miss Ambrose, who, during his viceroyalty was a great friend ... She lived to a great age and died in straitened circumstances in Eccles Street, Dublin, 1814, leaving directions that the painting should be left at the Castle ... it was allowed to knock about from room to room until 1870, when a valet objected to his apartments being disfigured by a picture so black & dirty ... The matter was reported to the Comptroller of the Household, Col. Caulfield (now Viscount Charlemont, C.B.), who thought there was much reason in the complaint and orders were given for its removal as lumber to the Board of Works Stores ... The frame ... attracted the Comptrollers attention, who said if allowed to

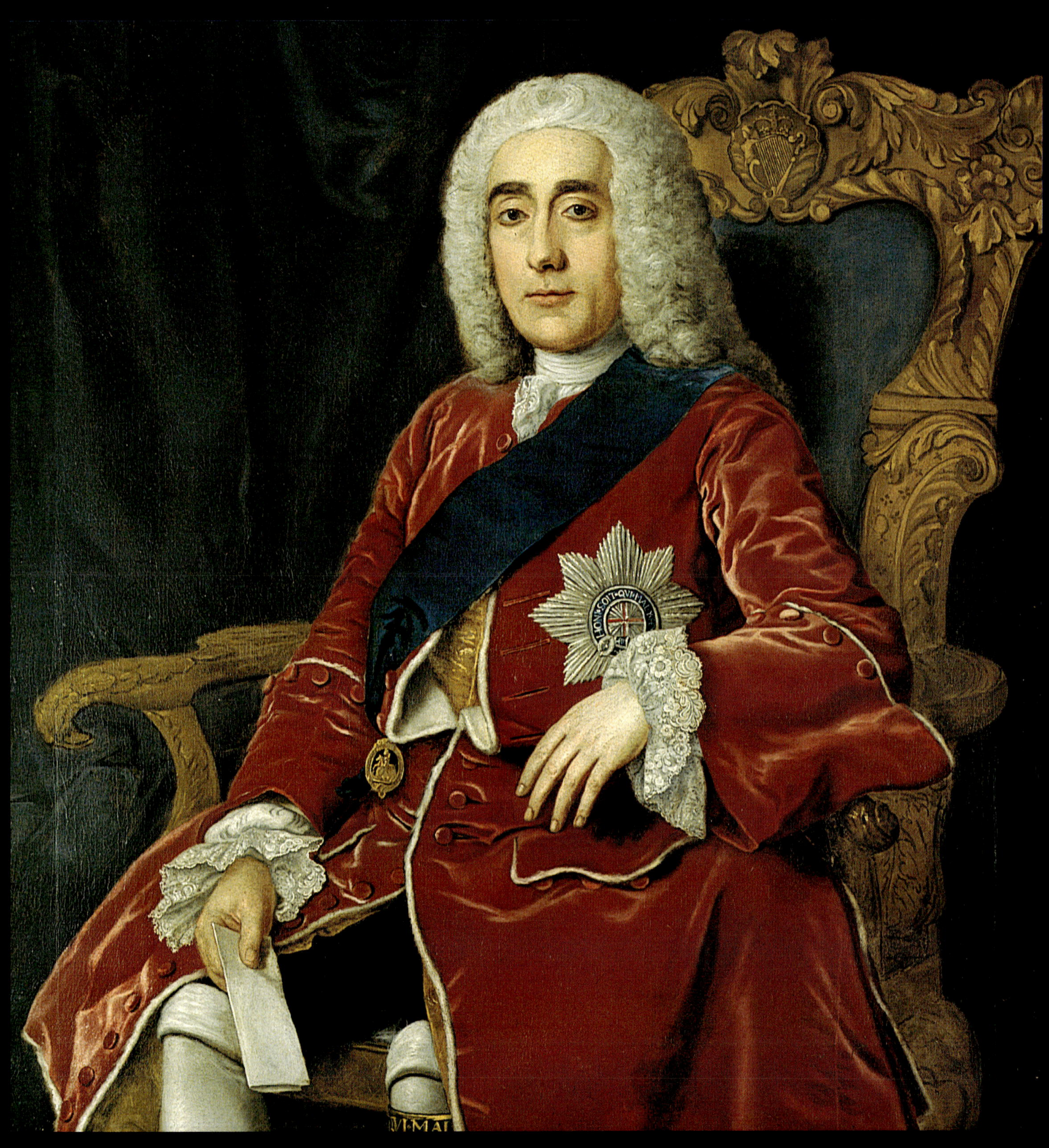

Thomas Hudson
Portrait of Philip Dormer Stanhope (1694-1773),
4th Earl of Chesterfield

appropriate it, he would have it cleaned and restored,* a request readily granted ... Sir Bernard Burke, at the time Ulster King of Arms ... at once recognised it as the picture of the Earl of Chesterfield.'

This rather far-fetched story is more credible when one considers that Chesterfield did indeed know a famous Catholic beauty in Dublin in the 1740s, Miss Eleanor Ambrose. She subsequently became Lady Palmer, and died in rooms in Henry Street, Dublin, in 1818. A visitor to her home shortly before her death left a description of a portrait which hung over her mantelpiece: 'It was a half-length portrait, and had, I believe, been given to her by the man of whose adoration she was virtuously vain ... a man who united so many accomplishments of manner and of mind, and [I] observed the fine intellectual smile, which the painter had succeeded in steeling upon the ... canvas ... She looked up at the picture of Lord Chesterfield with a melancholy smile.'†

PROVENANCE – In Dublin Castle in the 19th century. In the Viceregal Lodge, 1936.

LITERATURE
Richard Lalor Sheil, *Sketches, Legal and Political, by the late Right Honourable Richard Lalor Sheil*, 2 vols (London, 1855) i, 136, fn†
OPW 14882/28

I am grateful to Charles J. Burnett, Chamberlain of Duff House, for information on the Hudson portrait of Chesterfield formerly in that collection.

* There is a curious area in the lower right part of the painting where the details of the chair appear to have been crudely drawn rather than painted in. This gives the painting a rather flat appearance. An explanation for this could be 19th-century restoration work.

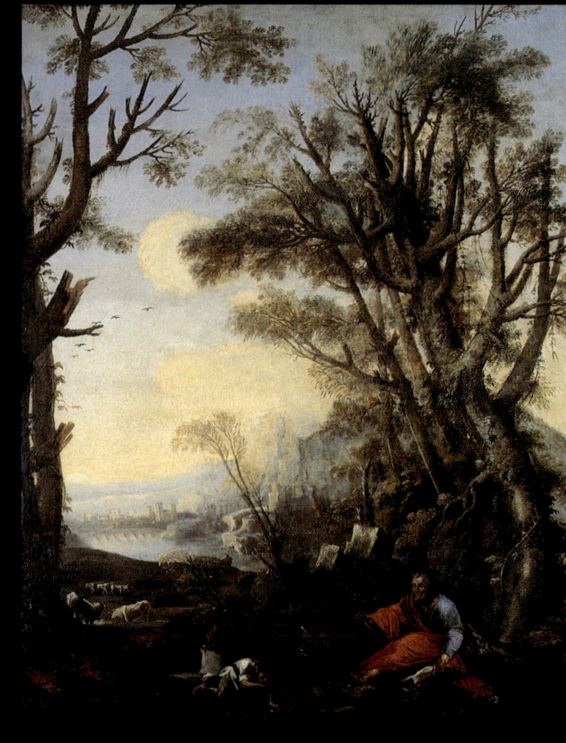

Italian, 17th century / early 18th century
Diogenes and his Bowl

attributed to Francis Johnston
Façade of Chapel Royal

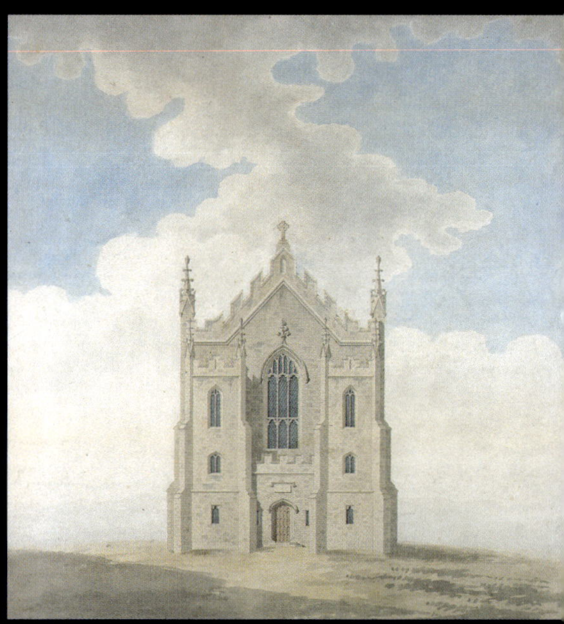

Italian, 17th century / early 18th century

Diogenes and his Bowl
oil on canvas, 188 x 158 cm

This painting is ostensibly a landscape in the style of the Italian painter, Salvator Rosa. The trees in the foreground, with their branches bent and damaged, are typical of his romantic style. The bearded figure of an old man seated by a river and dressed in blue and red can be seen in the foreground. With one hand he grips a large open book, while his other is extended as if in surprise. A stick appears to have fallen out of his grasp. Behind him on the bank is a bowl. In front of the old man, drinking from the stream, is a young boy.

The subject is difficult to decipher. The proximity of the boy and the reaction of the old man suggest that this is a depiction of the story of Diogenes and the bowl which occurs in 17th-century Italian painting. The Greek philosopher Diogenes was famous for the simplicity and frugality of his life. He lived in a barrel and had no worldly possessions. One day, upon seeing a boy drinking water from his cupped hands, Diogenes threw away his drinking bowl, realising that this was a luxury that he did not need. Diogenes was depicted a number of times by Salvator Rosa, including this particular story. He is usually situated in a wooded wilderness, surrounded by followers. But depictions of him in isolation are also known.

PROVENANCE – Unknown. No record of its purchase in this century. Does not fit descriptions of paintings in earlier lists and archives.

attributed to Francis Johnston (1860-1829)

Johnston was born in Armagh, the son of a prosperous builder/architect. In 1778 he began to work with the Dublin-based architect Thomas Cooley, and succeeded him as Primate of Ireland's architect in 1784. In 1805 he was appointed architect to the Board of Works and Civil Buildings, and spent the next fifteen years engaged in all kinds of public building projects, most notably the General Post Office. One of his most successful buildings, and one which has best survived, is the Chapel Royal at Dublin Castle, which was built from 1807 to 1814. This, and St George's Church in Hardwick Street, are the finest surviving examples of Johnston's ecclesiastical work.

Johnston retired in 1820, and his practice was taken over by his nephew and business partner William Murray. For the last nine years of his life, Johnston devoted his time to his extensive collection of artworks. He was a founding member of the Royal Hibernian Academy, and designed and built their premises on Sackville Street (destroyed in 1916) in 1824.

Façade of Chapel Royal

pencil and watercolour on paper, 49.3 x 44.5 cm

This is a detailed depiction of the façade of the Chapel Royal, Dublin Castle, which is situated in the Lower Castle Yard. It appears to have been a working architectural drawing rather than a piece of fine art. There is a scale at the bottom of the sheet, and marks on the surface of the paper suggest that it was used as a drawing for some time. It was framed by Combridges in Dublin during the first half of this century, and it may have been at this stage that it was hung in Dublin Castle.

PROVENANCE – Unknown. Possibly acquired from Combridges in the 20th century.

after Angelica Kauffmann (1741-1807)

Angelica Kauffmann was born in Switzerland and received her earliest training as an artist from her father. In the 1760s she lived in Italy, studying antique sculpture as well as the work of the Old Masters. She quickly established a reputation as a portraitist. In 1766 she settled in London, and in 1768 was a founding member of the Royal Academy to whose annual exhibitions she was a regular contributor. Kauffmann managed to become one of the most successful history painters and portraitists of her generation in an age when women were not considered suited to a career as a professional artist. Her gender does not seem to have impeded her progress, although it was targeted by Nathaniel Hone in his satirical attack on the academy, *The Conjuror* (1775, National Gallery of Ireland). Kauffmann was depicted nude in this work, although Hone was obliged to repaint this part of the painting.

She visited Ireland in 1771 when she was invited by the Lord Lieutenant, Lord Townshend, to paint his portrait and that of his family. She was the guest of a number of distinguished Irish families during her stay, including Lord and Lady Ely at Rathfarnham Castle, Lady Caroline Damer at Emo Park, and Mrs Clayton at St Stephen's Green. Apart from a small number of portraits, little of her work from this visit is known.

In 1781 Kauffmann married the Venetian painter Antonio Zucchi, and returned to Italy, where she continued to receive commissions for portraits and historical paintings. She befriended the German poet Goethe, and the artist Johann H.W. Tischbein. She was one of the most popular painters of the day. Many of her historical paintings were made into prints, and some of her designs were reproduced in decorative schemes and on furniture.

Andromache and Hecuba Mourning over the Ashes of Hector

c.1772, oil on canvas, 127 x 101 cm

This painting is a version of a painting which was exhibited at the Royal Academy in London the year after Kauffmann's return from Ireland. There is a mezzotint of the original by Burke in the British Museum, which was published by Ryland in March 1772, just before the exhibition. The subject is from Homer's *Iliad*, and depicts Andromache and Hecuba mourning over the ashes of Hector, the murdered commander of the Trojan army. Andromache is shown leaning on a large cinerary urn on which is inscribed the Greek letters of Hector's name. Their infant son Astyananx comforts his grandmother Hecuba. The scene takes place in a stark interior – the only decoration and source of light is the lamp in the background and a plaque on the wall behind it. The lamp recurs in another history painting – *Penelope Awoken by Eurykleia* (Vorlarlberger Landesmuseum, Bregenz) – which Kauffmann also exhibited at the RA in 1772.

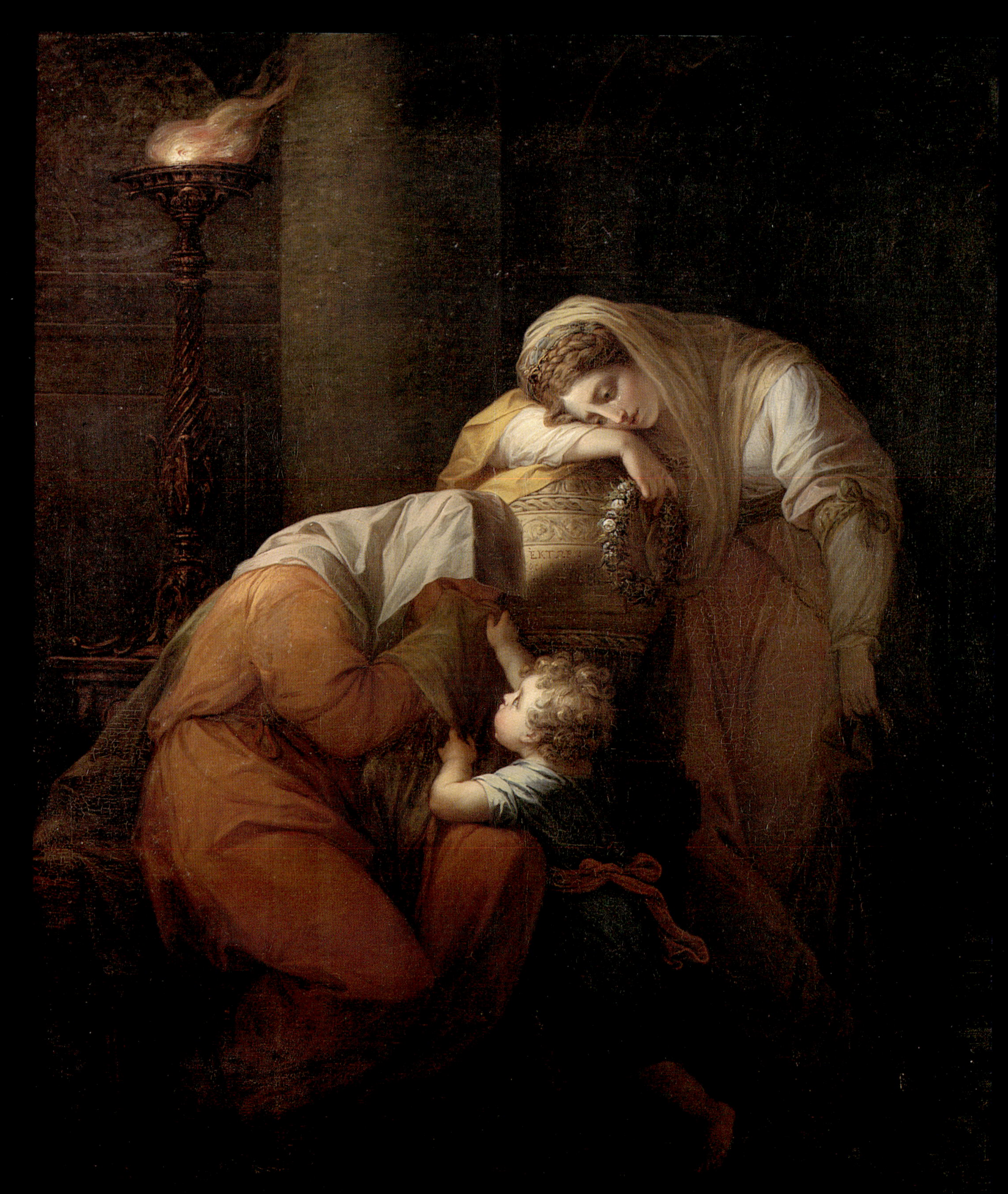

after Angelica Kauffmann , *Andromache and Hecuba Mourning over the Ashes of Hector*

This subject was a popular one among neoclassical painters. The Scottish artist Gavin Hamilton had an engraving of his version of the scene published in 1766, and Jacques Louis David ensured his entry into the French Academy after exhibiting a painting of the subject at the Salon in 1783. Kauffmann's depiction of the scene differs most notably from that of the two male artists in that she does not show the body of Hector, and her Andromache is remarkable for the restraint and quiet of her mourning. As in many of her works, she focuses on the different generations of the family; Hector's absence from the group is symbolised by the classical urn, but his family is shown united and supportive in their grief.

This delicately painted work appears to be a copy of Burke's engraving of Kauffmann's *Andromache*. Its subtle use of colour and line suggest that it is the work of an extremely competent artist who understood and appreciated the work of Angelica Kauffmann. (The whereabouts of the original Kauffmann painting is unknown.)

PROVENANCE – Purchased by the OPW from Naylor's, Liffey Street, Dublin, 1950s.

COMPARATIVE LITERATURE
Lady Victoria Manners and G.C. Williamson, *Angelica Kauffmann RA* (London, 1924) 40
Wendy W. Roworth (ed.), *Angelica Kauffmann – A Continental Artist in Georgian England* (Royal Pavilion, Art Gallery and Museums, Brighton, 1992) 173

I am grateful to Prof Wendy Roworth and Dr Judy Egerton for the attribution of this work, and for their comments on it.

A more detailed study of this painting and its provenance is being prepared by the author.

unknown, copy of Angelica Kauffmann

Diana and Actaeon

oil on canvas, oval-shaped mount, 33 x 40.7 cm
inscribed in pencil top right corner (covered by mount): Angelica Kauffmann R.A, top left (covered by mount): 1740

Venus Presenting Helen to Paris

oil on board, 49 x 37 cm
inscribed on frame: oil painting Major Birch R.A; label also on frame: J.D. Spence Picture Frame Makers, Dublin

The Flight of Paris and Helen from the Court of King Menelaus

oil on board, 49 x 37 cm
inscribed on frame: oil painting Major Birch R.A.; label also on frame: J.D. Spence Picture Frame Makers, Dublin

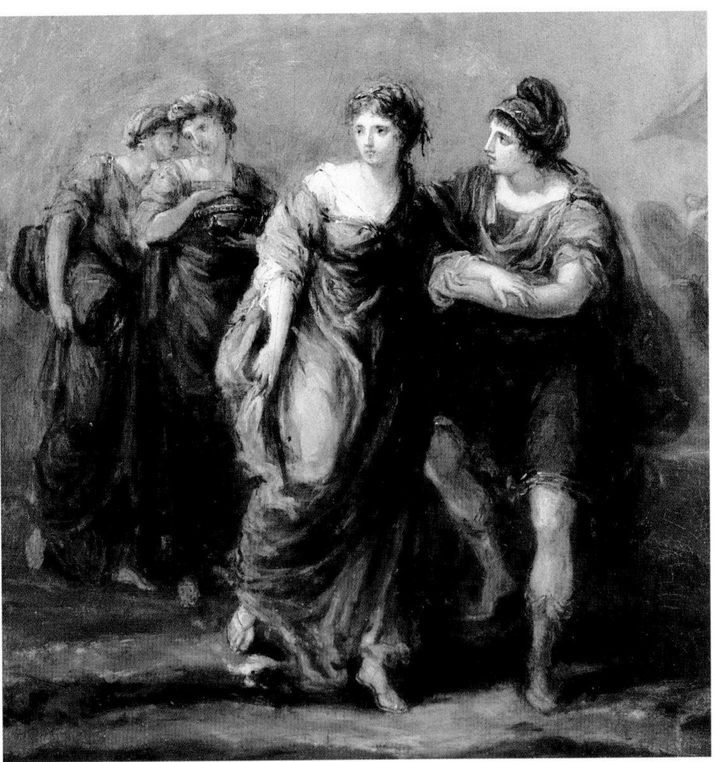

unknown, copy of Angelica Kauffmann
The Flight of Paris and Helen from the Court of King Menelaus (detail)

The above two subjects, in circular form, were engraved and published by Ryland, 1st January 1781. The two small paintings of Paris and Helen are copies, possibly from engravings, but in rectangular rather than circular form. They tell the story of the fateful meeting of Paris and Menelaus's wife Helen, and their subsequent flight which led to the Trojan war. They were possibly painted by Major Birch, in whose possession they once were.

PROVENANCE – Major General Birch, 1851. Purchased from D.M. antique shop, Nassau Street, Dublin, for £25 in 1955.

Henry Kirchhoffer (1781-1860)

Kirchhoffer was descended from a Swiss surgeon who came to Ireland with the Williamite army. His father was a cabinet-maker in Henry Street, Dublin. Kirchhoffer attended the Dublin Society Schools from 1797, and began exhibiting portraits in 1801. He worked as a miniature painter, mainly in watercolour, although oil paintings by him are known. His subjects are mainly landscape and portraits. He was one of the founding members of the RHA in 1826, and served as its secretary until 1830. In 1835 he settled in England, residing in Brighton for many years and exhibiting at the Royal Academy from 1837 to 1843. He died in London.

Sea Coast, Smugglers

1829, oil on canvas, 52 x 63 cm, signed (illegible inscription on tower)

This small oil painting depicts a Mediterranean port, with a prominent tower and mountain behind it. A merchant ship from which two Dutch flags are flying is moored in the bay, with smaller boats pulling alongside it. Exotically dressed figures stand on the quay, and are presumably meant to represent the smugglers. Dr Philip Smyly of the Maritime Museum has identified the scene as Martello in Corsica. The tower, which was blown up in 1796 by the English, with great difficulty, later became famous as the prototype for the Martello towers, which were built all over British-controlled coasts in the Napoleonic period.

A note in an OPW file dating to 1930 states that the painting has been restored and placed in the board room of the Commissioners of Public Works. According to the file, a signature was found on the painting: 'H. Kirchhoffer 1829'. Kirchhoffer did exhibit a painting entitled *Coast Scene, Smugglers* at the RHA in 1829. This work would seem to be a pastiche of 18th-century French marine painting, like that of Claude-Joseph Vernet or Lacroix de Marseille.

PROVENANCE – Unknown. In the dining room of the Viceregal Lodge in 1897 (OPW 5 6540/98). Appears in the 1909 inventory of paintings at the Viceregal Lodge, where it is described as being in the 'Morland style'. It hung in the board room of the Commissioners of Public Works in 1936 (A77/7/1/39, p.16).

LITERATURE
OPW 5 5147/30; OPW 5 6540/98; OPW A77/7/1/39

EXHIBITED
RHA 1829 (123)

I am grateful to Dr Philip Smyly of the National Maritime Museum, for his comments and help on the subject of this work.

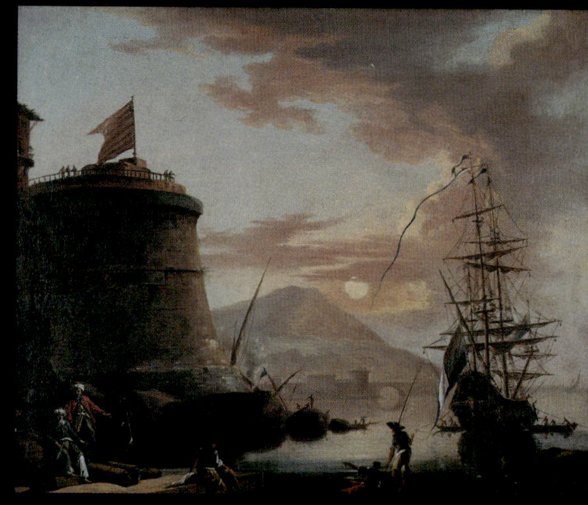

Henry Kirchhoffer
Sea Coast, Smugglers

Dermod O'Brien (1865-1945)

O'Brien came from Foynes, Co Limerick, the grandson of William Smith O'Brien MP. He was educated at Harrow and Trinity College, Cambridge, which he left before taking a degree. In 1887 he enrolled at the Antwerp Academy of Fine Art, where his fellow students included the painter Walter Osborne. In 1891 he moved to Paris, where he attended the Académie Julian. He lived in London from 1893 to 1901, studying at the Slade and sending paintings to the RHA in Dublin. After his return to Dublin he became known as a portrait painter, and took an active role in the RHA, of which he was elected president in 1910.

O'Brien was part of the Ascendancy, and was a frequent

Dermod O'Brien
Portrait of John Gordon Campbell (1847-1934), 7th Earl of Aberdeen

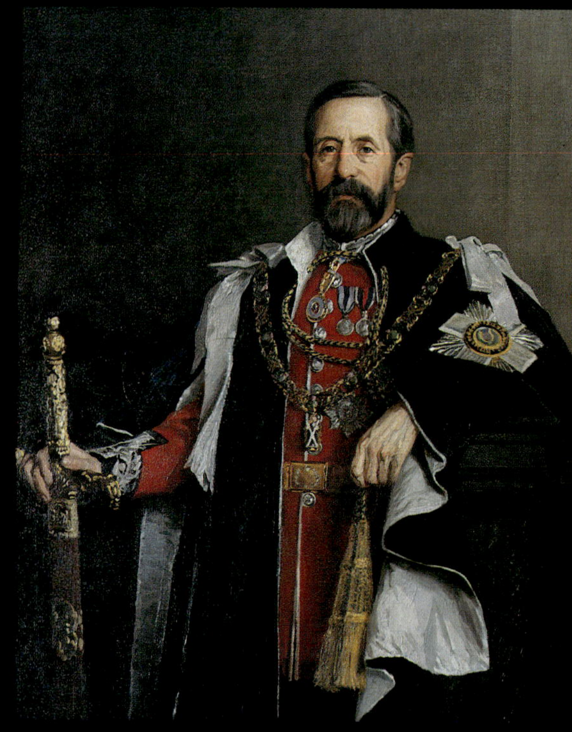

visitor of the Aberdeens. He served as Deputy Lieutenant of Limerick, and from 1916, High Sheriff of Limerick. After independence, he continued to take an active part in cultural affairs, and remained as president of the RHA until his death in 1945.

Portrait of John Gordon Campbell (1847-1934), 7th Earl of Aberdeen
1913, oil on canvas, 128 x 102 cm

This portrait was painted during the earl's second term as Lord Lieutenant (1906-15) and shows him wearing the collar and badge of the Order of the Thistle. The star of the Thistle is emblazoned on his cloak. Around his neck is the badge of St Patrick. This is a much more formal portrait than the earlier one of Aberdeen by Furse. He holds the sword of state in one hand, and stares intently at the viewer. Despite his involvement in the setting up of collections of modern art, O'Brien was staunchly academic in his own work, and resisted the contemporary pull towards impressionism, particularly in the realm of portraiture. *The Studio* praised his work of this period for its 'extreme sincerity, and for the feeling of form and balance which it displays', and this portrait does justice to this description.

Although nothing has yet come to light regarding the commissioning of the work, it must originally have been intended as part of the lord lieutenant series in the Picture Gallery. The dimensions of the painting are the same, but the frame of this work is quite different. It is likely that due to the outbreak of the First World War, and subsequent political events, it never became part of the group.

Provenance – Collection of the artist, 1913.

Exhibited
RHA, 1912 (68)
Whitechapel exhibition of Irish Art, 1913 (33)
Art of the State, 1993

style of David Roberts (1796-1864)

The Scottish artist David Roberts was widely known in the early Victorian period. Many of his paintings were reproduced in travel books, such as his *Picturesque Sketches in Spain* (1837) and *Italy, Classical, Historical and Picturesque* (1859). His landscapes are topographical in character and usually concentrate on architecture. Roberts had a tremendous sense of light and scale, and his views of the crumbling splendours of foreign climes, coupled with the inclusion of modern life, made his work very popular with the British public who shared the same romantic curiosity.

View in the Roman Forum looking North Eastwards, from the Temple of Saturn
watercolour on paper, 49 x 65 cm

The connection with David Roberts is made through an inscription, now missing, which was once on the back of the painting: 'Attributed to David Roberts, R.A. 1796-1864. View in the Roman Forum, looking north-eastwards, from the Temple of Saturn, towards the truncated mediaeval Fortress Tower, the Torre delle Milizie'.* Although the painting is in the style of Roberts, the details of this work, particularly in the foreground and in the depiction of the architecture, would indicate that it may be by an imitator. There is some damage to the sky and foreground, which also hinders accurate attribution.

Provenance – Unknown

Literature
OPW file A6/1/21, vol. II

* Dr Michael Wynne, who examined the painting in 1988, has given this recollection of the contents of the label. Its existence was noted in the files of that year, OPW file A6/1/21, vol. II.

Jan Baptiste de Saive (c.1540-1624), or studio of same

Very few biographical details of de Saive's life are known. He lived in Namur early in his career, and is sometimes known as Jean de Namur. In 1590 he was court painter in Brussels, and in 1603 he moved to Mechelen. He produced a number of religious paintings, usually altarpieces for churches in Brussels and other Belgian towns. He is more famous for his market scenes, which followed the style of the painter Joachim Beuckelaer. De Saive was unusual in that he attracted patronage from the aristocracy for his market scenes. In 1594, Archduke Ernest commissioned six market paintings representing the seasons, and in 1597 the court at Brussels also acquired a set of market paintings from him.

Fish Market
oil on canvas, 146 x 112 cm (cut down)

This work has been attributed to de Saive, or his studio, by Dr John Loughman of UCD and by Fred Meijer of the Rijksbureau voor Kunsthistorische Documentatie in The Hague. The original composition may have been taken from a much larger composition, which would have included a second set of market figures on the left, with a vista onto a Flemish town or market square in the centre. Dr Loughman has located the photograph of such a paint-

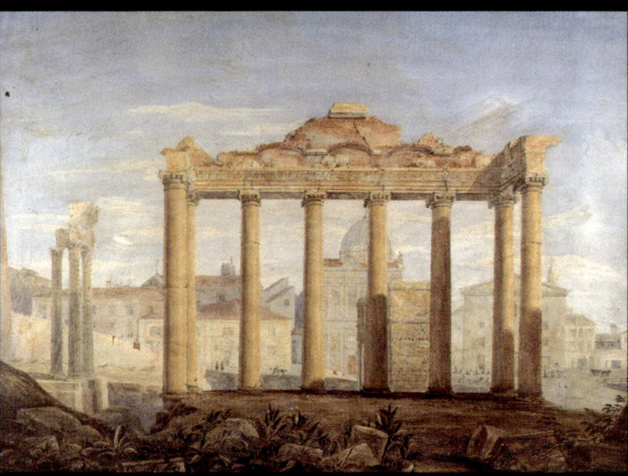

style of David Roberts
View in the Roman Forum looking North Eastwards, from the Temple of Saturn

Venetian school, 18th century
Sacrifice of Isaac

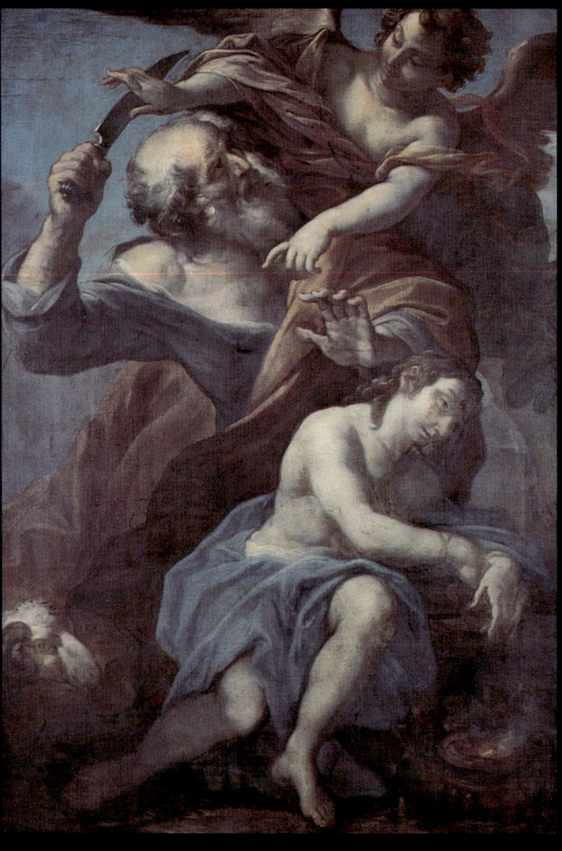

ing in a private collection in which the right-hand figures are very similar to the Dublin Castle painting.

The painting of market places began in 16th-century Antwerp with the painter Pieter Aertsen, who included religious subjects in the background of his seemingly secular works. Their appearance coincided with the economic expansion of Antwerp and Flanders, and with the decline of religious painting, especially after a ban on religious images was introduced. A new kind of patron emerged, usually middle class and urban, and as a result, artists began to specialise in particular kinds of subject matter. Market scenes were sometimes allegories of the times of the year, and the depiction of fish and shellfish usually represented March and April when oysters and mussels were plentiful. Here a remarkable range of fish is on display; it is likely that de Saive employed a specialist fish painter to do this part of the work for him. This work belongs to a transitional period in the development of genre painting, and there is a tension in it between the depiction of the figures in their peculiar costume and the display of goods in the foreground. This and the warm tonality of the colours adds to the charm of this painting.

PROVENANCE – Purchased by the OPW from Naylor's, Liffey Street, Dublin, 1950s.

COMPARATIVE LITERATURE
Alexander Wied, entry on De Saive in *Johnny van Haeften Gallery* catalogue (London) December 1987
E.A. Honig, *The Artist and the Market in Early Modern Antwerp* (Yale University Press, 1998)

I am grateful to Dr John Loughman for advice on attributing this work.

Venetian school, 18th century

Sacrifice of Isaac
oil on canvas, 172 x 119 cm

This work was at one time attributed to Pellegrini, but it is more in the style of his fellow Italian, Giovanni Battista Pittoni (1687-1776), whose work was widely collected in the 18th century. This work may be by a follower or imitator of this artist. It depicts the story of Abraham sacrificing his son Isaac. Isaac is seated with hands bound over an urn of burning embers. His father's knife is caught in mid-air by an angel who points to the ram, indicating that this should be sacrificed rather than Isaac. The paint is quite thin in parts, and the grouping of the figures is rather cramped. But the head of Abraham in particular is expressive, and is probably the most successful part of the painting.

PROVENANCE – Purchased by the OPW from Naylor's, Liffey Street, Dublin, 1950s

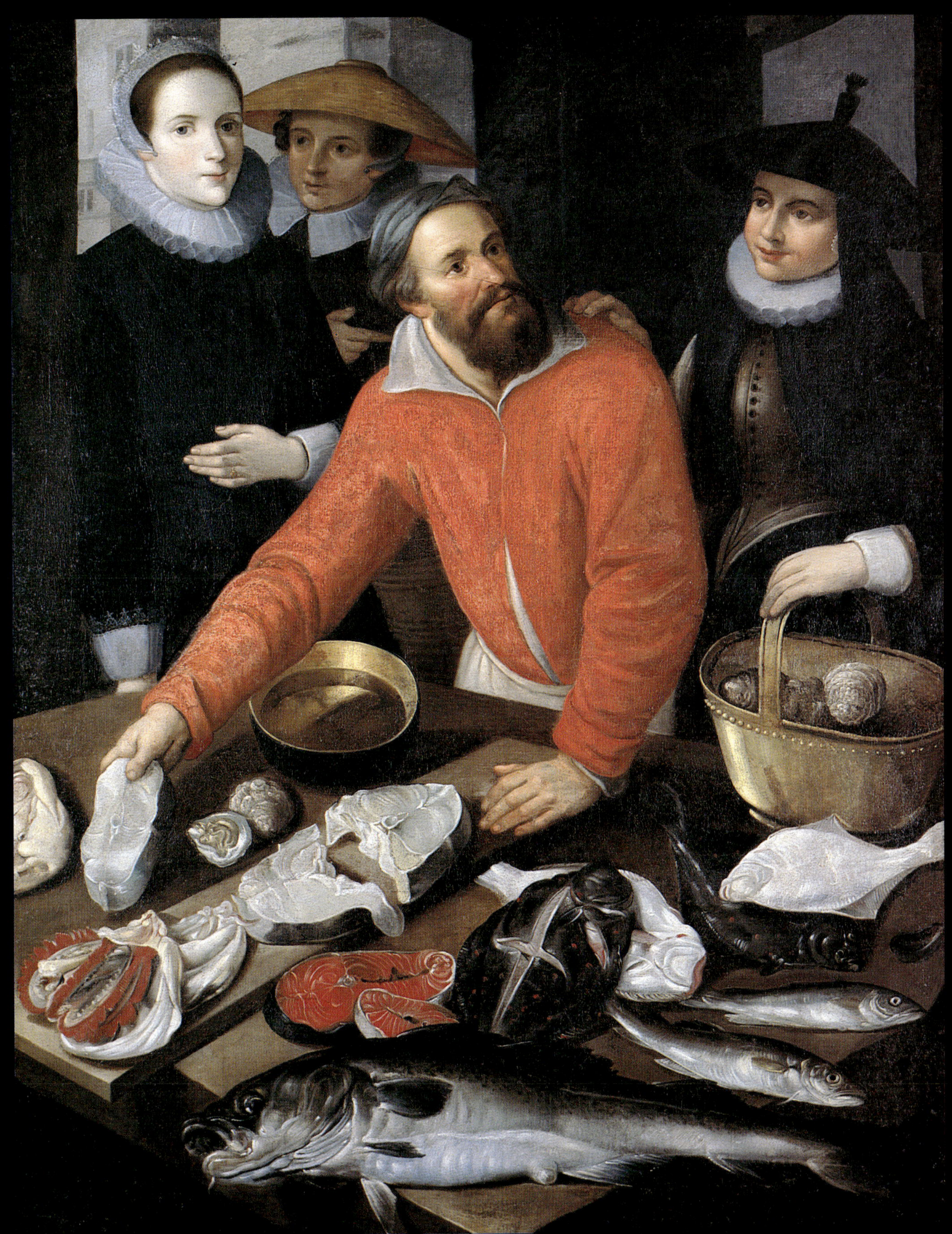

Jan Baptiste de Saive, or studio of same, *Fish Market*

Prints

R. Havell & Sons, after F.C. Pack (1750-1840)

Pack had a long and varied career. He was born in Norwich and came to London *c.*1781, where he spent a year working in Reynolds's studio. He arrived in Ireland in 1787, apparently on the recommendation of Reynolds to the Duke of Rutland. Pack concentrated on landscape and view painting, and exhibited at the Society of Artists in the early 1800s. He finally left Dublin for London in 1821, having had to subsidise his living through teaching. He died in London.

East View of the Giant's Causeway, no.1
coloured aquatint, 49 x 66 cm (proof copy)
signed bottom right: F.Chris. Pack
marked: F.C. Pack esq. Pinx. Engraved by Havell & Son. Proof. (dedication: To his Royal Highness, George Prince of Wales, Regent of the United Kingdom. These views of the Basalt District, in the County of Antrim, Ireland, are with permission most respectfully dedicated to his Royal Highnesses devoted Servant Faithful Christopher Pack.)

West View of the Giant's Causeway, no.2
coloured aquatint, 49.5 x 67 cm (proof copy)
signed bottom right: F. Chris. Pack 21
marked: F.C. Pack Esq. Pinx. Engraved by Havell & Son. Published Nov. 9 1819, by F.C. Pack, Dublin, and Mr. Ackermann, Printseller, Strand, London. Proof. (dedication: Select views of the Basalt District, in the County of Antrim, Ireland.)

Strickland describes these prints as 'among the scarcest of Irish views'. He himself owned signed proof copies. The Giant's Causeway is one of the most popular tourist sites in Ireland, and was often depicted by artists. The prismatic formations of basalt were caused by volcanic activity along the north Antrim coast. Molten basalt was ejected from the earth, and its cooling process resulted in the strange shape of the rock. Dr William Hamilton published a book on the subject of its origin in 1786, which added to the public's curiosity.

LITERATURE

W.G. Strickland, *A Dictionary of Irish Artists*, 2 vols (Dublin, 1913) ii, 213

R. Havell & Sons, after T.S. Roberts (c.1760-1826)

Thomas Sautell Roberts was a pupil of the Dublin Society Schools from 1777. He was apprenticed to the architect Thomas Ivory, but decided to become an artist. After a few years in London, he settled in Dublin in 1799. He exhibited Irish and English views at the Royal Academy from 1789 to 1811, and again in 1818. His early views were painted in watercolour, and he had them engraved. Many were published as part of a series, *Illustrations of the Chief Cities, Rivers and Picturesque Scenery of the Kingdom of Ireland.* From 1800 to 1821 he exhibited with the Society of Artists in Dublin. At the inaugural exhibition of the RHA in 1826, Roberts was on the selection committee. According to Strickland, he injured his shoulder while travelling by coach in England, and had to give up painting. He committed suicide in his home in Richmond Street, Portobello, very shortly afterwards.

View of Lower Castle Yard, Dublin Castle
aquatint, 43 x 61 cm
label on back: Castle of Dublin. Dedicated by permission to the Right Hon.ble Charles Earl Whitworth, G.C.B. Lord Lieut. of Ireland and Grand Master of the Order of St Patrick. In the centre is seen the New Castle Chapel, on the Right the Treasury, to the left the Entrance to the Ordnance Office, and Avenue leading to Gt. Ship Street. Published 1816 by Del Vecchio, Westmoreland St, Dublin.

This print has, at some point, been varnished to make it look like a painting. It is a delightful view of the Lower Castle Yard, from where the modern Stamping Building is now situated. The label on the back (see above) outlines the main buildings visible in the view. The Castle chapel, or Chapel Royal as it is usually called, dominates the composition. This had only been completed two years before the print was published. The print is dedicated to Lord Lieutenant Whitworth, and it is known that Roberts was patronised by the Dublin Castle establishment. Lord Lieutenant Hardwicke and Chief Secretary, Charles Abbott, owned landscapes by him.

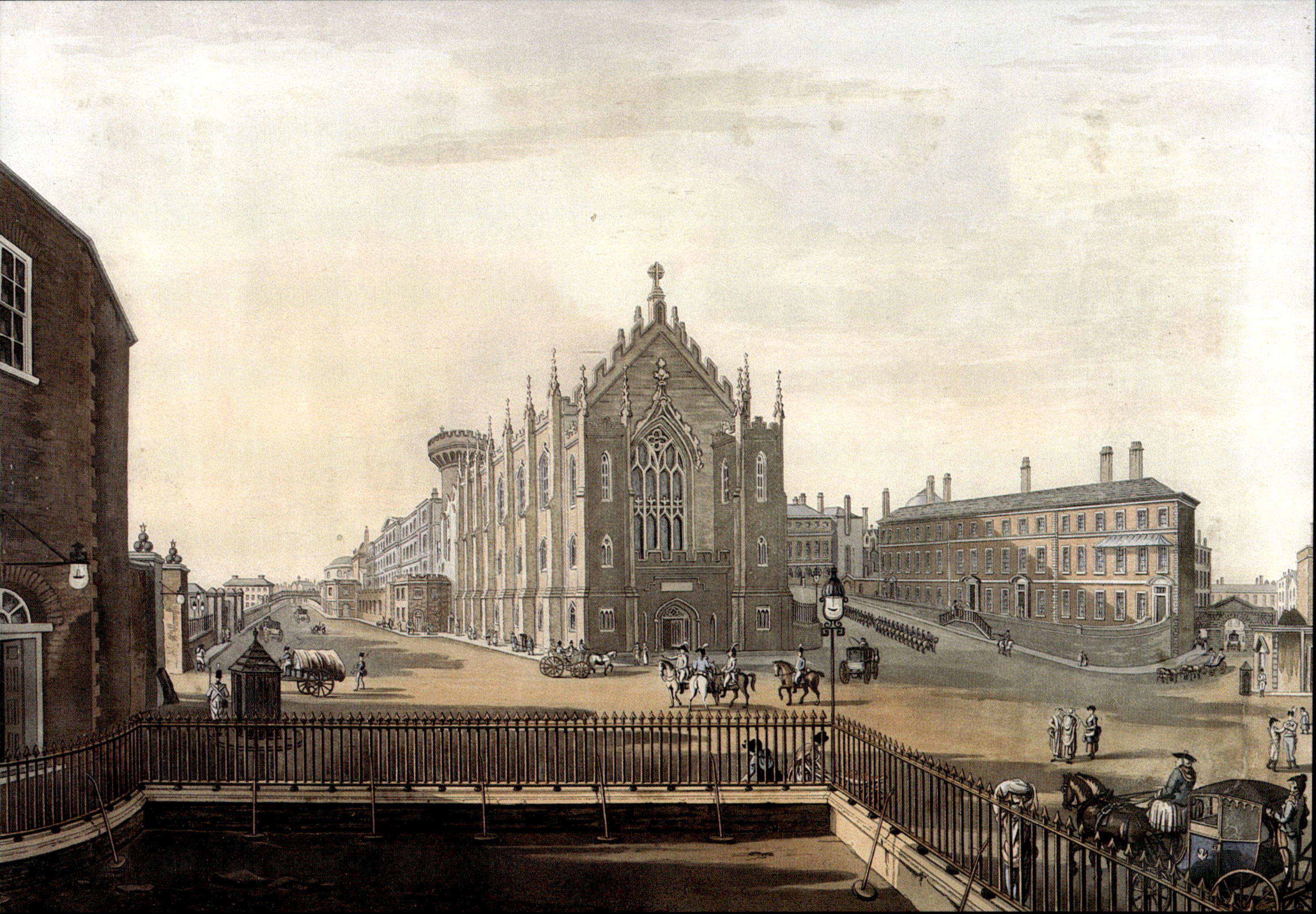

R. Havell & Sons, after T.S. Roberts
View of Lower Castle Yard, Dublin Castle

bottom left
R. Havell & Sons, after F.C. Pack
East View of the Giant's Causeway, no.1

bottom right
R. Havell & Sons, after F.C. Pack
West View of the Giant's Causeway, no.2

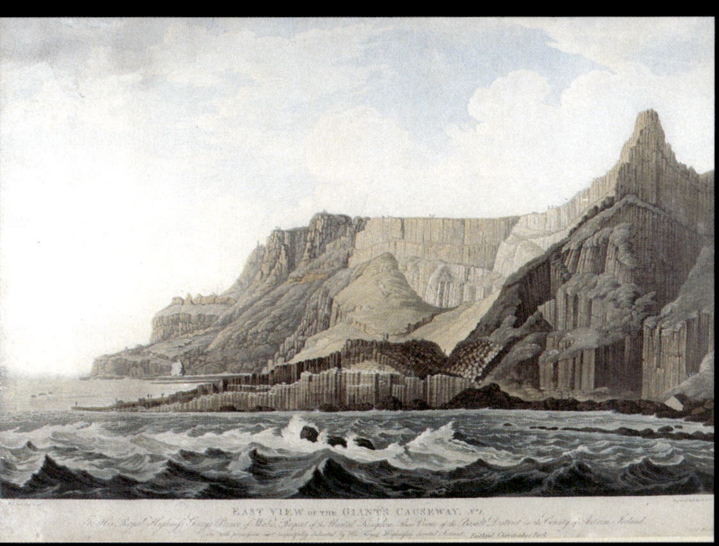

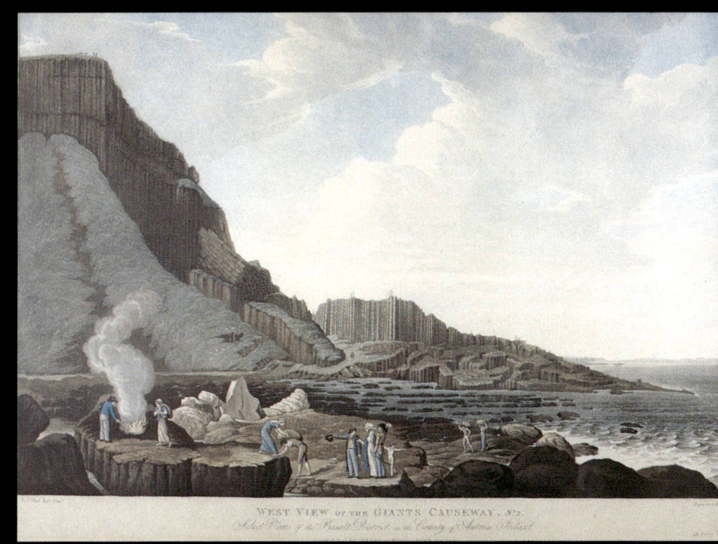

Sculpture

(See also under Granard gift)

after the antique

Arrotino (Knife Grinder)
marble, 37.5 cm (including base)

The *Arrotino* or *Knife Grinder* is a widely copied piece of sculpture whose subject matter was interpreted very differently over the centuries. The fact that the figure seems to be listening intently has led many to speculate on his identity. The 18th-century scholar Agostini solved the mystery when he recognised the composition from an antique gem. According to his findings, it represents the knife-grinder awaiting instructions from Apollo to begin flaying alive the god's rival, Marsyas.

PROVENANCE – Unknown

Dying Gladiator
bronze, 29 cm; marble plinth: 4.5.cm

This is a copy of the celebrated antique sculpture the *Dying Gladiator*. The original marble sculpture was discovered in the 17th century, and acquired by Pope Clement XII in 1737, since when it has been in the Capitoline Museum in Rome. It was widely copied by artists for its depiction of the male anatomy and also for the expression of exhaustion. The gladiator wears a torc around his neck, and his unclassical features indicate that he is a Gaul or Celt. He is shown lying on his shield, with his sword, belt, and what appears to be a Celtic trumpet on the ground.

PROVENANCE – Purchased by the OPW at the sale of Courtown House, Kilcock, Co Kildare, 1963 (lot 364).

Dying Gladiator
marble, 28 cm

This figure is based on the antique sculpture of the *Dying Gladiator* (see previous entry).

PROVENANCE – Unknown

Albert Carrier-Belleuse (1824-1887)

Carrier, who changed his name to Carrier-Belleuse in 1868, was a leader in the baroque revival in the decorative arts in France in the mid-19th century. He was committed to the production of good quality decorative art which could be produced in editions, rather than unique fine art pieces. Carrier began making statuettes for commercial manufacture in the 1840s. He produced portrait busts, small figures and groups to be produced in almost every possible material, including terracotta, porcelain and bronze. From 1850 to 1854 he worked for the Minton porcelain works in England.

He began exhibiting at the Salon in 1854, and in 1863 the Emperor bought his *Bacchante* for the Tuileries. He contributed sculptural work to many of the buildings being erected or refurbished under Baron Haussmann's direction, including the Louvre and the Opera. He continued to produce small decorative pieces and monumental sculpture throughout his career, and from 1876 was director of the Sevres porcelain factory. He exhibited his work at international exhibitions, and held public auctions on a regular basis. His assistants included Rodin and Mathurin Moreau.

Orpheus
c.1867, bronze on marble base, 53 x 65 cm (including base)
signed: Boyer Carrier

Orpheus was a poet and legendary musician. It was said that he could charm wild animals with his music. Seated on a classical chair draped with an animal skin, he holds a lyre in one hand – given to him by his father Apollo. The melancholy disposition of Orpheus is probably a reference to the loss of his wife Eurydice, whom he had followed into the underworld but lost forever by disobeying the gods and looking back towards Hades. Orpheus was a male equivalent to Sappho, who is also shown seated with a lyre. Both figures were widely depicted in the 19th century, providing images of the tragic figure of the artist, doomed to a life of unhappiness. Offenbach's opera *Orphée aux Enfers*, which was first performed in 1858, added considerably to the popular interest in the story.

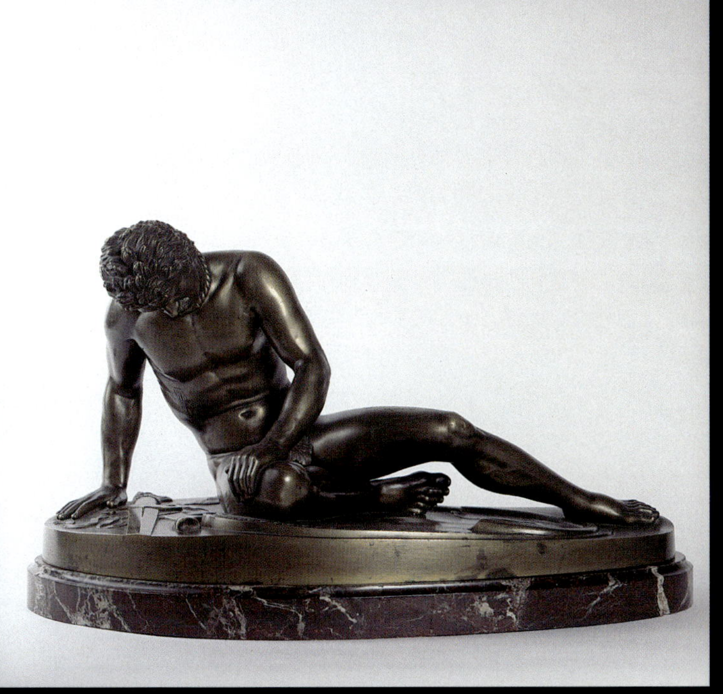

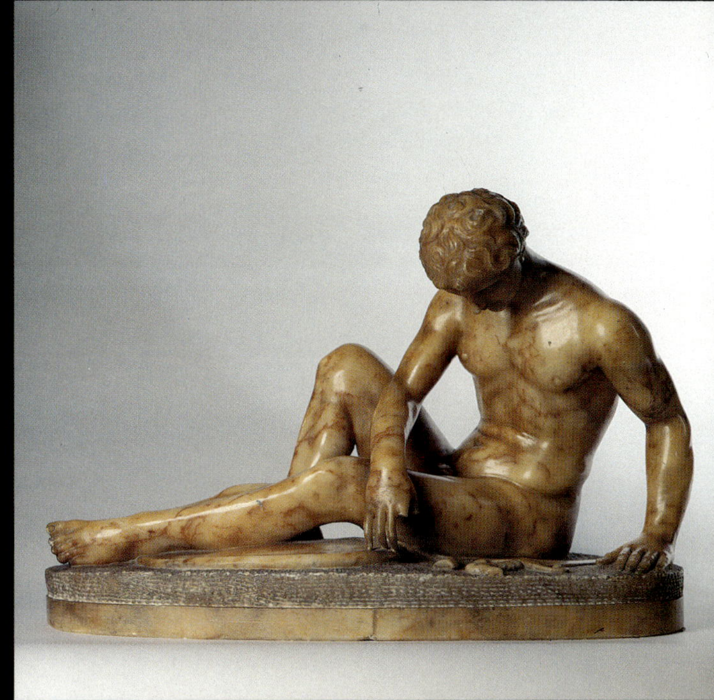

after the antique
Dying Gladiator

after the antique
Dying Gladiator

after the antique
Arrotino (Knife Grinder)

Albert Carrier-Belleuse
Orpheus

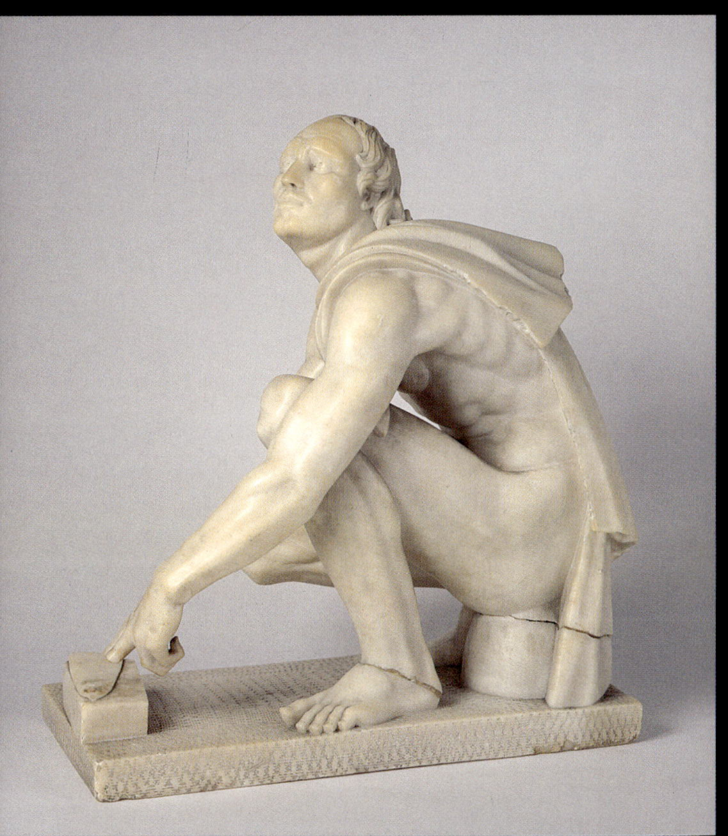

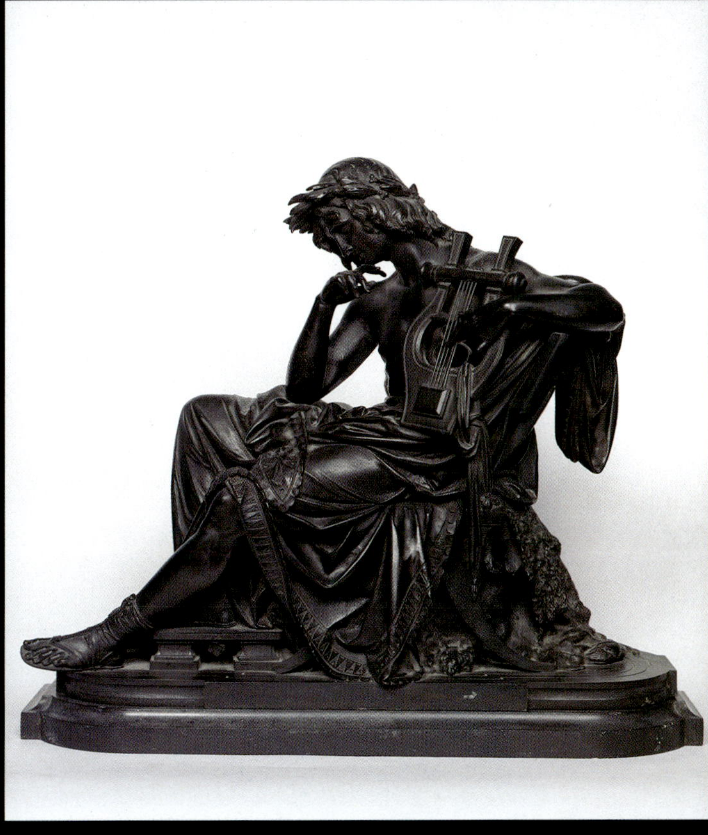

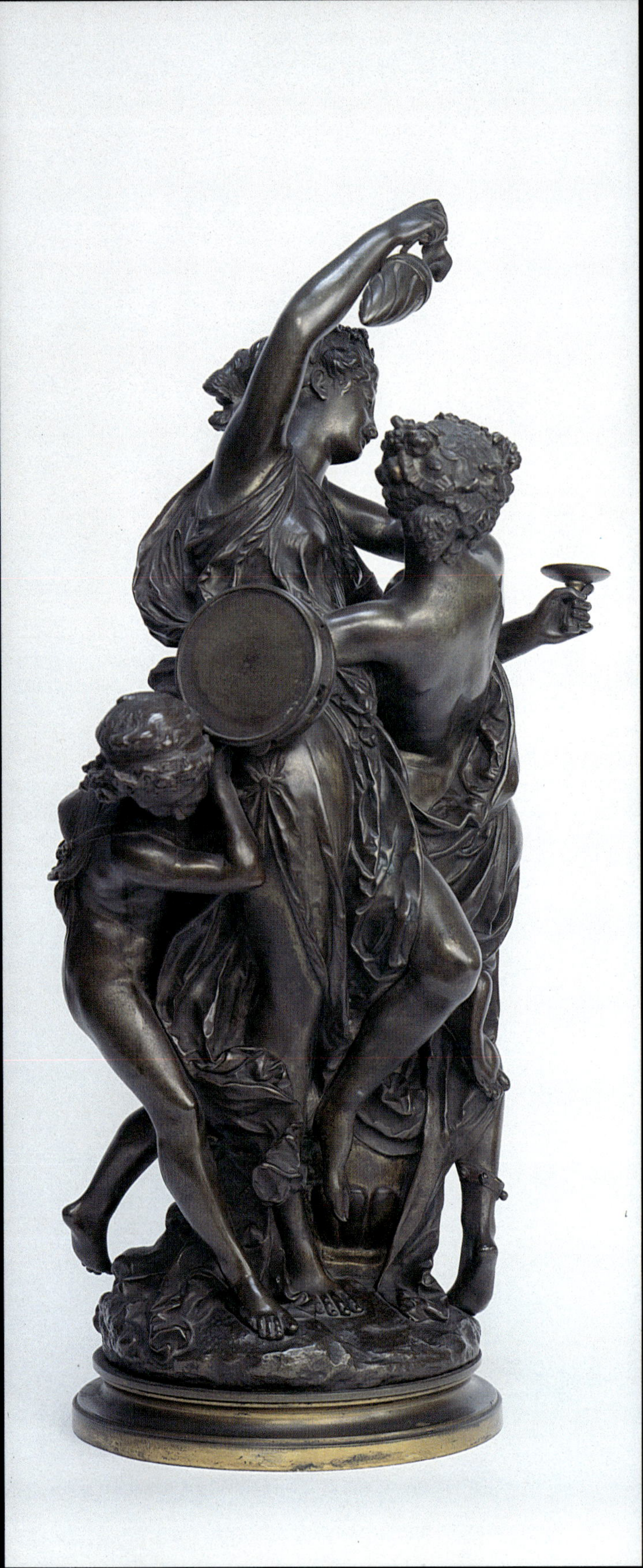

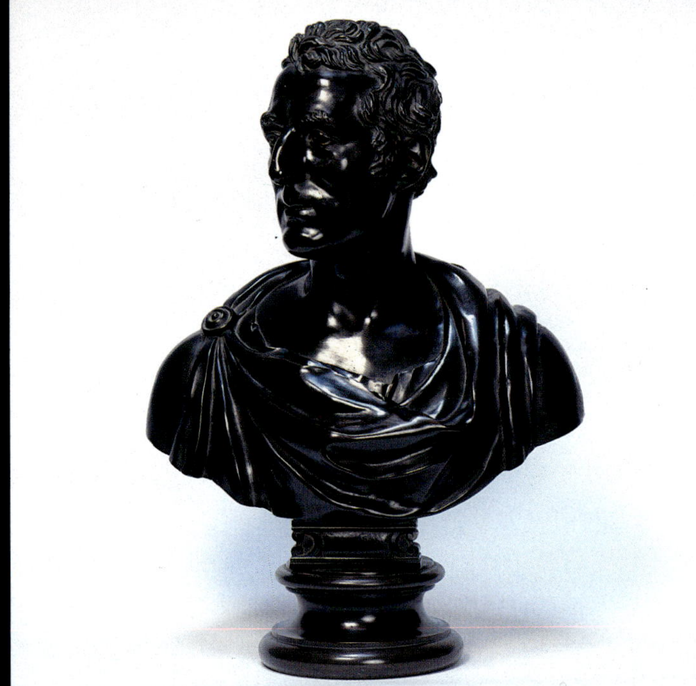

attributed to Lawrence Gahagan
Arthur Wellesley (1769-1852), 1st Duke of Wellington

Albert Carrier-Belleuse
Bacchantes Dancing

English / continental school, 17th century
Bust of an Unidentified Nobleman

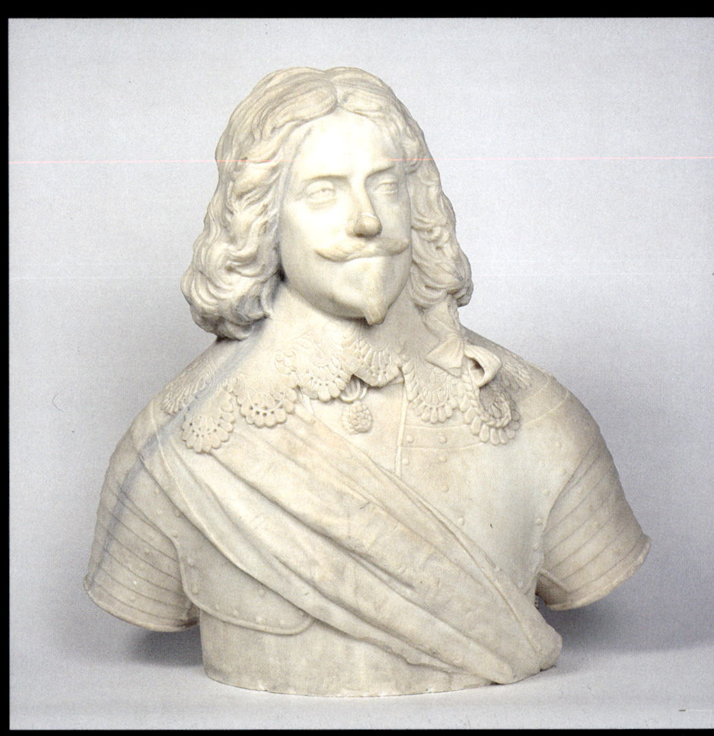

The foundry mark of Boyer gives some indication of the date of the figure. Boyer exhibited a bronze Orpheus by Carrier-Belleuse at the 1867 *Exposition Universelle*. The original maquette for the work was made by 1863, as a photograph of it dating to this time is known. A gilt-bronze version of the figure was included in the 1980 Los Angeles County Museum exhibition, *The Romantics to Rodin*. A piece with Boyer's mark, like the Dublin Castle one, is in the Cleveland Museum of Art.

PROVENANCE – Unknown. In Dublin Castle since late 19th century (visible in photographs of State Apartments); in dining room of State Apartments, Dublin Castle (1908 inventory: 'One Bronze figure representing Music on shaped marble plinth').

COMPARATIVE LITERATURE
P. Fusco & H.W. Janson (eds), *The Romantics to Rodin* (Los Angeles County Museum, 1980) 161-63. (I am grateful to Dr Paula Murphy for drawing my attention to this reference.)

Bacchantes Dancing

bronze: 69 cm, signed: A. Carrier

This work is typical of the kind of decorative art sculpture produced by Carrier and his contemporaries, Clodion and Carpeaux, c.1860. It shows a group of bacchantes dancing and drinking, their heads entwined with grapes. A large urn, which was once gilt bronze, forms the centre of the piece.

PROVENANCE – Unknown

English / continental school, 17th century

Bust of an Unidentified Nobleman

c.1640, marble, 61 cm

This bust is not mentioned in any inventories or descriptions of the Castle. It was located in the basement of the Castle in 1992, when it was first put on display. The costume of the sitter dates him to the 1640s, but there is no indication of who it might be. The most striking feature of his dress is the plait of hair which is tied with a ribbon on his left shoulder. This occurs in a number of portraits of Charles I and in at least one bust of Charles II as a child. It is apparently a rather flamboyant fashion which was adopted by the king and one or two courtiers.

The quality of the carving is quite fine and unlike the kind of sculptural work being done in Ireland in the 17th century. Most of the work being produced in Ireland and Britain in this period was monumental tomb sculpture. A portrait bust such as this is quite rare. It is possible that it was brought to the Castle from England by an official at some point, and relegated to storage in the basement. While it has not been possible to attribute the piece to any particular artist, it is very similar to the work of François Dieussart (1622-1661), an influential sculptor who worked at the court of Charles I in England and for the House of Orange in Holland.

PROVENANCE – Unknown. Located in basement of Castle in 1992.

attributed to Lawrence Gahagan (fl.1756-1820)

Gahagan was born in Ireland and was a pupil of the Dublin Society Schools, where he won a medal in 1756. He moved to London where he won a prize at the Society of Arts in 1777 for a six-foot-high relief of Alexander exhorting his Troops. He concentrated on small portrait busts, many of which he exhibited at the Royal Academy from 1796 to 1817.

Arthur Wellesley (1769-1852), 1st Duke of Wellington

bronze on bronze pedestal, 56 cm (73 cm with pedestal)

Sir Arthur Wellesley, later Duke of Wellington, was Chief Secretary for Ireland from 1807 to 1809. Born in Dublin, the third son of the Earl of Mornington, he became one of the most famous men in 19th-century Britain. His political career began as MP for Trim (1790-95), and ended as Prime Minister from 1828 to 1830. He was a hero of the Napoleonic Wars, having lead the allied defeat of Napoleon at Waterloo.

The bust shows the duke as a young man wearing a toga which is fastened on his left shoulder with a round brooch. He looks slightly to the left. This bust is related to the marble busts of the duke by the sculptor Joseph Nollekens (1813/14). However there are slight differences, particularly in the shoulder area, which is uncovered in the Dublin example.

There are two variations of this bust: one was based on Lawrence Gahagan's 1809 bust which was engraved in 1812; the later version was copied and displayed at Apsley House, Woburn Abbey and Stratfield Saye. The Dublin Castle bust is a variation of this earlier version. There are some differences especially around the shoulder. An identical plaster version of the Dublin Castle bust is in the collection of the American Philosophical Society (photograph in the Heinz Archive, National Portrait Gallery, London).

PROVENANCE – Listed in the 1908 inventory of the State Apartments: located in St Patrick's Hall.

attributed to John Houghton (fl.1741-1775)

Houghton worked as a woodcarver in Dublin in the mid-18th century. In 1739 he and another sculptor were paid for carving a coat of arms and other decorations at Carton, Co Kildare. The Dublin Society awarded him prizes for his sculpture in 1741 and 1742, the latter for a piece of sculpture based on Raphael's cartoon of St Paul preaching at Athens. He worked on frames, including that of Bindon's portrait of Jonathan Swift, which is in the Deanery of St Patrick's, and on several of the frames in Trinity College, Dublin. With David Sheehan, he made a number of important funeral monuments. In the 1740s he was employed on the decoration of the State Apartments in Dublin Castle.

Marcus Aurelius (carved overmantle)

c.1751, oak and pine, 223 x 233.5 cm
inscribed: Marcus Aurelius Germanis Parthius Supplicibus, ac sese Dedentibus Dextram porrigit at que in suam fidem recipit

This overmantle is one of the earliest original artworks in Dublin Castle. The architectural historian Frederick O'Dwyer believes that it was originally made in 1750/51 for the ante-drawing room, which is no longer in existence. It was situated in what is now part of the State drawing room, next to the Throne Room, and was destroyed in the 1941 fire in the State Apartments. Fortunately, the overmantle had been placed outside on the Battleaxe landing many years before. In 1952 it was removed from over the chimney piece on this landing, when a new door into the Throne Room was put in place.

The design of the overmantle derives from that of another overmantle which is in the Stone Hall in Houghton Hall, England, where it is executed in marble. The design was published in Isaac Ware's *The Plans, Elevations and Sections of Houghton, Norfolk* (1735). The architect, Ware, had connections with Dublin, and worked for the Earl of Kildare at Leinster House and for his brother-in-law at Castletown in the 1750s. He may indirectly have influenced Lord Chesterfield's schemes for the refurbishment of the State Apartments in the 1740s, and in the design of the ante-drawing room. The influence of Ware's designs in Dublin in this period can be seen in another similarly carved overmantle, which is in the inner hall of Iveagh House, St Stephen's Green. This, which is based on another Houghton Hall overmantle, is also attributed to Houghton, although the quality of the carving is quite different to the Dublin Castle piece; it is much less three-dimensional and smoother in execution. Houghton, the most prominent woodcarver of the time, is recorded as working at Dublin Castle in this period. He was responsible for the fitting-out of the ballroom and the Council Chamber in 1749, and it is possible that he also undertook work on the ante-drawing room. His name, however, does not appear among those craftsmen who received payment for the 'fitting up of the Castle of Dublin, for the Reception of his Grace the Duke of Dorset' (i.e. the refurbishment of the ante-drawing room).*

The scene depicted on the overmantle is from the life of Marcus Aurelius, the Roman emperor who ruled from AD 161-180. Gibbons places him at the apex of the Roman Empire just before its decline. He is noted for his interest in stoic philosophy, which he tried to use in his rule, and which was at odds with the autocratic ideas more usually associated with his position. He insisted on sharing power with Lucius Verus, who died in 169. From his tutor, Fronto, he learned rhetoric and developed his literary tastes. His *Meditations*, a series of books which he wrote in Greek, contain his enlightened ideas of leadership. They were translated into English in 1634. The choice of a scene from the life of Marcus Aurelius would seem to be eminently suitable for the ante-chamber of the Throne Room. However the inscription on the overmantle is militaristic in style, and refers to Marcus Aurelius as conquering emperor rather than enlightened leader. A rough translation of the inscription is 'Marcus Aurelius ruler of Germany and Parthius, he, himself, strikes down his enemy with his right hand, and receives them into his own faith'.[†]

PROVENANCE – Part of the ante-drawing room decor, 1751.

LITERATURE

* House of Commons Journals, v, appendices ccxxxvi, ccxxxvii (1751-52)
H. Leask, *Dublin Castle, A Short Descriptive and Historical Guide for the Use of Visitors* (Dublin, 1944)
Frederick O'Dwyer 'The Ballroom in Dublin Castle' in Agnes Bernelle (ed.), *Decantations – A Tribute to Maurice Craig* (Lilliput Press, Dublin, 1992) 162-63

† I am grateful to Dr Ann Neville for translating this inscription and explaining its meaning.

John Hughes (1865-1941)

Hughes was born in Dublin and studied at the Metropolitan School of Art, where he won a scholarship to the Royal College of Art in London. Here he came into contact with the ideas of French realism, and later studied in Paris where this style had originated. In 1894 Hughes returned to Dublin and took up a teaching position at the Metropolitan School. In 1898 his monument to Charles Kickham was unveiled in Tipperary by the Fenian John O'Leary. Two years later, Hughes resigned from the School of Art, and in 1901 moved to Paris, where he remained for the rest of his life. In 1910 he was commissioned to do a monument to Gladstone, which never made it to its intended site in the Phoenix Park. It was erected in Gladstone's home town of

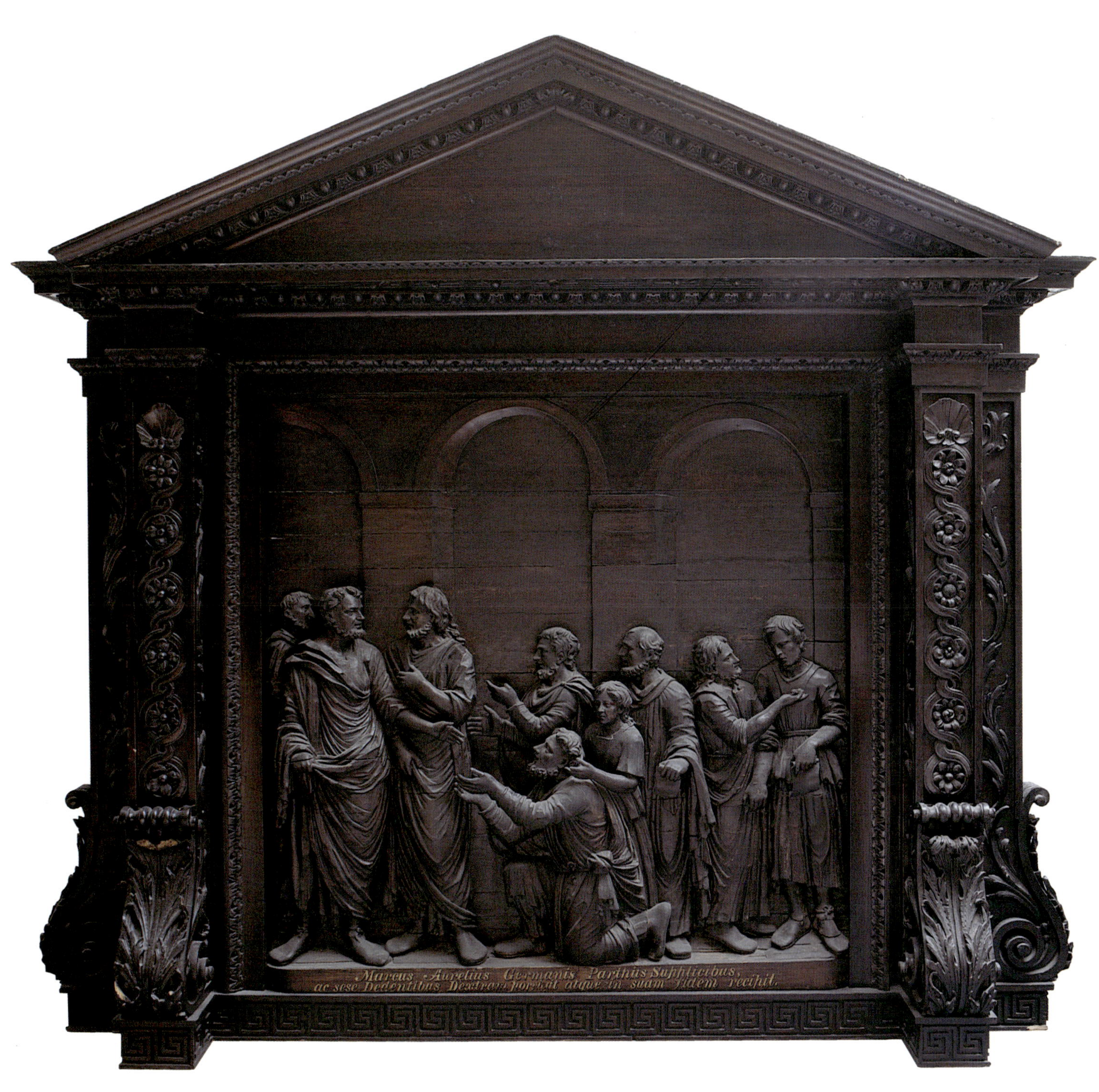

attributed to John Houghton
Marcus Aurelius (carved overmantle)

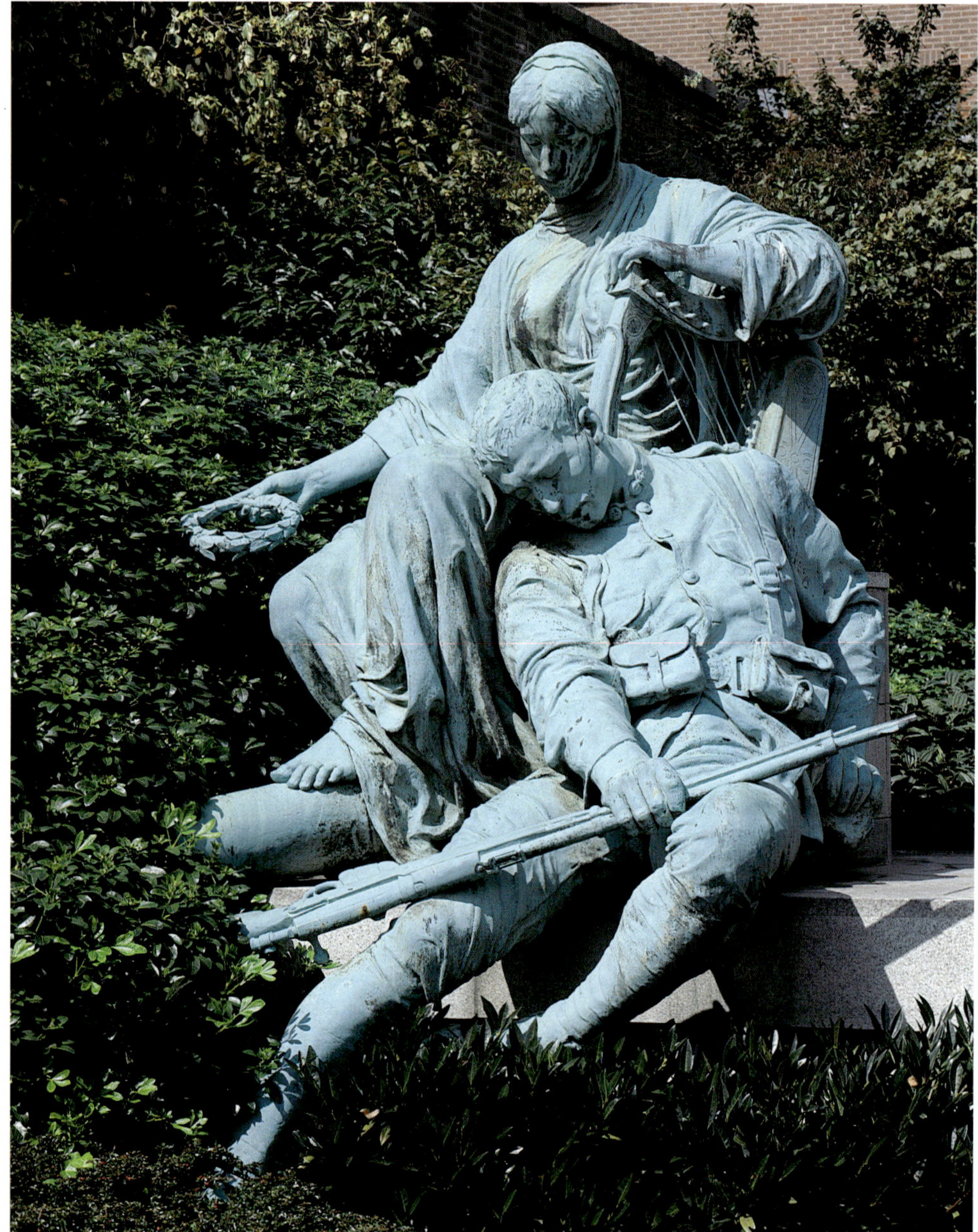

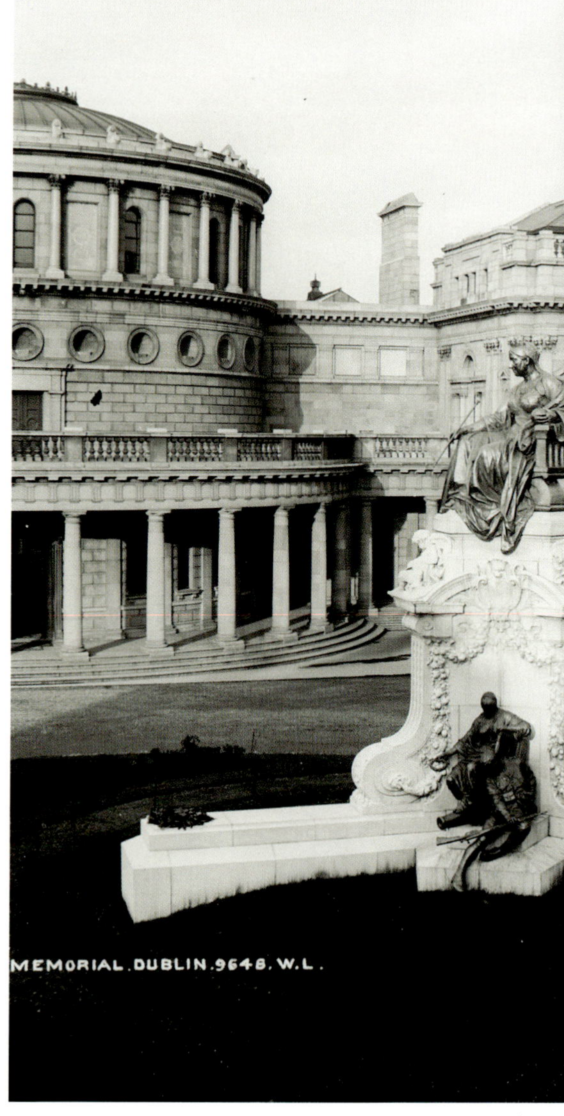

John Hughes
Figures from the Monument to Queen Victoria: (left) *Victory*, (right) *Fame*

Hawarden, North Wales, in 1925.

Along with Oliver Sheppard, Hughes introduced a new type of monumental sculpture into Irish art. His Parisian training brought him into contact with a tradition of large-scale ambitious public sculpture that combined realistic detail with the use of allegory. The monument to Queen Victoria was the most ambitious undertaking of his career, and he devoted more than five years of his life to it.

Figures from the Monument to Queen Victoria: Victory
1908, bronze, 319 cm

This group depicts Erin tending a dying soldier. Erin, presented as a young woman, holds out the laurel crown of victory in one hand, while her other arm rests on an Irish harp. The soldier is a reference to the recent Boer War in which many Irishmen had fought. Hughes has depicted him in contemporary uniform. His half-closed eyes and slouched body indicate that he is dying, but he grips onto his rifle firmly, while his other hand clasps onto a rock behind him.

This figure demonstrates Hughes's keen understanding of anatomy and modelling. The group manages to be realistic and contemporary in detail while retaining a monumentality and pathos appropriate to the subject.

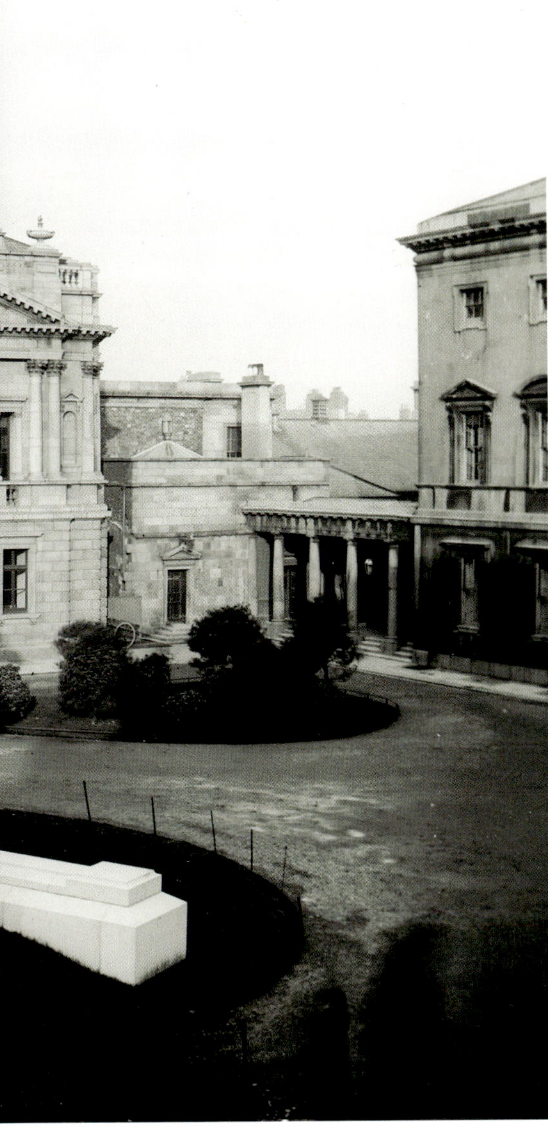

Lawrence Collection photograph of the Queen Victoria Monument outside Leinster House

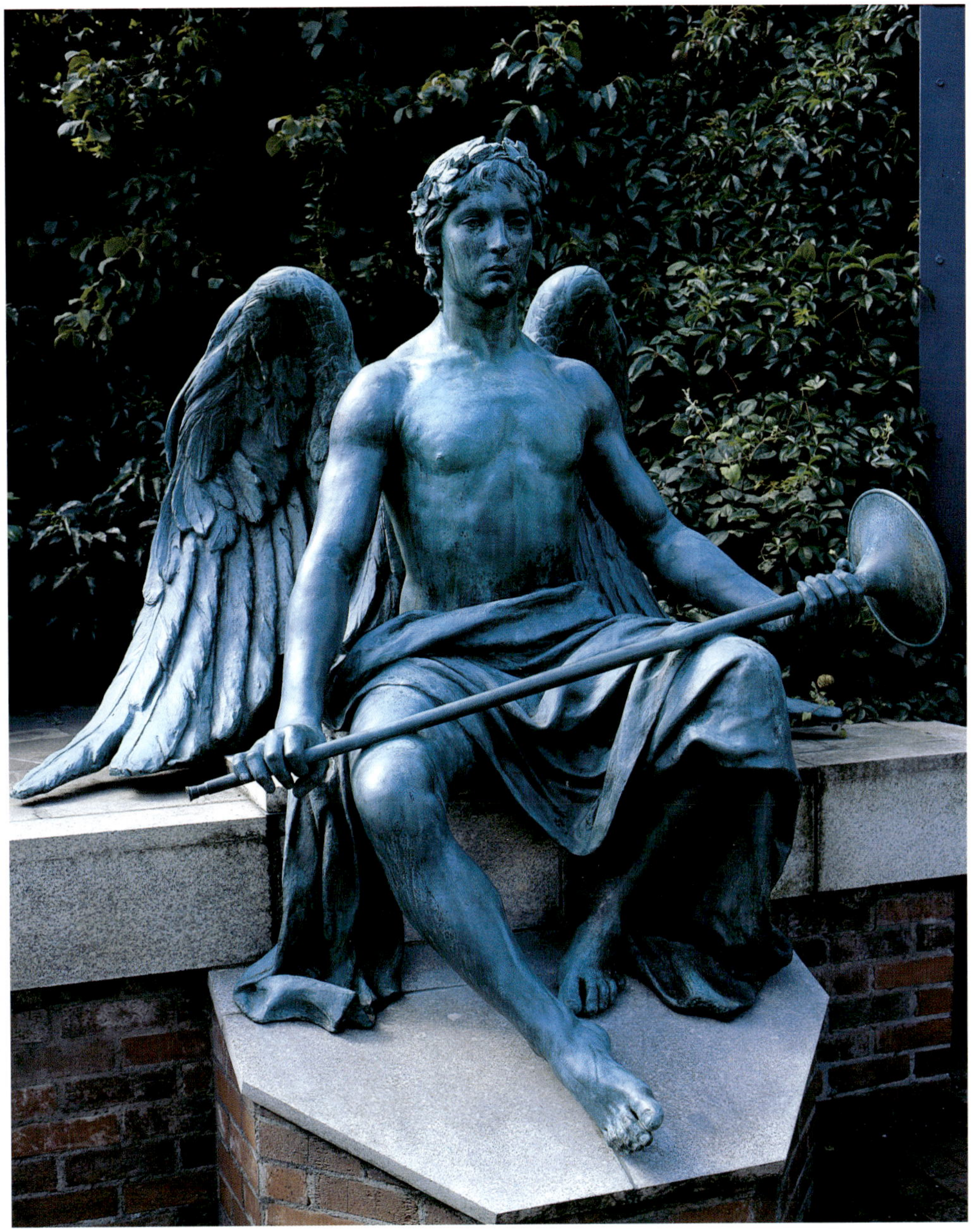

Figures from the Monument to Queen Victoria: Fame
1908, bronze, 180 cm

This is a classical winged figure with a laurel crown. It was obviously intended to balance the two figure groups which originally accompanied it on the Victoria monument. It appears to be symmetrical with the trumpet balanced across its knees. The tension in the muscles of the arms and legs of the figure has been closely observed and replicated in the piece.

The monument, of which these two bronzes were once a part, was first proposed by the Royal Dublin Society in 1900, after the last visit of Queen Victoria to Ireland. It was paid for by public subscription, under the supervision of the Commissioners of Public Works who were responsible for the grounds of Leinster House, where it was to be erected. In 1903 the commission was given to the Irish sculptor John Hughes, who moved to Paris after signing the contract and made the sculpture abroad. It was shipped back and reassembled on the lawn of Leinster House, then the premises of the RDS in 1908. Lord Aberdeen, Lord Lieutenant, unveiled the statue on 15th February at an elaborate ceremony.

This enormous piece of public sculpture consisted of a stone plinth surmounted by a formidable bronze sculpture of Queen Victoria. The two bronze groups, now in Dublin Castle, were placed at ground level on two plinths underneath the figure of the queen. A third group representing Peace, temporarily at the Castle, is to be placed at Leinster House. The figures relate directly to the Boer War (1899-1902). Indeed, part of the function of the sculpture was a memorial to the dead and wounded of this war. The groups depict Erin tending a dying soldier; Fame carrying a trumpet, and Peace, represented by two allegorical figures of Agriculture and Industry.

John Turpin has described the monument as 'a combination of world-wide imperialist celebration, affirmation of Irish unionism and a war memorial to fallen Irish soldiers carrying all the emotion that a war memorial attracted'. In their now disjointed situation, the sculptures are more a curiosity than any grand statement. Seen at much closer range than originally intended, the beauty of Hughes's work can be better appreciated, although the full impact of the work has been lost.

The figure of Victoria, which was not as successful, became even more of an embarrassment after independence when the RDS moved out of Leinster House and it became the home of the new Dáil and Senate. In 1948 the monument was dismantled, and for many years the different components were stored in the Royal Hospital, Kilmainham, and at Daingean in Co Offaly. In 1992 the bronze groups were given a less formal setting in the courtyard at the back of the conference centre in Dublin Castle. The figure of Queen Victoria was moved to Sydney in 1987.

PROVENANCE – Commissioned by the OPW and erected at Leinster House in 1908. Put into storage in 1948. Re-erected at Dublin Castle in 1992.

LITERATURE

Paula Murphy 'The Politics of the Street Monument', *Irish Arts Review Yearbook 1994*, vol. 10 (Dublin, 1993) 202-08

John Turpin, 'Nationalist & Unionist Ideology in the Sculpture of Oliver Sheppard and John Hughes, 1895-1939', *The Irish Review*, 20, spring/summer 1997

Judith Hill, *Irish Public Sculpture – A History* (Four Courts Press, Dublin, 1998) 145-47

Joseph Robinson Kirk (1821-1894)

Kirk was the son of the sculptor Thomas Kirk. He studied sculpture with his father, and began exhibiting at the RHA in 1840. At the same time he was a student at Trinity College, Dublin, graduating in 1843. He spent the following year in Italy. He made a number of important pieces of public sculpture and portrait busts. The four allegorical figures on the top of the campanile in Trinity College are by Kirk, as is the monument to the Marquis of Downshire at Hillsborough, Co Down.

His mythological and genre figures, such as Andromeda, were made popular by the Art Union in the 1840s, when they purchased several pieces and gave them as prizes to subscribers. Kirk lived in Bray, Co Wicklow, and is buried in Mount Jerome cemetery, where he had made a number of monuments, including the female figure over the tomb of his father.

Sappho

1858, marble, 116 cm; marble pedestal 78 cm
signed: JR Kirk. RHA/Sculptor/Dublin.1858.

This sculpture was made for Benjamin Lee Guinness, and was situated at the main entrance of Iveagh House when the building was handed over to the Irish state in 1939. (Another piece called *Sappho* by Kirk was sold at the 1865 *International Exhibition of Art and Manufactures* in Dublin, when it was bought by Lord Gough.)

Sappho, the ancient Greek poetess, is seated on a outcrop of rock with waves of water lapping up against its edges. She holds her lyre in one hand, and leans on the rock with her head tilted to one side in a melancholy attitude. According to one legend, Sappho was said to have fallen in love with a boatman who abandoned her, and in her grief she threw herself from her chamber window and dashed herself against a rock in the sea below. She was frequently depicted in this type of tragic pose in the Victorian period. This is an excellent example of Kirk's skill in creating different textures and movement with marble – for example, in the foam of the waves and in the folds of the figure's classical dress.

PROVENANCE – Commissioned by Sir Benjamin Lee Guinness 1858. Presented along with other contents of Iveagh House to the Irish state in 1939.

LITERATURE

OPW A41/23/18/43

W.G. Strickland, *A Dictionary of Irish Artists*, 2 vols (Dublin, 1913) i, 586

EXHIBITED

Dublin Exhibition of Arts, Industries and Manufactures, 1872 (11)

John van Nost, the Younger (fl.1750-1787)

John van Nost was the dominant sculptor in Dublin in the mid-18th century. His uncle, John van Nost the Elder, was a leading sculptor in London during the early 1700s, and had made an equestrian sculpture of George I for Dublin (1717), now in the Barber Institute, Birmingham. Van Nost the Younger came to Dublin around 1750. He was commissioned to make a number of public sculptures by Dublin Corporation, the lord lieutenant, and other bodies. One of his earliest commissions was for the two sculptures for the gateway of the Castle. In 1758 his statue of George II was erected in St Stephen's Green. The following year

Joseph Robinson Kirk
Sappho

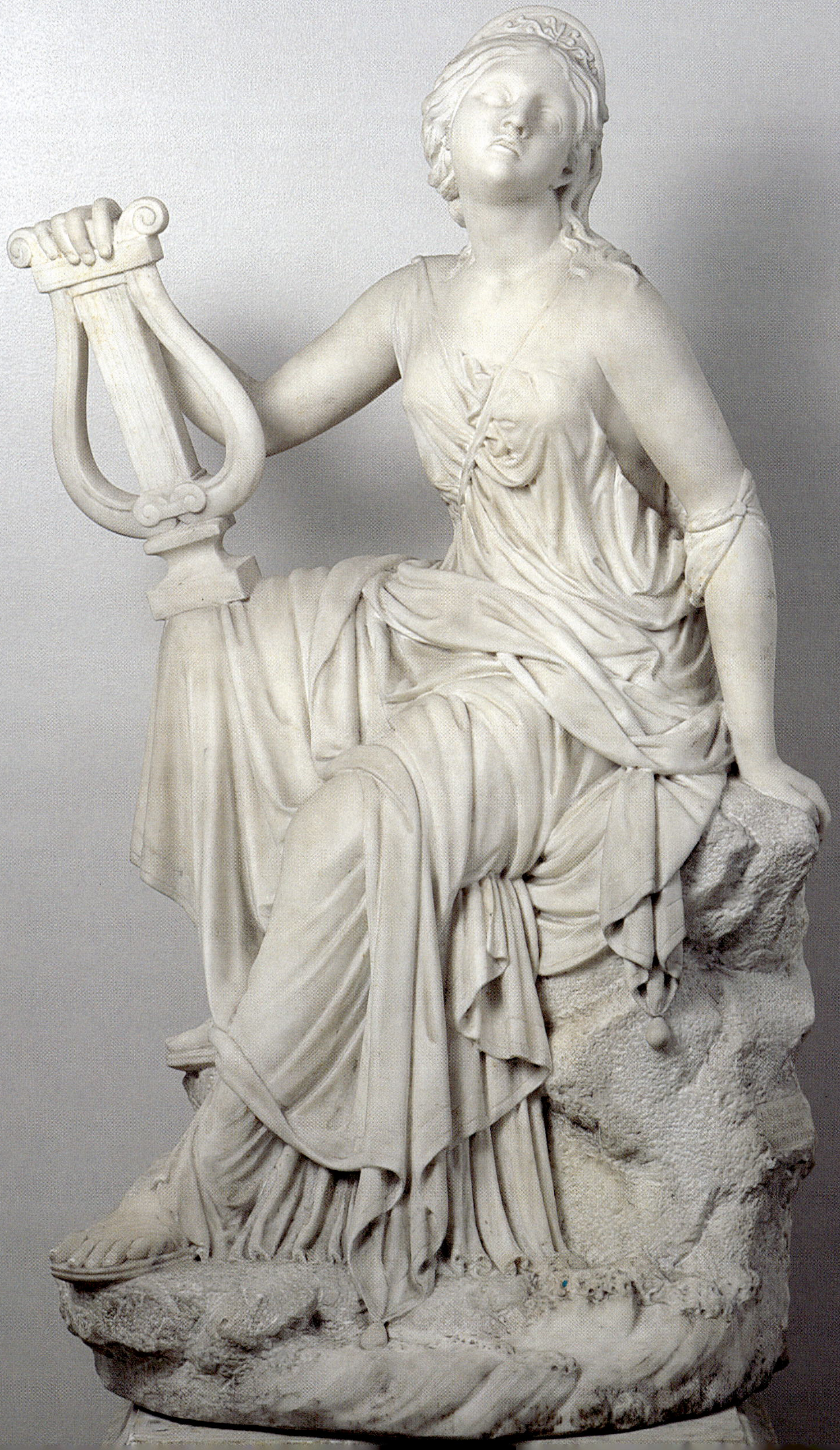

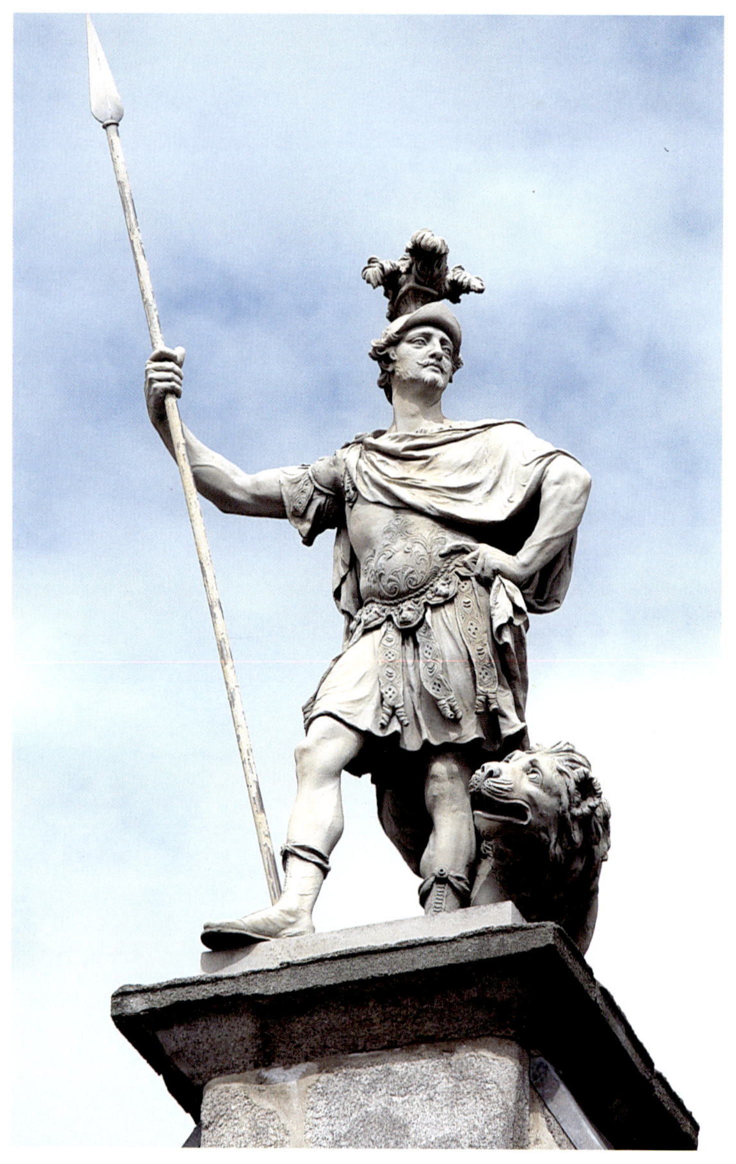

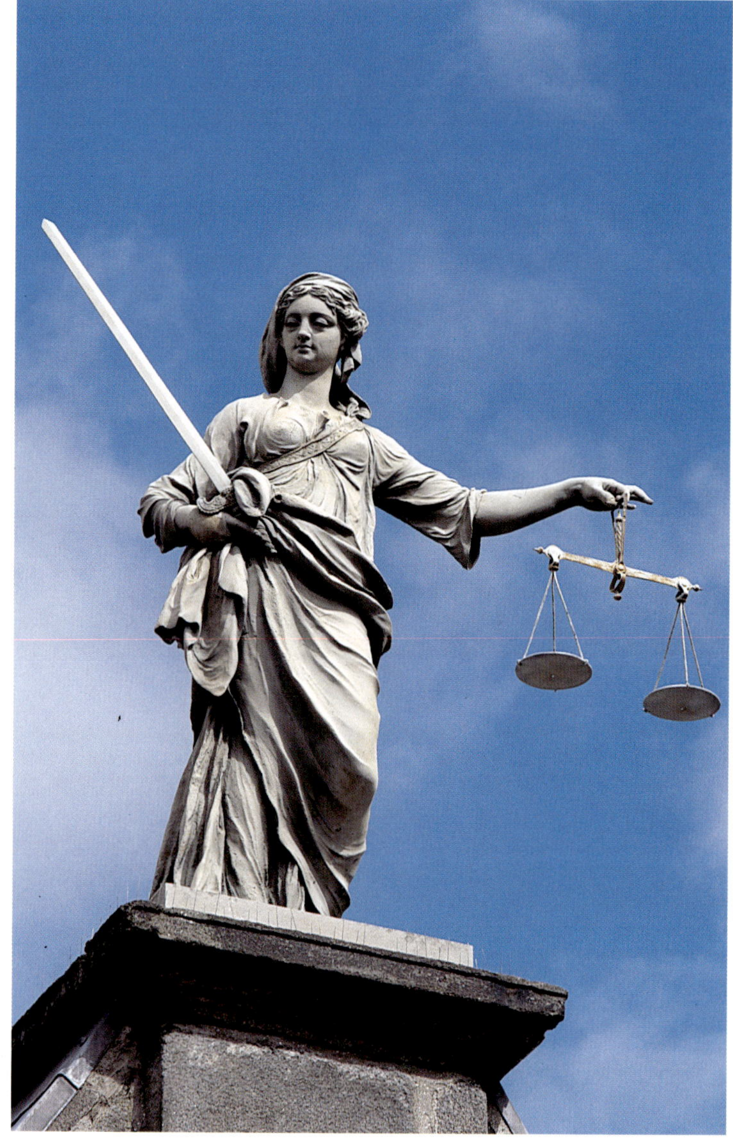

left
John van Nost, the Younger
Fortitude (Mars)

right
John van Nost, the Younger
Justice

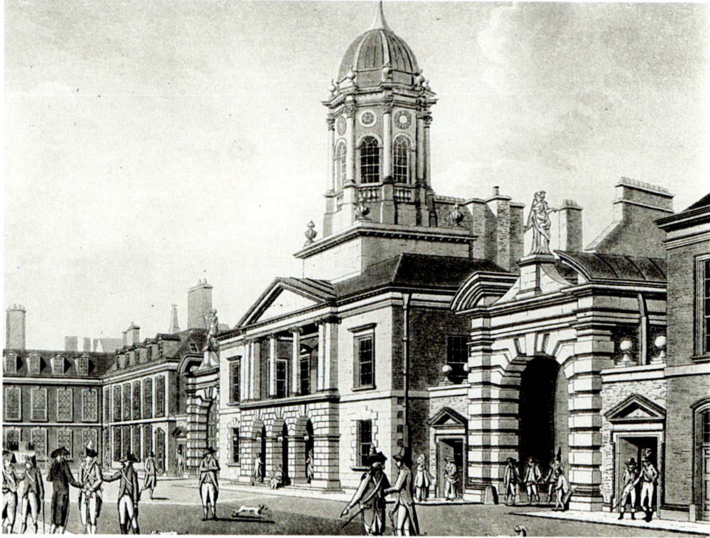

James Malton
Great Court Yard, Dublin Castle
(detail, showing pedimented gateways surmounted by figures of Fortitude and Justice)

his sculpture of General Lord Blakeney was placed in the central mall of Sackville Street. His classical sculpture of George III, which the Duke of Northumberland presented to the merchants of Dublin in 1765, is now in the National Gallery of Ireland.

Fortitude (Mars)
1753, lead, 240 cm

Mars is shown with a plumed helmet and classical armour. A lion, a symbol of his courage, is at his feet.

Justice
1753, lead, 240 cm

Justice stands in classical dress, with the scales of justice in one hand and the sword of vengeance in the other. The scales indicate her impartiality and the sword, her power.

Very few pieces of public sculpture from the 18th century have survived in Dublin. *Fortitude* and *Justice* have probably done so primarily because of their subject matter – they are allegorical figures, whereas most public sculpture of that period depicted monarchs or political figures, and thus became the target for the public's anger or disapproval. Van Nost's first piece of public sculpture for Dublin, also made of lead, was a statue of George II for the newly built Weaver's Hall in the Coombe (*c.*1750). This was still in existence in the 20th century, when it disintegrated on being moved.

The figures of Justice and Fortitude were, along with Prudence and Temperance, the four 'cardinal virtues' of civic life, and they are frequently depicted in or on public buildings. Justice was often considered to be the most important of the four because she regulated the behaviour of the citizens. She has been given the more prominent position at Dublin Castle – she stands over the 'real' gateway into the Castle. The other gateway, on which Fortitude is situated, was blind for most of its history. The two gateways were built *c.*1750 to flank the new Bedford Tower. This complex of buildings completed the north range of the Upper Castle Yard which had been in a dilapidated state. A large castellated entrance is shown on the site of the tower in Charles Brooking's 1728 map of Dublin. Van Nost's sculptures relate visually to the relative delicacy of the cupola and dome of the central tower. Although made out of lead, they are painted to look like stone. Lead was quite a common material for outdoor sculpture in the 18th century. It could be painted to look like stone or bronze, or occasionally it was gilded. It has a natural patina of its own which is very attractive. The primary reason for using the material, however, was probably economic; it is cheaper than bronze or marble.

The most striking aspect of the van Nost sculptures is the fact that they have their backs to the city – a feature which Dubliners have not failed to comment on. The reason for this is probably to do with the surrounding streetscape of the Castle in the 18th century in which the building was largely obscured from view. (The vista onto the gate from Cork Hill was not created until the Wide Streets Commissioners cleared housing behind it in the 1760s.) Another reason is the function of the statues themselves. They were commissioned to complete an architectural scheme which was centred on the Upper Castle Yard on to which they face. Justice, in particular, looks down into the Castle, and it would appear that she is there as an example to those working within the offices below, rather than relating to the citizens outside the Castle walls.

During the refurbishment of the Castle in 1986, the sculptures were removed and restored by Naylor Conservation in England. They were in a poor state of repair and were covered with layers of paint – thirty layers in the case of Justice, which split in two while being taken down. The sculptures were fitted with new stainless steel armatures and placed on new Portland stone bases. Fortitude was given a new spear, as the original one was missing, and Justice was given a new stainless steel blade for her sword. The restoration revealed the detail of van Nost's work. Although the lead was quite crude with other materials mixed in, it had withstood over two hundred years of smog and Irish weather. Both figures are finely modelled – the veins in Fortitude's arms and legs and the detail of his armour have been carefully depicted. Justice, whose pose is a perfect counterpoint to that of her companion, delicately extends the scales of Justice and balances her sword rather precariously against her hip. Photographs of the newly restored Justice also reveal the holes bored in the pans of her scales, which allow the rain water to drain away. A popular story recounts that when first erected, the rain water gathered in one of the scales weighing them down on one side. To avoid further embarrassment, the Castle authorities apparently had the holes drilled in them so that the water could drain away and the scales of Justice appear balanced.

PROVENANCE – Commissioned by the Castle authorities, and erected in November 1753.

LITERATURE

Richard Lewis, *The Dublin Guide* (1787) 38
J. Warburton, J. Whitelaw & R. Walsh, *History of the City of Dublin* (London, 1818) 470
L. Weaver, *English Leadwork – Its Arts and History* (London, 1909) 148-49
W.G. Strickland, *A Dictionary of Irish Artists*, 2 vols (Dublin, 1913) ii, 480, 487
Maurice Craig, *Dublin 1660-1860* (Dublin, 1952) 167
J. Cornforth, 'Dublin Castle – III', *Country Life*, 20th August 1970
Judith Hill, *Irish Public Sculpture – A History* (Four Courts Press, Dublin, 1998) 51-2

Louis François Roubiliac (1705-1762)

Roubiliac was born in Lyons. He trained with the German sculptor Balthasar Permoser, who had been a pupil of Bernini. In 1730 he was awarded a prize for his sculpture by the French Academy, and shortly after that date he moved to London. He established his reputation there with a marble statue of Handel, which was one of the first examples of rococo sculpture in England. He executed many fine portrait busts of contemporary writers and artists such as Hogarth, Pope and Voltaire, as well as a number of important tomb monuments in Westminster Cathedral. His work was characterised by its realism, and he is considered to have been one of the most important sculptors working in England in the 18th century.

Bust of Earl of Chesterfield

1746, bronze on marble socle, bust: 43 cm; socle: 16 cm
inscribed: Phillippus Stanhope Comes. [Ch]esterfield Prorex Hiberniae.
Anno 1746 – Rubillac F[ecit]
(page 95)

This bust of Chesterfield is a bronze version of a marble bust which was made in London in 1745, just before Chesterfield took up his position as Lord Lieutenant of Ireland in July of that year. The marble bust is now in the collection of the National Portrait Gallery in London. It is likely that Chesterfield had a small number of bronze busts made around the time he returned to London in April 1746.* The Dublin bust is mentioned as being in the Castle in Dr Maty's edition of Chesterfield's letters, published 1777. Maty states that the bust 'was fixed with public acclamations, and out of part of the savings of the public money'.†

Chesterfield would have been familiar with Roubiliac's work through his busts of contemporary and classical writers. He is said to have declared that, in his opinion, 'Roubiliac only was a statuary, the rest stone-cutters.'

Roubiliac's image of Chesterfield is one of the most flattering of the sitter. He has presented the earl without a wig, or any costume, in the style of classical portrait sculpture. The modelling of the face, while quite lifelike, retains an air of authority. His expression is extremely naturalistic, with the trace of a smile in the tensed muscles around his mouth and right side of his face.

Chesterfield was interested in the classical revival. In May 1745, at about the time Roubiliac modelled the bust, Chesterfield acquired a bust of Cicero for his library, possibly also by Roubiliac but after the antique. Very conscious of the antique tradition, he would have wanted to emulate it in presentations of himself.

Provenance – In State Apartments 1777; dining room, Dublin Castle (1908 inventory). According to OPW memo of P.S. O'Cearnaigh, Director of Public Monuments Branch, 10th May 1968, 'it was transferred at some time to the Viceregal Lodge and removed during the late Dr. Hyde's presidency by order of his Secretary. It was taken into Coleraine House Furniture Store where it came to my notice in 1956 and I had it returned to the State Apartments.'

Literature

Lord Chesterfield, *Miscellaneous works of the late P.D. Stanhope, Earl of Chesterfield, to which are prefixed memoirs of his Life by* M. Maty, 3 vols (Dublin, 1777) i, 167†

Frederick O'Dwyer, 'The Ballroom at Dublin Castle' in Agnes Bernelle (ed.), *Decantations – A Tribute to Maurice Craig* (Lilliput Press, Dublin, 1992) 162

Sotheby's European Sculpture and Works of Art, 16th December 1998 (150)

Comparative literature

Katherine A. Esdaile, *The Life and Works of Louis François Roubiliac* (London, 1928)

John Kerslake, *Early Georgian Portraits* (National Portrait Gallery, London, 1977) i, 49; ii, plate 139

Gordon Balderston 'Roubiliac and Lord Chesterfield', *Apollo*, March 1985, 189

* Three bronze versions of this bust are known: the Dublin Castle example, one in the Victoria and Albert Museum, and one which was on sale in Sotheby's in 1998. The latter belonged to Nathaniel Clements, the Ranger of the Phoenix Park, and builder of what was to become the Viceregal Lodge. This bust, like the Dublin Castle example, has a marble socle with a gilt-bronze mount, bearing Chesterfield's coat of arms. It is also dated 1746.

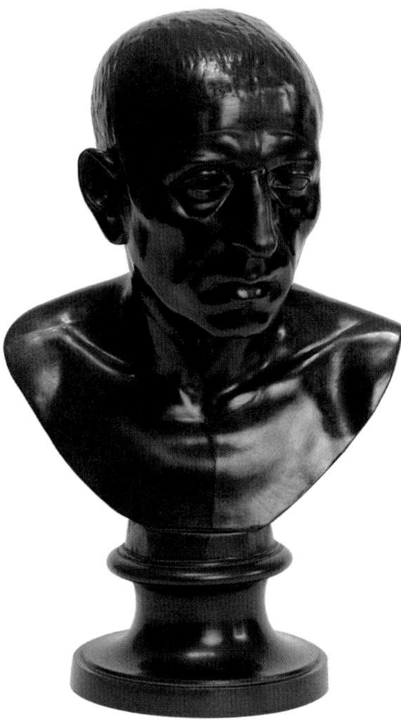

19th-century cast of 18th-century original

Bust of Cicero

bronze, 36 cm (49 cm including base)

According to the notes in the records of the OPW, this bust represents the 18th-century French philosopher Voltaire. In fact it is a depiction of Cicero. The nature of the casting of this bust suggests that it is one of a series produced to furnish a library or study.

Provenance – Unknown. Probably acquired in the 20th century.

I am grateful to Philip Ward-Jackson of the Conway Library, Courtauld Institute, London, for his assistance in identifying the subject.

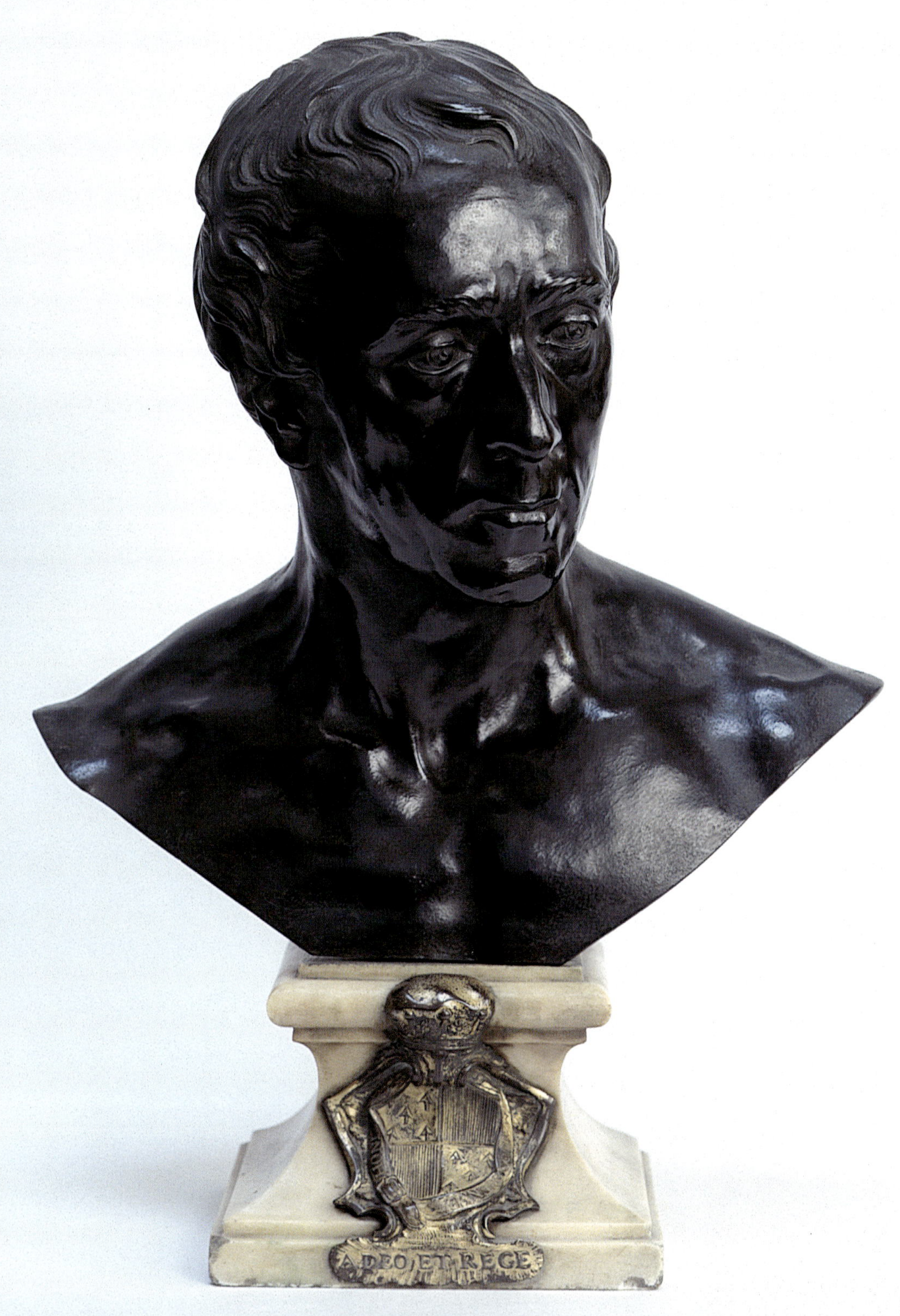

Louis François Roubiliac
Bust of Earl of Chesterfield

Marble from the collection of Lord Cloncurry at Newcastle Lyons

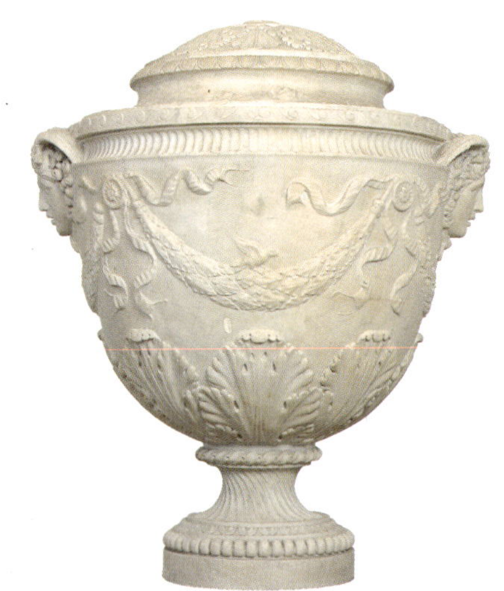

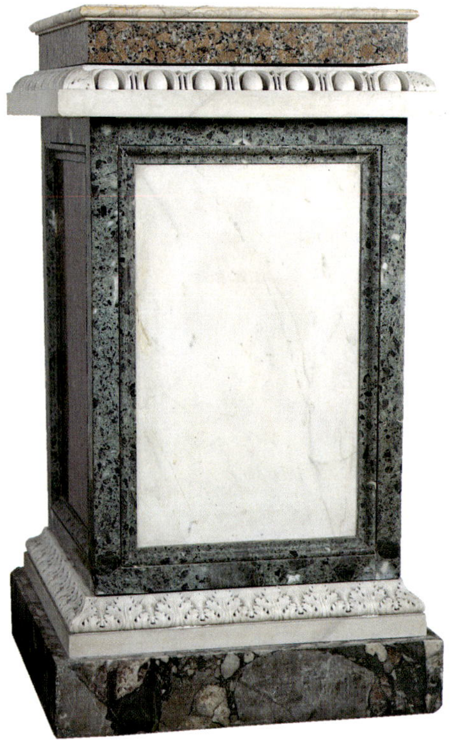

Italian, 18th century
Marble urn on marble plinth

A number of important pieces of sculpture were acquired by the OPW for Dublin Castle in 1962 at the sale of Lyons, Co Kildare. Newcastle Lyons was the seat of Valentine Lawless (1773-1853), 2nd Baron Cloncurry, who was born in Dublin and educated at Trinity College. In 1795 he became a United Irishman, and shortly afterwards moved to London to study law. His connection with the United Irishmen, which was not very active, resulted in his arrest in May 1798 and his subsequent imprisonment from 1799 to 1801. After his release from prison, his father and grandfather having died in the interim, he put the family estate in order and travelled on the continent. He settled at Newcastle Lyons upon his return to Ireland in 1805, and remained there for the rest of his life. He was a supporter of Catholic Emancipation and Repeal of the Act of the Union, and was on familiar terms with Daniel O'Connell and the Marquis of Anglesey.

His collection at Newcastle Lyons was probably one of the most important collections of sculpture in Ireland in the 19th century. Most of the pieces were acquired by the baron on his visit to Italy from 1803 to 1805, when he was planning the decoration of his home in Ireland, on which the architect Richard Morrison was then at work. He was in contact with many important scholars and artists while in Rome, including Canova and Baron von Humboldt, and is known to have taken part in a number of excavations of classical sites. Pieces of sculpture, including antique marble columns, were shipped back to Dublin from Rome during this period, and incorporated into the design of his house in Kildare.

In 1962 Newcastle Lyons was sold and became the premises of UCD's agriculture faculty until 1990. A number of important pieces were bought at this sale by the OPW, who were then restoring Dublin Castle. Apart from the pieces outlined below, the two scaglia marble columns which support the central beam of the ceiling in the Marble Hall, opposite the entrance to the Erin Room, were also acquired at this sale (lot no. 2: 'Pair of Statuary Marble and Brescia Corinthian Columns').

Dr Lynda Mulvin of the Department of History of Art at University College Dublin has kindly given a commentary on each of the vases from a classicist's point of view.

Italian, 18th century

Marble urn on marble plinth
urn: Carrara marble, 74 cm; plinth: marble (various), 110 cm

'The vase is likened to a form that was made for funerary vessels. In antiquity vessels such as these carried ashes of the dead. It has a fluted pedestal foot, is ornate with spiralled fluting and acanthus leaves in relief decorating the base. Swags decorate the body of the ves-

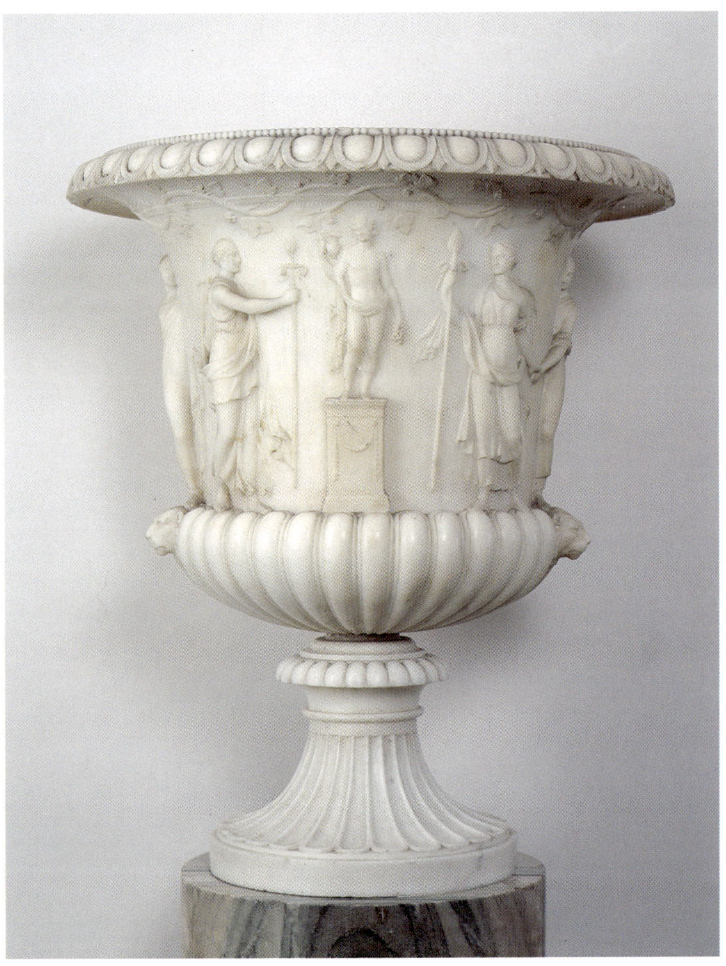

Italian, 18th century
Pair of marble urns: Bacchanal (vase A)

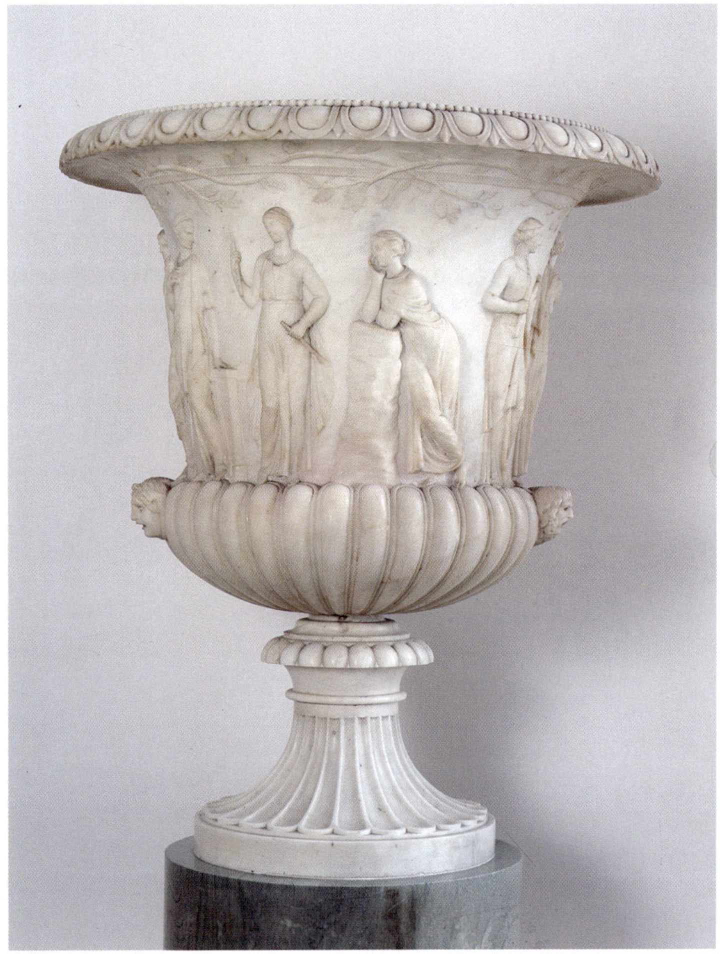

Italian, 18th century
Pair of marble urns: Apollonian Muses (vase B)

sel. It has pan-like horned faces, which act as handles.' (Dr Lynda Mulvin)

The marble plinth on which the urn stands is made up of a number of interesting pieces of stone including Carrara, jasper, porphyry and Tinos marble. The cornice is incised with a deep egg and dart moulding. The piece was located on the first floor corridor of Newcastle Lyons in front of a window.

PROVENANCE – Purchased by OPW for Dublin Castle at Lyons House sale, October 1962 (lot 567).

LITERATURE
Jackson Stops McCabe, *Important Sale at Lyons House, Celbridge, Co Kildare*, 23rd October 1962

Pair of marble urns: Bacchanal (vase A) and Apollonian Muses (vase B)

Carrara marble (on green-veined marble pedestals), 87 cm, pedestal: 128 cm

These vases were originally situated in the dining room of Lyons House, where they were commented on by visitors to the house. In 1826 John Norris wrote of the 'two large vases, excellently sculptured', and in Bernard Burke's account of the great houses of Britain and Ireland (1854), he wrote: 'The dining parlour presents two splendid vases of choice sculpture, one representing Apollo and the muses, the other a Bacchanalian dance.' They were probably acquired by Lord Cloncurry in Italy at the beginning of the 19th century. It is possible that he commissioned them with the decor of Newcastle Lyons in mind.

'The shape of both vases is an adapted form of the Calyx Krater with a broad body and a wide mouth, a fluted pedestal base and egg-and-dart moulding on the up-turned rim. By the Roman period these vases were purely decorative and Bacchic subject matter was especially suited to its shape since a krater was a vessel used for mixing wine and water. It had handles placed horizontally, close to the base to facilitate carrying.

'In the case of these vases, the handles have been reduced to figurative projections: panther heads on one and dramatic masks on the other. In the case of vase A, the vine together, with the panthers, are attributes usually associated with Dionysus/ Bacchus and the scene that is represented is a Bacchanalia or Dionysic rite. Vase B has a climbing fruit branch filling the space above the figures which suggests an outdoor pastoral scene and when viewed together with the theatrical face masks, these attributes are usually associated with Apollo and the Muses.

'The Bacchanalia scene on vase A depicts a youthful Bacchus/Dionysus standing on a plinth. He is accompanied by the Maenads (followers of Dionysus) holding a thyrsus (a long fennel stalk wreathed in ivy and vine leaves with a pine cone at the top). Dionysus was a common theme for Attic Greek vases. On Vase A, he is depicted as a half-naked youth with his lower torso covered in light drapery. He holds an amphora raised in his right hand to his shoulder. This is a pose not commonly adopted for Dionysus in antiquity and a rare example is the François vase c.570 BC where he is depicted carrying a large amphora on his shoulder.* This would suggest that the source for vase A was possibly an unknown Roman copy of a Greek original and is a loose interpretation of the Bacchanalia after antiquity in a conventional classicising style.

'Vase B appears to depict the Muses. In Greek mythology they were the daughters of Zeus and Mnemosyne (memory) the goddess of literature, music and dance and later of all intellectual pursuits. In the Roman period they each presided over a particular art form such as Calliope, epic poetry and Clio, history. Each carry attributes such as Erato carries the lyre and presides over lyric poetry and Euterpe carries the flute and presides over lyric poetry. They were often associated with Apollo and the contest with Marsyas. On vase B, the relief figures all carry their varied attributes. The figure leaning on the pedestal is reminiscent of the central figure's pose in the Aldobrandini wedding wall painting (Vatican Museum), and could have been a possible model for such a figure. This is a fairly common theme for 18th century copies of antique original vases.' (Dr Lynda Mulvin)

PROVENANCE – Purchased at Lyons House, Celbridge, Co Kildare, 1962 (52).

LITERATURE

Jackson Stops McCabe, *Important Sale at Lyons House*, Celbridge, Co Kildare, 23rd October 1962

Patricia Cashen, *Valentine, Lord Cloncurry and his Collection at Lyons House*, unpublished MA thesis, UCD, 1986

June Eiffe, 'Lord Cloncurry's Roman Collection', in *New Perspectives in Art History* (Irish Academic Press, Dublin, 1987)

* T.H. Carpenter, *Art and Myth in Ancient Greece* (London, 1991) 12ff. The François vase was discovered in an Etruscan tomb in 1844 by the Italian Alessandro François.

Decorative vase

Carrara marble, 31 cm

'This is like the form of a funerary vase. Although without a cover, the narrow neck could have held a stopper or lid. It has a fluted pedestal foot, and is decorated with palm fronds. Ram's heads project as handles. The garlands are linked to the rams rather like the bucrania swag pattern (bull's heads) which was a decorative moulding in antiquity.' (Dr Lynda Mulvin)

PROVENANCE – Purchased at Lyons House, Celbridge, Co Kildare, 1962 (100). Described in catalogue as 'an Adams [sic] style vase'.

LITERATURE

Jackson Stops McCabe, *Important Sale at Lyons House*, Celbridge, Co Kildare, 23rd October 1962

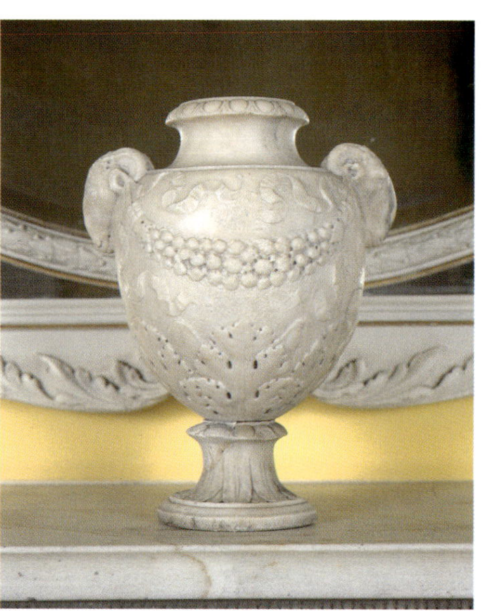

Italian, 18th century
Decorative vase

Decorative Ware

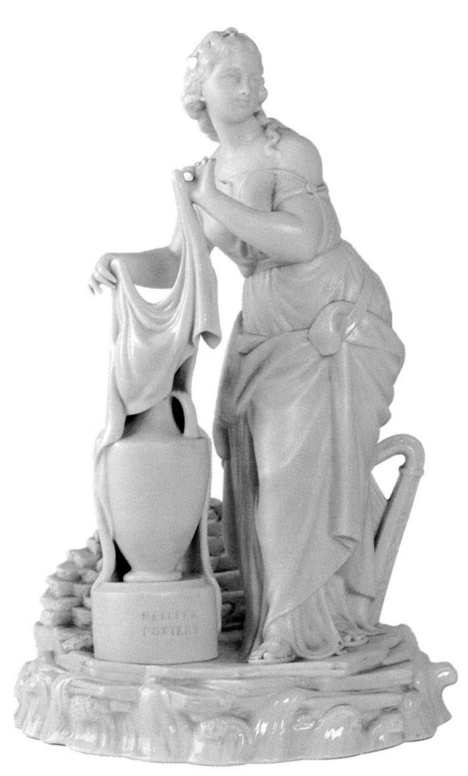

William Boyton Kirk (for Belleek)
Hibernia, Awaking from her Slumbers

Belleek

The Belleek pottery was founded in 1858 at Belleek, Co Fermanagh, by three men – a local landlord, J.C. Bloomfield, a ceramics expert, R.W. Armstrong, and a wealthy businessman, D. McBirney. Bloomfield hoped that the factory would help alleviate the poverty of the locals. It went into production in 1863, when a dozen potters from Staffordshire were brought over to Ireland to train the new workers. It made a wide range of ceramic ware, including the now famous and collectable decorative range.

William Boyton Kirk (1824-1900) (for Belleek)

Kirk was the brother of Joseph Robinson Kirk. He attended the Dublin Society Schools, and began exhibiting at the RHA in 1844. He designed a number of figures for Belleek and the Shakespeare dessert service for the Worcester China works in England, where he lived for a number of years.

Hibernia, Awaking from her Slumbers
post 1860s, parian ware, 43 cm
base has black stamp depicting round tower, wolfhound, harp and word 'BELLEEK'

The young woman, who can be identified as Hibernia from the Celtic cross and harp, is unveiling a classical urn. The waterfall of Belleek can be seen beneath the stones she stands on. The piece, really an advertisement for the Belleek factory, is a good example of the growing popularity of Celtic symbols in late 19th-century decorative art.

LITERATURE
Máiread Reynolds, *Early Belleek Wares* (National Museum of Ireland, Dublin, 1973)

after Bertel Thorwaldsen (1768-1844)

The Danish sculptor Thorwaldsen lived in Italy from 1796 to 1838. There he became part of the circle of neoclassical artists, and his work was heavily influenced by antique art and by his contemporary, Canova. He executed many fine funerary monuments, including that of Pope Pius VII in St Peter's, and Schiller in Stuttgart.

Night
19th century, plaster, circular form, 78.5 cm

Day
19th century, plaster, circular form, 78.5 cm

These two works are plaster copies of two marble reliefs which Thorwaldsen made in Rome and Copenhagen in 1815. There are a number of these to be seen on the interior walls of houses in Dublin, including the Oscar Wilde house on Merrion Square, and the premises of the Royal Dublin Society in Ballsbridge. The designs were apparently reproduced widely soon after Thorwaldsen produced them. Eugene Plon states that they were engraved on shells, cameos and gems, and moulded in plaster and biscuit.

The original sculpture of *Night* was made in Rome. It shows a female figure, the goddess of night, carrying two infants in her arms – Death and Sleep. Its companion piece, *Day*, shows Eos flying through the air, scattering flowers. A putto holds on to her shoulders and carries a lighted torch.

PROVENANCE
Transferred from 51 St Stephen's Green to Dublin Castle in 1952, according to OPW memo of P.S. O'Cearnaigh, Director of Public Monuments Branch, 10th May 1968.

COMPARATIVE LITERATURE
Eugene Plon, *Thorwaldsen: His Life and Works* (London, 1874)

after Bertel Thorwaldsen (1768-1844) right
left *Night* right *Day*

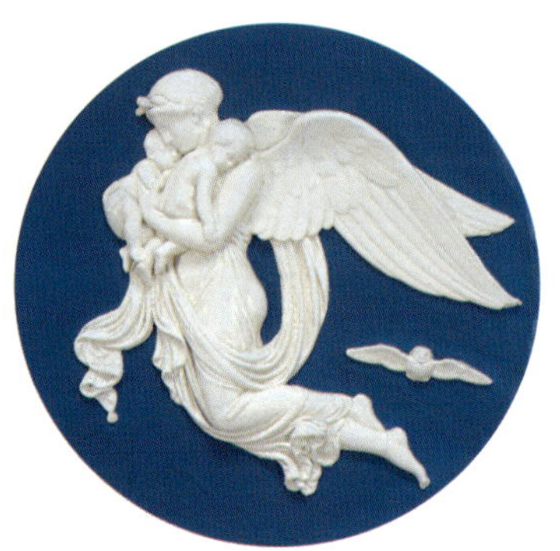

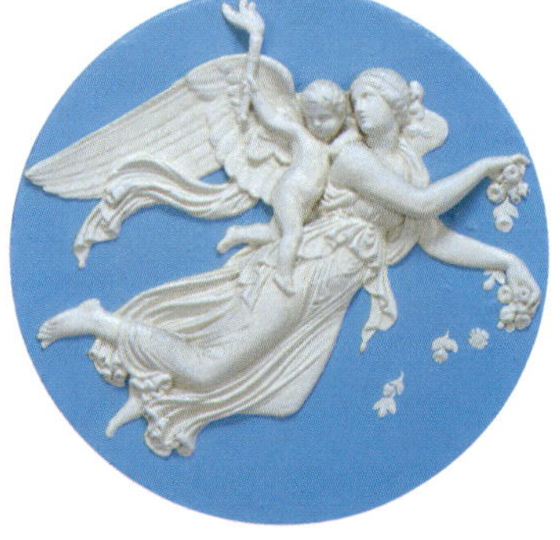

Josiah Wedgwood (1730-1795)

Josiah Wedgwood opened his first ceramic works in Burslem, Staffordshire, in 1759. After the success of his 'Queen's ware' in 1765, he built a new factory, Etruria, where he specialised in manufacturing ranges of ornamental ceramics. His shrewd understanding of marketing and contemporary taste, as well as his technical ability, made him one of the most successful ceramicists of all time. Leading artists were employed to supply designs based on antique sculpture,vase painting or cameos for both three-dimensional and bas-relief pieces.

The four Dublin Castle plaques, discussed below, are made of black basalt – a ceramic technique developed by Wedgwood c.1767 using a distinctive black colouring only available in Staffordshire, known as 'Egyptian black clay'. This consisted of a black iron oxide, which was found in water which had been drained from the local coal mines. Wedgwood refined its appearance and quality, until he produced 'basaltes', which he hoped would look as if they were made of 'Etruscan bronze', thus cashing in on the contemporary vogue for all things antique and classical.

It is difficult to attribute any of Wedgwood's ceramics to specific designers. He deliberately promoted the name of the company above that of the individual artist. All four plaques at Dublin Castle were bought as the designs of Flaxman. However only two are based on his work.

John Flaxman (1755-1826) (for Josiah Wedgwood)

Flaxman began designing for Wedgwood in 1775, and with his support, travelled to Italy in 1787, where he lived for seven years. After his return to England he concentrated on monumental tomb sculpture. He also produced outstanding book illustrations which were influential among artists in the early 19th century.

When working for Wedgwood, Flaxman would send him a drawing which Wedgwood would correct and annotate and return to the artist. Once the design was agreed on, Flaxman would send a wax model of the piece to Wedgwood. The model was adapted for reproduction by specialised craftsmen in Etruria (Wedgwood's factory), and a plaster cast of the model taken. Progressive firings of this plaster cast would be made, reducing the size of the original model. Finally, plaster of Paris moulds would be made to be used on the different types of vessels and plaques as required.

Hercules strangling the Lion (1st Labour of Hercules)
black basalt ware, oval, 19 x 14 cm, stamped on reverse: WEDGWOOD

Hercules and the Erymanthian Boar (4th Labour of Hercules)
black basalt ware, oval, 19 x 14 cm, stamped on reverse: WEDGWOOD

The story of the twelve labours of Hercules recounts the tasks of bravery and strength which Hercules was forced to undertake for the King of Tiryns, Eurystheus. In the first labour, Hercules is shown strangling the lion of Nemea which had been terrorising the citizens of that city. The second plaque shows the fourth labour, in which Hercules, with the skin of a lion draped over his shoulder, is carrying the Erymanthian boar, which he captured alive and brought back to Eurystheus.

attributed to William Hackwood (for Josiah Wedgwood)

Night or *Venus and Cupid (Ceres and Triptolemus)*
black basalt ware, oval, 16.5 x 13 cm, stamped on reverse: WEDGWOOD

This shows a dancing female figure carrying two poppies in her hands which the child is trying to grasp. The subject comes from an illustration of an antique gem in Agostini's *Gemmae et Sculpturae Antiquae* (1685) (plate 116) called *Venus and Cupid.* The motif is also published in Montfaucon's *L'Antiquité Expliquée* (1722) i, plate 54. Wedgwood sometimes called this motif 'Night' or 'Ceres and Triptolemus' – a reference to the antique myth of how Ceres, the earth goddess, gave poppies to the child Triptolemus. Although attributed to William Hackwood, the design is a direct transcription of an existing motif. It was widely used on Wedgwood wares in the late 18th century.

attributed to John Bacon (1740-99) (for Josiah Wedgwood)

John Bacon worked for Derby porcelain as well as Wedgwood. He executed a number of fine tomb monuments, including Dr Johnson's monument in St Paul's Cathedral, London.

Day or *Erato*
black basalt ware, oval, 16.5 x 13 cm, stamped on reverse: WEDGWOOD

Erato, one of the muses of Apollo, is associated with love and lyric poetry. Her attribute is the lyre. Like its companion piece, the design is based on an illustration of an antique gem – plate 115 in Lionardo Agostini's *Gemmae et Sculpturae Antiquae*. In this case, the designer/artist made certain changes to the original. Here the goddess has been clothed and a lyre placed in her hands. The altar behind her has also been added.

PROVENANCE – Purchased in Dublin, 1952.

LITERATURE
Wolf Mankowitz, *Wedgwood* (London, 1953)
David Buten, *18th Century Wedgwood – A Guide for Collectors and Connoisseurs* (Buten Museum of Wedgwood, 1980) 116
E.B. Adams, *Dwight & Lucille Beeson Wedgwood Collection at the Birmingham Museum of Art* (Alabama, 1992)

COMPARATIVE LITERATURE
David Bindman (ed.) *John Flaxman* (Thames and Hudson, London, 1979)

John Flaxman (for Josiah Wedgwood)

Hercules strangling the Lion
(1st Labour of Hercules)

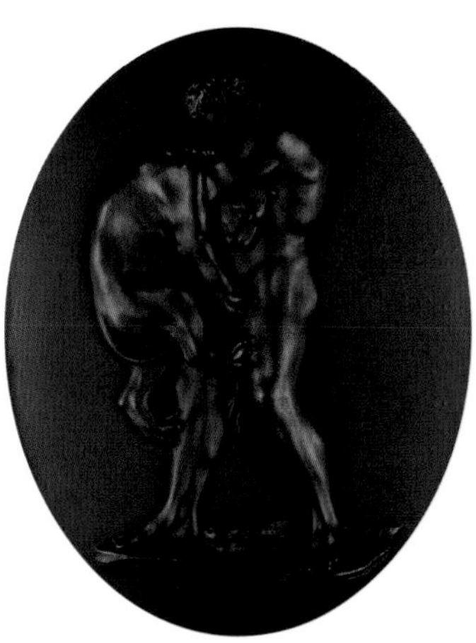

Hercules and the Erymanthian Boar
(4th Labour of Hercules)

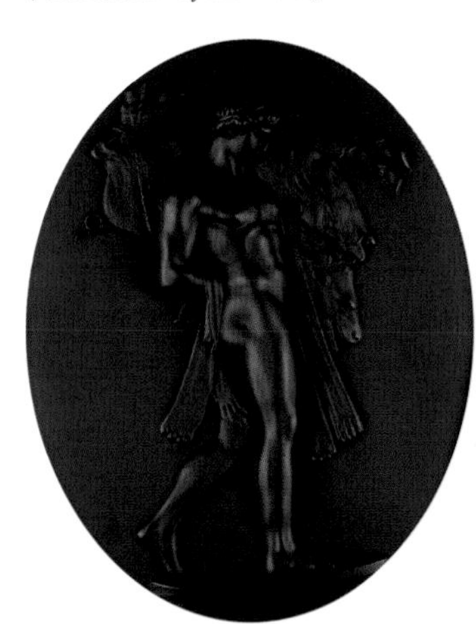

attributed to William Hackwood

Night or *Venus and Cupid*
(Ceres and Triptolemus)

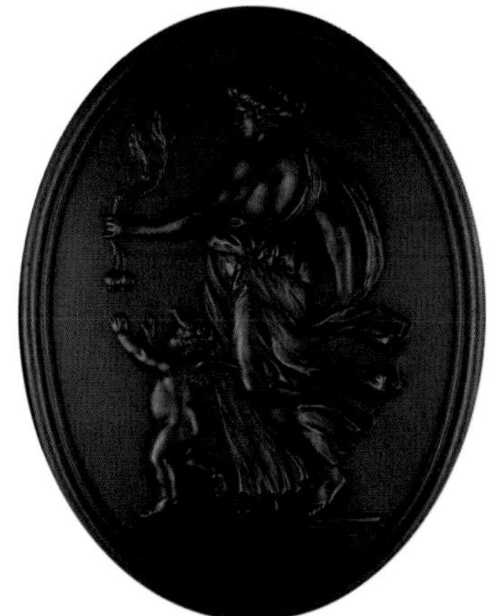

attributed to John Bacon

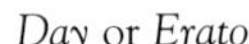

Day or *Erato*

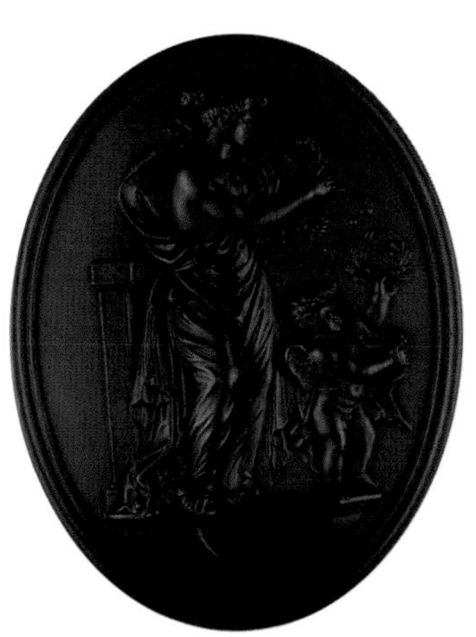

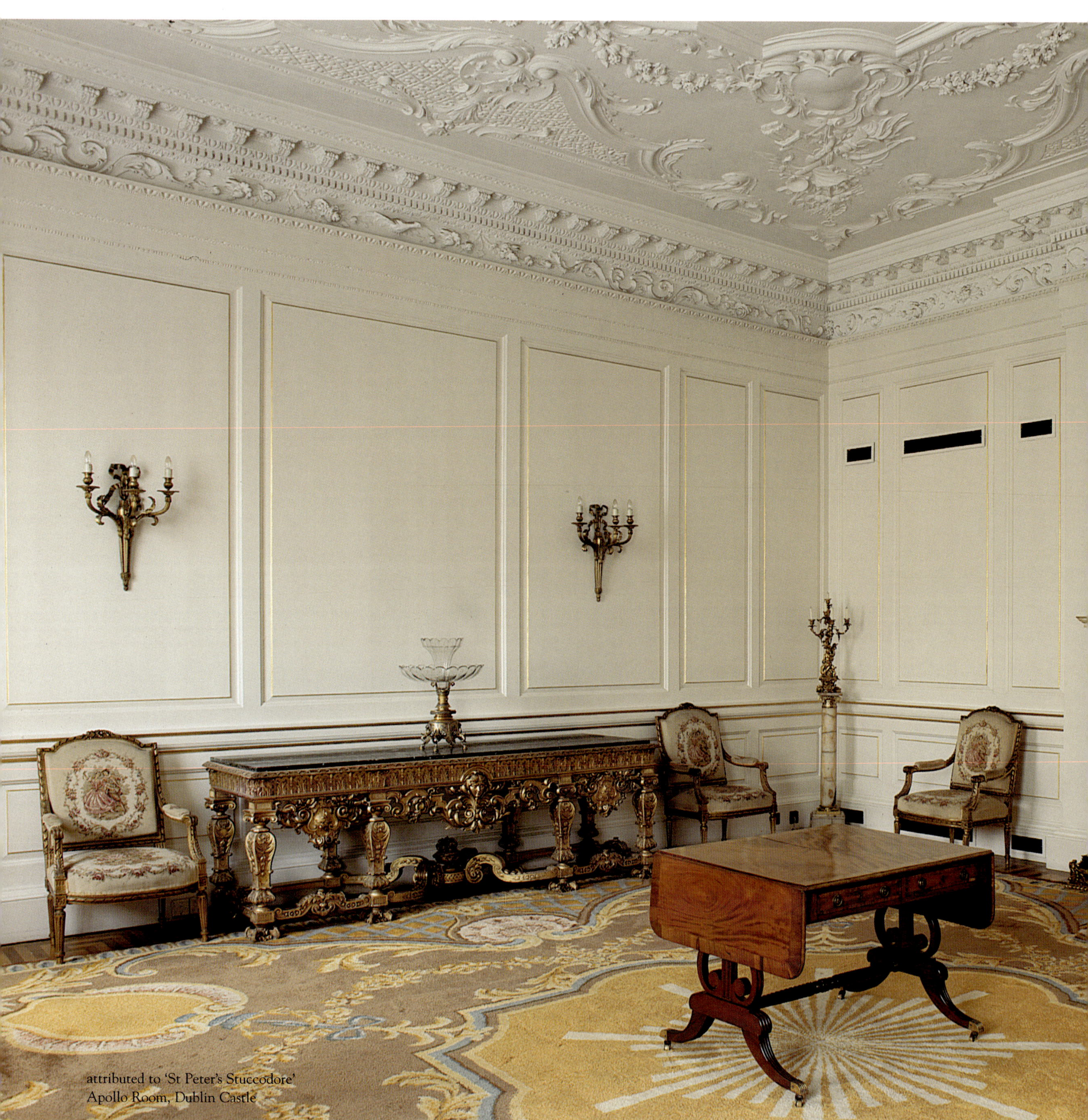

attributed to 'St Peter's Stuccodore'
Apollo Room, Dublin Castle

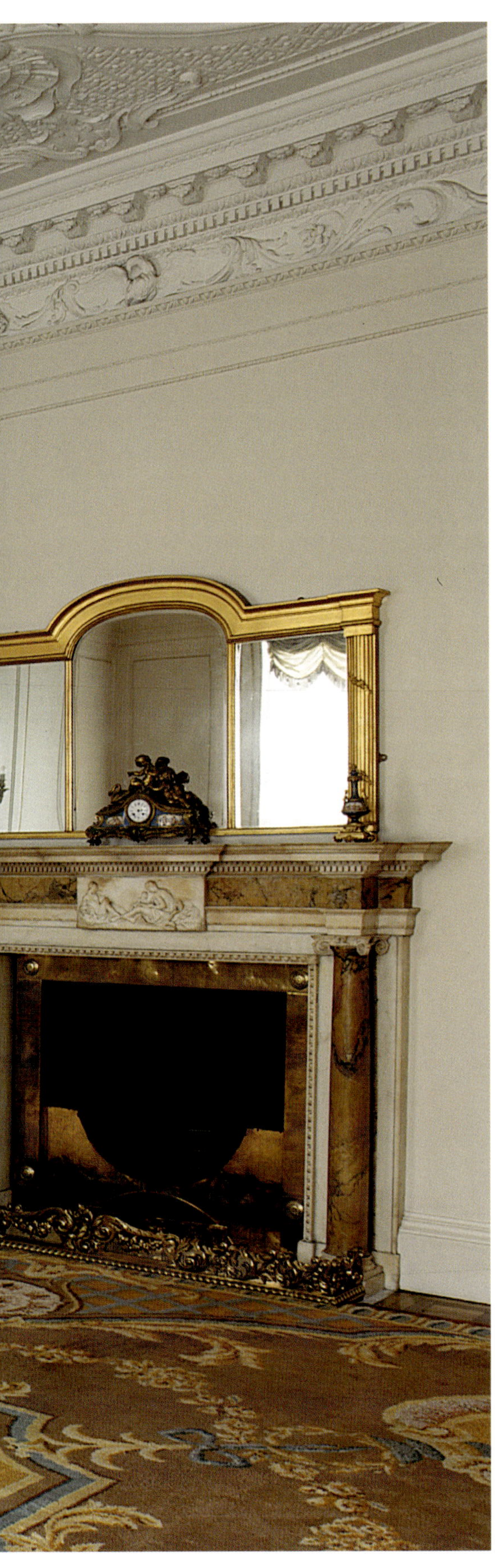

Stuccowork Ceilings

Bartholomew Cramillon (fl.1755-1772)

Bartholomew Cramillon came to Dublin around 1755, and introduced a German rococo style into Irish stuccowork. His most important work, and the best documented, is the chapel of the Rotunda Hospital, which he executed in 1755. The expert on Irish stuccowork, Joseph McDonnell, believes his style is also evident in the ceilings of Mespil House and Belvedere House. Cramillon abandoned the idea of compartmentalised ceilings, which was the preferred format for stuccoed ceilings earlier in the century. There is a tremendous delicacy in the execution of his work. He used new motifs associated with the advent of the rococo style. The shell-like forms in the Medicine ceiling at Dublin Castle are typical of this work. They have an organic quality and a subtle sense of movement, which makes the design appear fluid and natural.

Medicine with Arts and Sciences

c.1750, stuccowork ceiling (originally in Mespil House)

This ceiling was acquired by the OPW in 1952 when Mespil House was demolished. According to C.P. Curran, the Irish Assurance Company gave the three Mespil House ceilings to the State. Two were installed in the Castle, a third one, depicting the Elements and Seasons presided over by Jupiter, is at Áras an Uachtaráin.

Mespil House was originally situated near Leeson Street, close to the Grand Canal. It was built around 1751 for the celebrated Cork physician and man of letters, Dr Barry. Barry was an eminent scholar, a founder member of the Physico-Historical Society, and Professor of Physics at Trinity College. In 1775 he published a treatise on ancient wine and the properties of water. He died in Bath in 1776. The house was later the home of the artist, Sarah Purser, who died in 1943. After her death, the area around her house was developed and Mespil House demolished, the stucco ceilings having been removed.

This ceiling was made for Dr Barry's ground-floor study/dining room, which was quite a different shape to the present room in the State Apartments. It had a bay window, which extended the ceiling out towards the garden. It was in this space that the scene depicting Medicine, now on the rear wall, was situated. This consists of a winged putto supporting an oval, which shows a female figure representing Medicine and holding the knotted rod of Aesculapius entwined with a serpent, her right arm embracing a cockerel. From ribbons beneath the design hang a book and a flask. This obviously refers to Dr Barry's profession and to the work which he did in this room. Indeed, it is likely that the doctor took a personal interest in the iconography of the stuccowork, and as C.P. Curran has suggested, drew the stuccodore's attention to such reference books as Ripa's *Iconologia* (first published in 1593), a widely used book on the subject of gods, goddesses, and their symbols and emblems.

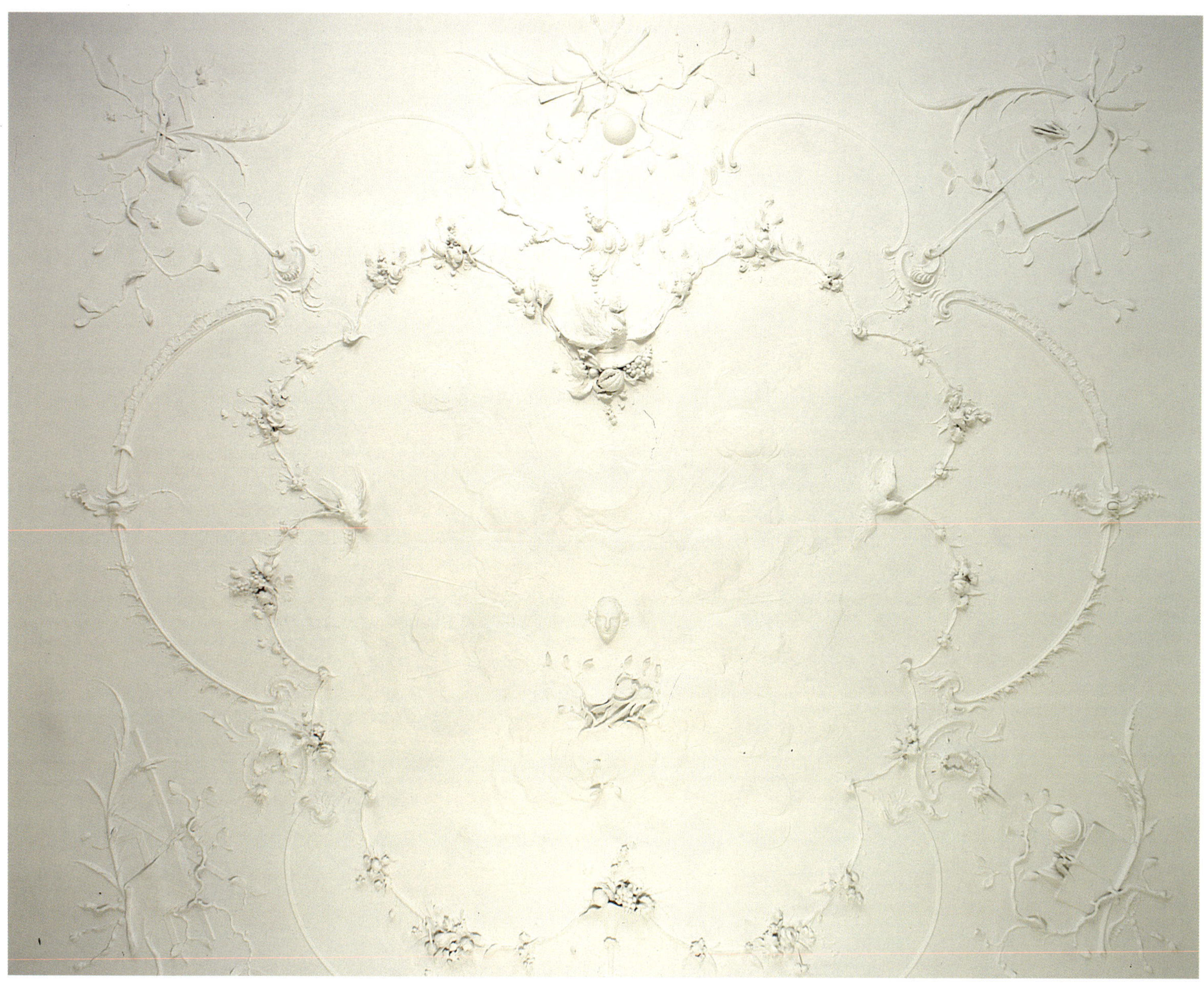

The main part of the ceiling is dedicated to Apollo, the Roman god associated with the arts and sciences – another reference to the interests and pursuits of Dr Barry. At the centre of the design is the head of Apollo, which appears surrounded by the rays of sun in the midst of clouds. Each corner of the ceiling has emblems of the arts of painting (palette, brushes and a drawing of a figure), sculpture (bust, hammer and chisel) and architecture (set square, ruler and an architectural plan, which refers to Mespil House), and the study of astronomy and geography (globe, compass and map). These elements are united by a garland with fruit and flowers, which is carried in the beaks of doves. A second motif of rolling waves and coral and shell-like forms draws the elements of the design together. This is the rocaille, which gives the rococo style its name.*

PROVENANCE – Acquired by the OPW from Mespil House and re-erected in Dublin Castle in 1952.

LITERATURE

C.P. Curran, *Dublin Decorative Plasterwork* (London, 1967)

Joseph McDonnell, *Irish 18th Century Stuccowork and Its European Sources* (National Gallery of Ireland, Dublin, 1991)

* Joseph McDonnell has noted the similarity between motifs on this ceiling and that of the ceiling of the Norfolk House Music Room (now in the Victoria and Albert Museum, London). He has suggested that Cramillon may have been employed on this before coming to Ireland. Joseph McDonnell is currently engaged in research on this stuccodore.

Minerva introducing the Arts to Hibernia
c.1750, stuccowork ceiling (originally in Mespil House)

This ceiling came from the front section of the drawing room at Mespil House, and corresponds with the Medicine stuccowork (part of the previous entry) which was in the room beneath it. It consists of an oval medallion, held aloft by two putti. The medallion seems to be fastened by a ribbon to a branch, from which dangles one of the putti. The bottom part of the medallion appears to be weighed down by a basket of flowers and fruit; another putto awkwardly holds it in place. On either side, birds hold aloft garlands of flowers and fruit in their beaks. This charming device has, at its centre, the scene of Minerva introducing the Arts to Hibernia. Hibernia stands with arm outstretched on the seashore leaning on a harp. Minerva descends from the clouds with three female figures, representing sculpture, painting and architecture. Sculpture extends her hand to Minerva and holds a bust. Architecture sits with her back to the viewer, but her compasses and a sheet of drawing paper are visible. Painting stands behind with her palette and brushes.

This is a delightful and witty depiction of such a high-minded subject. The stuccodore has varied the depth of the stucco quite dramatically: Hibernia's arm is extended right out into space, as is the ribbon from which the medallion supposedly hangs, while the group of figures around Minerva is in low relief. It is a tribute to the craftsmen who moved the ceiling to the State Apartments that these details have not been lost.

PROVENANCE – Acquired by the OPW from Mespil House and re-erected in Dublin Castle in 1952.

LITERATURE

C.P. Curran, *Dublin Decorative Plasterwork* (London, 1967)
Joseph McDonnell, *Irish 18th Century Stuccowork and Its European Sources* (National Gallery of Ireland, Dublin, 1991)

opposite
Bartholomew Cramillon (fl.1755-1772)
Medicine with Arts and Sciences

bottom left
Bartholomew Cramillon (fl.1755-1772)
Medicine with Arts and Sciences – Aesculapius

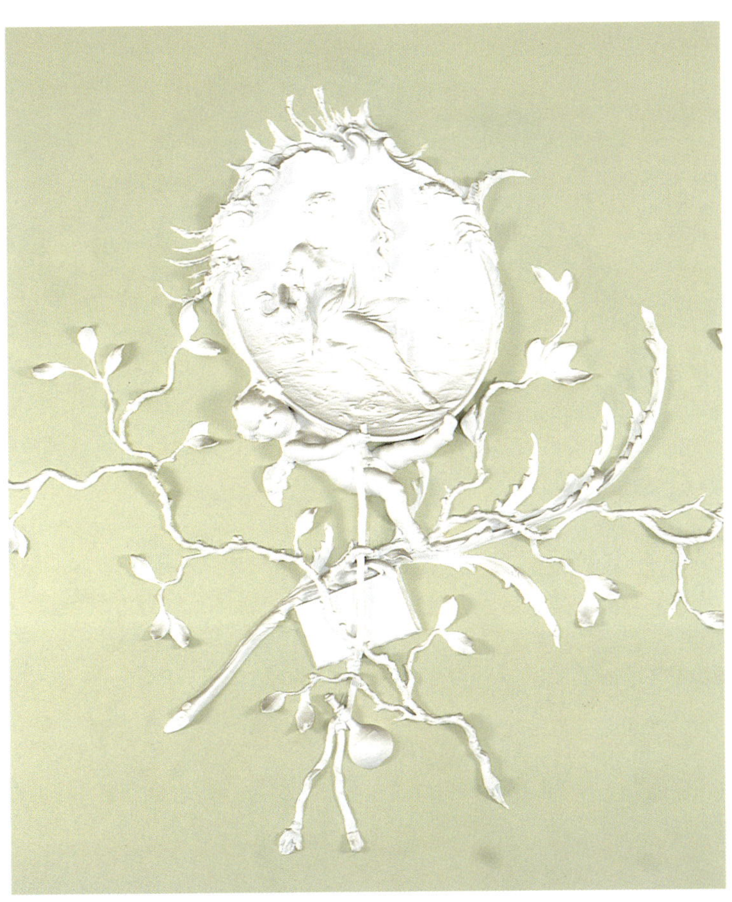

bottom right
Bartholomew Cramillon (fl.1755-1772)
Minerva introducing the Arts to Hibernia

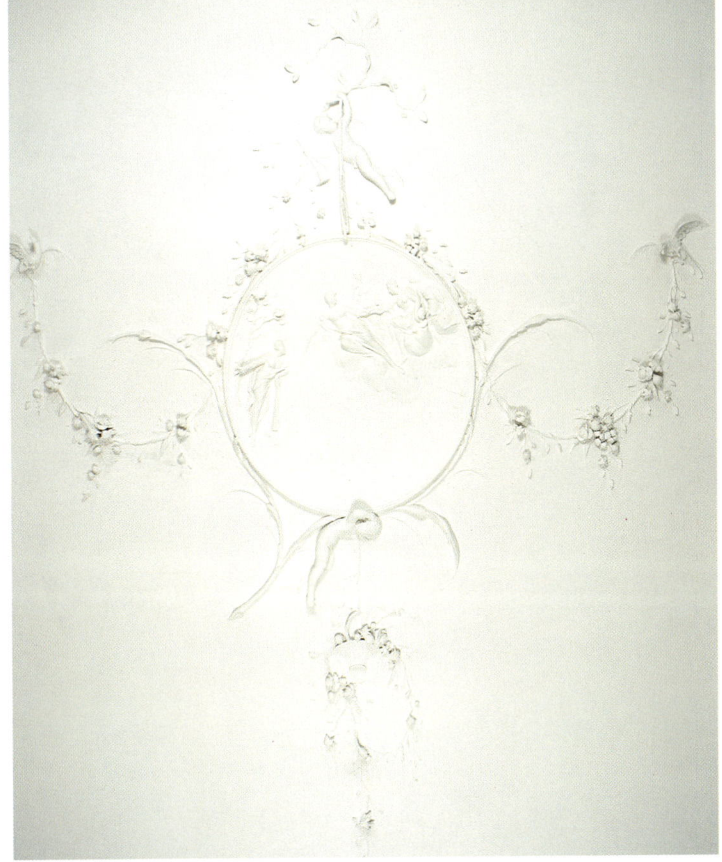

attributed to 'St Peter's Stuccodore'

Joseph McDonnell, in his recent study of Irish 18th-century stuccowork, has attributed the design and execution of this ceiling to an anonymous stuccodore known as 'St Peter's Stuccodore', because of his decoration of the Church of St Peter in Drogheda (*c.*1752). His origins are unknown, but it is likely that, like a number of other leading stuccodores, he came from the continent to work in Ireland. He also worked at Russborough, Co Wicklow, and at Bellamont Forest, Co Cavan.

Apollo Ceiling
stuccowork ceiling and frieze, inscribed: 1746
(originally in Tracton House, 40 St Stephen's Green, Dublin)

Tracton House at 40 St Stephen's Green was built in 1746 for the Surveyor-General of Ireland, Arthur Jones Neville MP, a man who coincidentally was involved in the building of Dublin Castle. Neville was an enlightened patron of the arts, who paid for the young Irish painter Jacob Ennis to travel in Italy and become familiar with continental art. His own career ended in disgrace after he was dismissed for embezzling State funds.

The original back drawing room of Tracton House formed the Apollo Room. The house was demolished in 1912 to make way for the new Bank of Ireland premises. At this time, the Apollo ceiling, along with the cornice, wall panelling and joinery, were taken out and re-erected in the National Museum. During the Second World War, the room was dismantled and put into storage. In 1966 the OPW incorporated the ceiling and cornice into a reconstruction of the original Tracton House room in the State Apartments. This room was created entirely for the incorporation of the Apollo Room. Before the 1941 fire, this space formed part of the State drawing room. The wall panelling in the room is a replica of the original, which did not survive its chequered history. The chimney piece (which is later in date) comes from the original Tracton House room. In the tablet in the centre of its lintel is a scene depicting Venus and Mercury teaching Cupid. Joseph McDonnell has identified this as a copy of an engraving after Boucher.

The ceiling is a spectacular example of mid-18th-century Irish stuccowork. In the centre is the figure of Apollo holding a lyre, and beneath him are arrayed the signs of the zodiac. From each of the four corners of the ceiling, cartouches with trophies representing music, the arts, war and the hunt are suspended, as if fastening the central image of the floating Apollo to the walls of the room. These are closely based on a series of engravings by Jacques Dumont le Romain, which were published in Paris in the 1730s.* Festoons of flowers and elaborate scrolling link the elements together. The date 1746 is inscribed on the group representing the arts. Lower down, the frieze contains scrolls, fruit, flowers and birds, depicted in a much less formal manner than the ceiling.

PROVENANCE – Made in 1746 for Tracton House. Moved to National Museum of Ireland, 1912. Put into storage *c.*1939. Reinstated in Dublin Castle 1966.

LITERATURE

Aubrey J. Toppin, 'The Apollo Room in the Museum', *Museum Bulletin*, iii (Dublin, 1913) 6-8

C.P. Curran, *Irish Decorative Plasterwork* (London, 1967)

J.B. Maguire, 'Dublin Castle: Three Centuries of Development', *JRSAI*, vol. 115 (Dublin, 1985)

Joseph McDonnell, *Irish 18th Century Stuccowork and Its European Sources* (National Gallery of Ireland, Dublin, 1991) 20-21*

Joseph McDonnell 'The Influence of the French Rococo Print in Ireland in the 18th century', *Bulletin of the Irish Georgian Society*, xxxvi (Dublin, 1994) 63-74

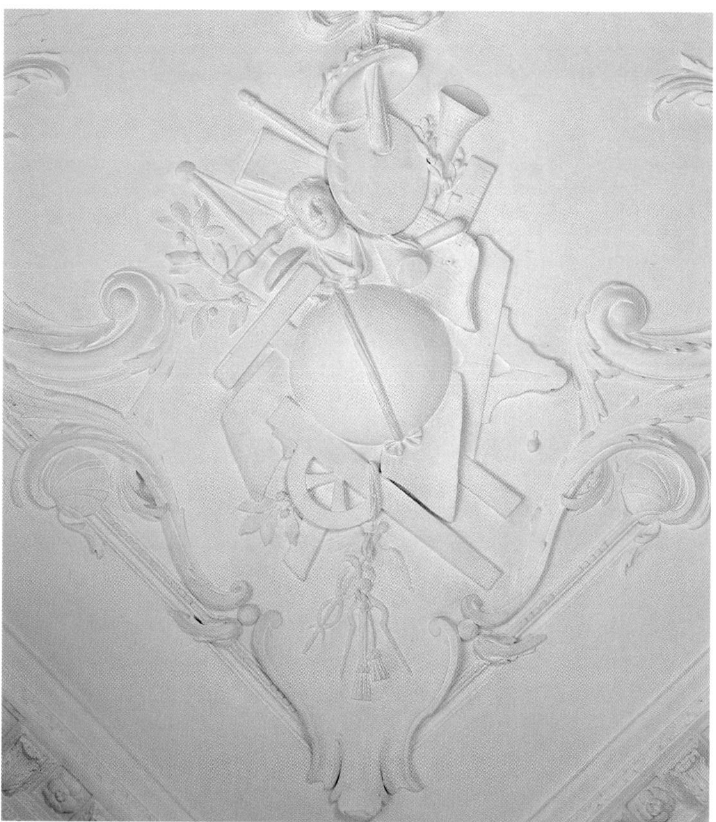

attributed to 'St Peter's Stuccodore'
Apollo Ceiling
Arts cartouche
opposite Apollo

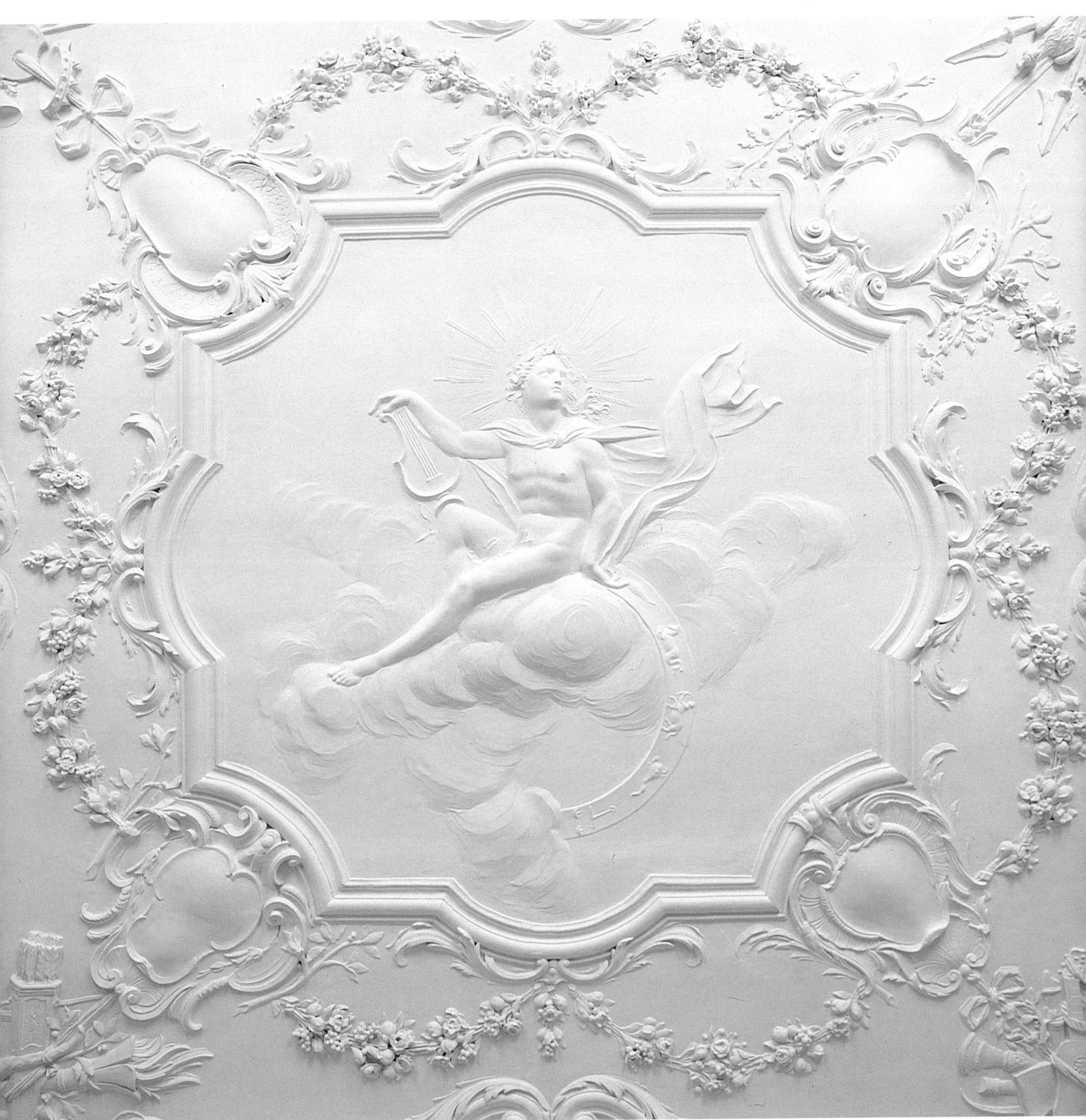

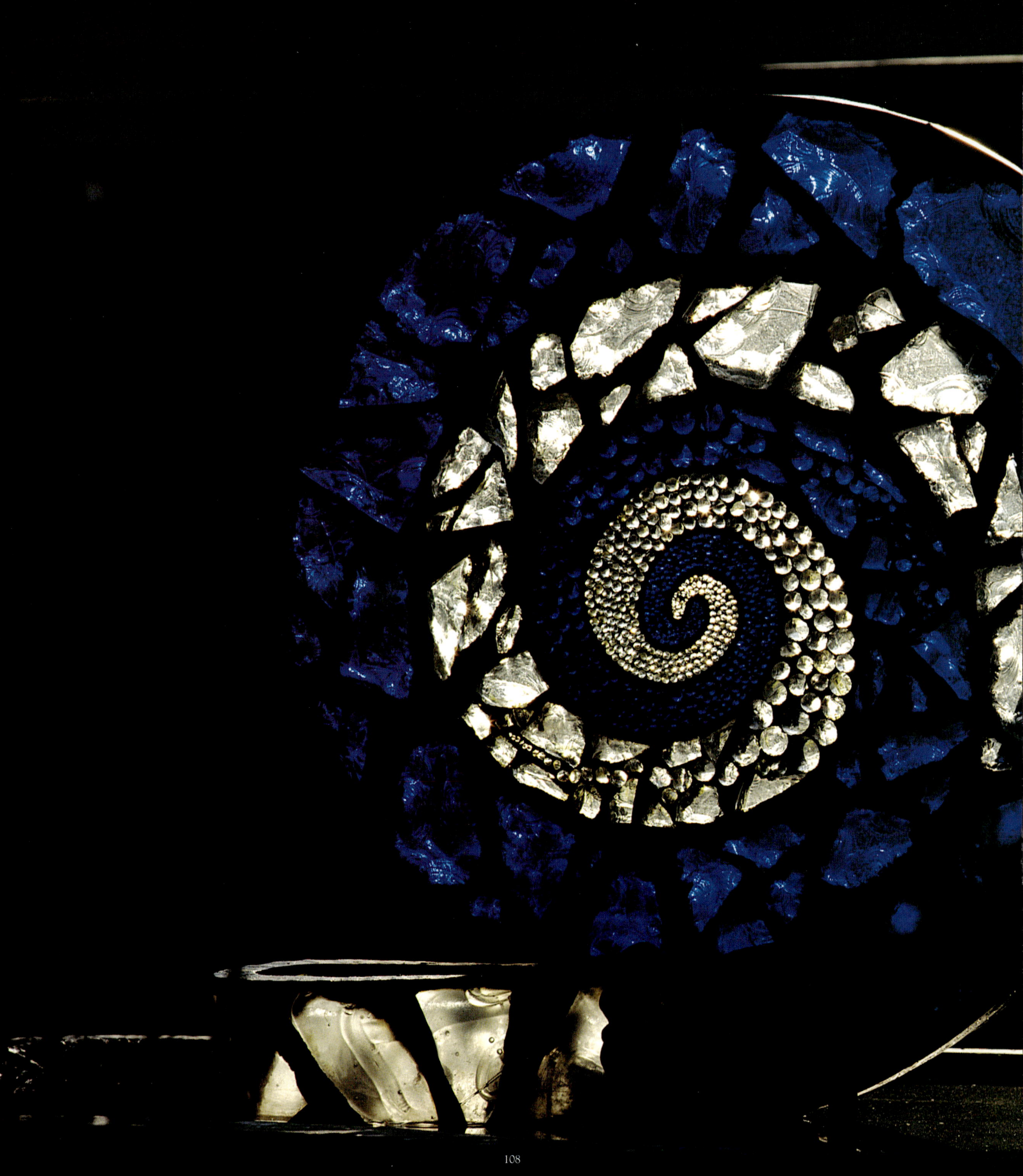

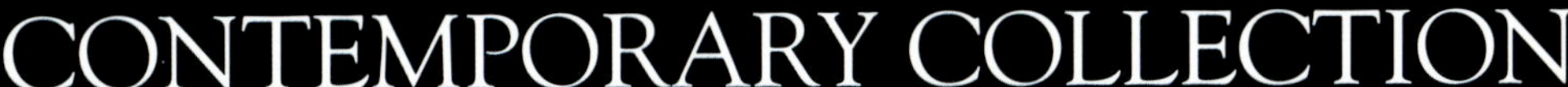

CONTEMPORARY COLLECTION

This section concentrates on artworks which were specifically commissioned for Dublin Castle or acquired for specific locations within it. Apart from the works catalogued here, there are numerous other paintings and prints located in the complex. These are part of the State collection and, as such, can be moved to other offices outside the complex as required. (They are currently being catalogued and published by the OPW's Art Management Group in the *Art in State Buildings* series.)

The artworks in this section must be seen within the context of the major refurbishment of the Castle in the 1980s and early 1990s. As has already been outlined in the introduction, from 1922 onwards many of the buildings in the complex fell into a relative state of dereliction, or were used for a wide range of often inappropriate purposes. This was partly a result of the requirements of the new State, which, with limited funds, needed to house diverse Government departments in whatever space was available. It was also partly due to a lack of interest in the history of Dublin Castle, which was seen as symbolic of British rule in Ireland. Aside from the State Apartments, part of which had been rebuilt in the 1960s, and the modernist style Stamping Building (1974) in the Lower Castle Yard, the whole complex was, by the early 1980s, in need of urgent attention.

OPW architects drew up an architectural report on the Castle in 1982. This highlighted the importance of a more select use of the buildings, and the need to encourage the general public into and around the complex. This, it was felt, would result in a wider understanding of Dublin Castle and its historical and architectural importance. The first and most major step in the rehabilitation of the Castle was the rebuilding of the Upper Yard in the late 1980s. The architectural team was subsequently involved in the commissioning of many of the artworks which accompanied the architectural refurbishments. These paintings, sculptures and installations have a very specific and important role in the development of a new image for Dublin Castle. Their prime function is to mediate between the architectural space and the visitor.

The commissioning of artworks was made possible through the Percent for Art scheme, which was initiated by the Government in 1978. This allows for the allocation of 1% of the cost of a building project to be spent on work by living artists. Most of the money raised in this way went to commissioning new works which were made for specific locations. They connect with the architectural space, which they emphasise, interact with, and provide a focus for beyond the purely functional. While some of the Percent for Art's budget was spent on acquiring suitable works directly from galleries or artists, most of it went to work which was selected through a careful commissioning process. The architects of the OPW, under the direction of the Art Management Group, were assisted in this by the Arts Council. Artists were shortlisted, and asked to submit proposals and sketches or models. Out of this the final work was chosen. Careful consideration had to be given to materials, the technical difficulties of installing the work, and its future maintenance. The finished works show a range of responses to the Castle: some engage with its history, the majority with its present or even future use.

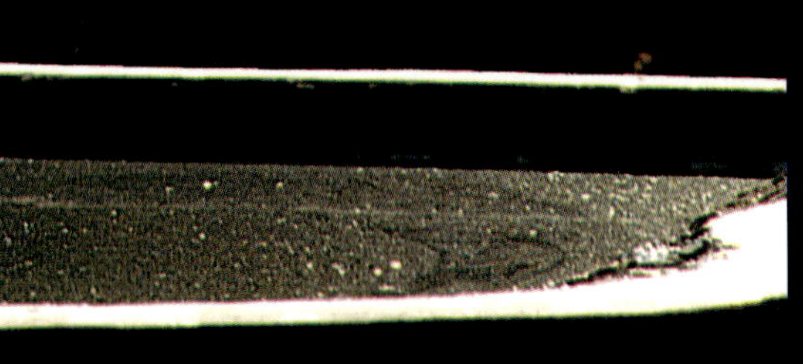

Dublin Castle is (and always was) a working building. It encapsulates not just the State Apartments, but other, less formal uses. At present, the Comptroller and Auditor-General, the Revenue Commissioners, the National Drug Unit, and two State tribunals of inquiry are located in the Castle. The Chester Beatty Library will open in the Clock Tower building in the year 2000. EU presidencies and other official meetings are held in offices in the Upper Castle Yard, where a modern and busy conference centre is located. Increasingly, Irish people associate Dublin Castle with events in modern political life rather than with the legacy of the British administration. This is partly the result of the major refurbishment and development of the Castle in the last twenty years, and the determination of the government to transform the complex into a useful resource.

THE CONFERENCE CENTRE

This is situated in the north-west corner of the Upper Castle Yard, behind the 18th-century façade of the original building. It was built in 1986-89, after the demolition of various buildings in this part of the Castle and a comprehensive archaeological excavation. One of the spurs to complete this purpose-built conference centre was the fact that Ireland was due to host the EC presidency in 1990, meetings of which were to be held in the centre. A small part of the budget that went into this massive project was put towards the commissioning of four major works of art by Irish artists. Shortlists of suitable artists were drawn up by the OPW architects with the advice of the Arts Council and the Sculptors' Society of Ireland, which were also represented on the selection committees. In all of these commissions, artists were encouraged to consider the history of the Castle, the present use of the surrounding space, and the specifics of the site itself.

Maud Cotter

Maud Cotter was born in Co Wexford and attended the Crawford College of Art & Design in Cork, where she studied under the sculptor John Burke. Cotter began to experiment with stained glass around the time she left college in 1978. During the following years, she became, along with James Scanlon, one of the most innovative stained-glass artists working in the country. She brought a new vitality to glass-making, using the medium to express a range of ideas and emotions which previously had been thought to belong only to the more obvious fine art media.

She deliberately avoids figurative imagery, which she feels is too often associated with the medium of stained glass, relying instead on a use of strong colour and abstract design, worked out in advance through preliminary drawings and collages. Her work is influenced by natural processes: 'I do portraits of processes in nature. I'm very conscious of decay and growth,' she said in 1986. She also recognises the connection between architecture and stained glass, and the potential of the latter to elucidate space.

During the 1990s, Cotter lived and worked in London for a number of years. Her more recent sculptural work uses a wide range of materials, including cardboard and textiles. She sees a connection between this work and the earlier stained glass – all have a strong physicality. They filter and transform light, and therefore connect very directly with the perception of the viewer. A more recent example of her work, *Absolute Jellies make Singing Sounds* (1994), can be seen in the Green Building in Temple Bar, just a few hundred yards from the Castle, a work which uses steel, glass, perspex, copper and lead.

That Sound Meets Sense, Straight as Lemons Meet Fish

1988, stained glass window, 287 x 58 cm
Castle Hall, Conference Centre

This window was the first work of art commissioned by the OPW after the building of the conference centre in 1988. It is situated in the north wall of Castle Hall on Castle Street, a building which straddles the old and new parts of the building. In the brief for the work, Cotter was asked to take into consideration these two aspects of the space, which, while modern in its interior, from the outside maintains some of the features of the 18th-century Guard House.

The artist's starting point for the piece came from the connection between sound and sign-making. From illuminated manuscripts, she was conscious of the discrepancies between the sign or letter and the spoken word. In this work she has used all kinds of primitive scripts, from Egyptian hieroglyphs to Assyrian cuneiform to the central line of Ogham which extends up to the Pythagorean symbol of growth at the top. The actual symbols she uses do not mean anything in particular; they are symbolic of communication in general. Cotter sees drawing and art-making as closely connected to this need for communication. She has used layered flashes of colour to emphasise a sensuality which appears at odds with the logic of language. The varying intensity of the colours, which is possible because of the technique, creates a floating effect and adds another layer of meaning to the piece. The formal layout of the design in grids, which is at odds with the painterly effect of the colour, is another reference to rational thought befuddled by the reality of communication. There is a sensual and humorous quality to the work which plays on the idea of language and script. While making the piece, the artist was conscious of the forthcoming use of the space by the European Union, and the idea of different nationalities meeting together.

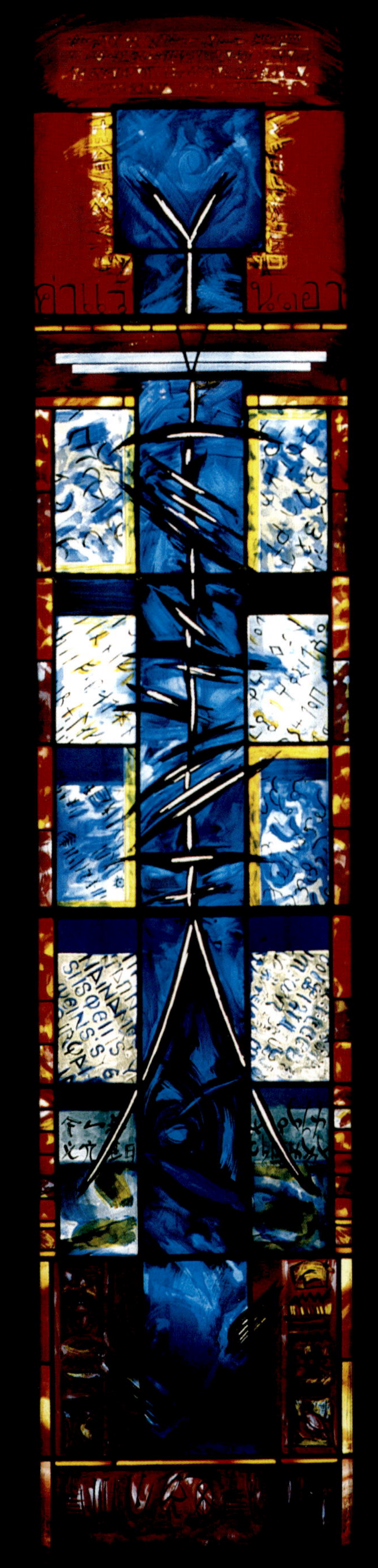

PROVENANCE – Commissioned by the OPW in 1988 for Castle Hall, Conference Centre, and installed on 26th August 1988.

LITERATURE
Art in State Buildings 1985-1995 (OPW, Dublin, 1997) 105. ART 01558.

COMPARATIVE LITERATURE
Nicola Gordon Bowe, *Stained Glass, Painting and Drawing* (Crawford Municipal Art Gallery, Cork, 1983)
Nicola Gordon Bowe, John Montague, *Maud Cotter – My Tender Shell* (Gandon Editions, Kinsale, 1991)
John O'Regan (ed.), *Profile 8 – Maud Cotter* (Gandon Editions, Kinsale, 1998)

That Sound Meets Sense
(preparatory drawing)
1988, charcoal on paper, 29 x 58 cm
Bedford Hall

This drawing was the preliminary design for the window submitted by Cotter. Drawing is extremely important to her. While a student in Cork, she was encouraged to draw constantly – a practice to which she still adheres. In the case of the Dublin Castle commission, the artist had no say in the proportions of the window so she used a full-size drawing to give her a sense of its scale and dimensions. The body is central to her work, so the drawing allowed her to become physically aware of the space. She also saw an inference of the scale and size of the body in the work.

Cotter is at pains to point out that she does not use drawings as the blueprint for her sculptural work. She sees them as conceptual tools, and once she begins to work in glass, that medium takes over. In this way, Cotter's approach to glass-making is completely different from traditional stained-glass artists who follower the initial cartoon very closely.

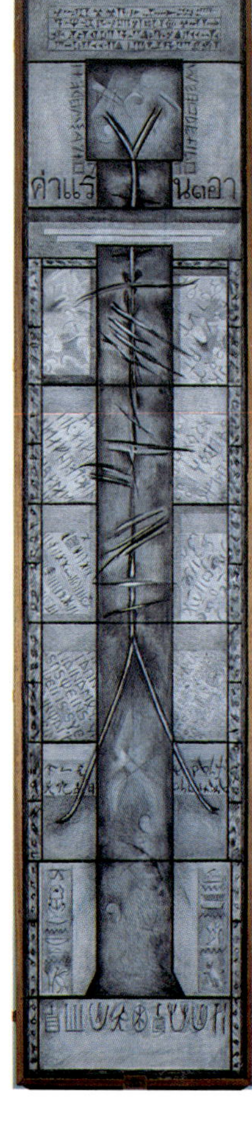

PROVENANCE – Gift from Mahon McPhillip, 1988.*

LITERATURE
Art in State Buildings 1985-1995 (OPW, Dublin, 1997) 22. ART 01874.

* Mahon McPhillip were one of the main contractors for the restoration and conference facilities contract for Dublin Castle, 1986-88.

Cecily Brennan

Cecily Brennan studied at the National College of Art & Design, Dublin, and was a founder member of the Visual Arts Centre in Dublin. In 1991 she was elected a member of Aosdána. She held her first solo exhibition at the Project Arts Centre in 1982, when her interest in painting and landscape was apparent. This theme developed in her work over the next fifteen years or so. Her more recent work has been in sculpture. Brennan was one of the most critically acclaimed Irish painters of the 1980s. In her work of this period, she concentrated on landscape, and produced works based on Irish and Icelandic terrains. The large scale and dramatic colour of her landscapes emphasises the sublime energy of nature. The battle between chaos and control is a pivotal theme in her painting; this is evident in the Dublin Castle work.

Garden Pathway
1989, oil on canvas, 320 x 557cm
Conference Centre

In October 1988, the OPW selected Cecily Brennan's proposal for an artwork for the north wall of the conference centre. It was to be the largest painting undertaken by the artist. It consists of three separate canvases and measures 3.2 by 5.5 metres. The subject is based on a small garden, which the artist has painted in close up so that the viewer is confronted by the colours and textures of the plants, rocks, and the central pathway which leads the eye upwards but not out of the painting. Despite the title *Garden Pathway*, there is a chaotic wildness about this landscape which contrasts with the regularity of the surrounding architecture. The swirling shapes of the elements add to this idea. The colours are vibrant and primitive, and suggest the power and energy of nature. The painting is situated opposite the stairway and next to the glass wall, which looks out on to the moat of the Castle. It connects with the natural world outside, and opens up the interior space in a very dramatic manner.

PROVENANCE – Commissioned by the OPW for the conference centre in 1988. Installed in June 1989.

LITERATURE
Art in State Buildings 1985-1995 (OPW, Dublin, 1997) 19, 53

COMPARATIVE LITERATURE
Aidan Dunne, review of show at Taylor Galleries, *Magill*, 18th April 1985
John Hutchinson 'Cecily Brennan', *Irish Arts Review*, vol. 3, no. 3, Autumn 1986
Luke Gibbons and Penelope Curtis, *Cecily Brennan* (Douglas Hyde Gallery, Dublin, 1991)
Peter Murray (ed.) *0044 – Irish Artists in Britain* (Crawford Municipal Art Gallery, Cork, 1999)

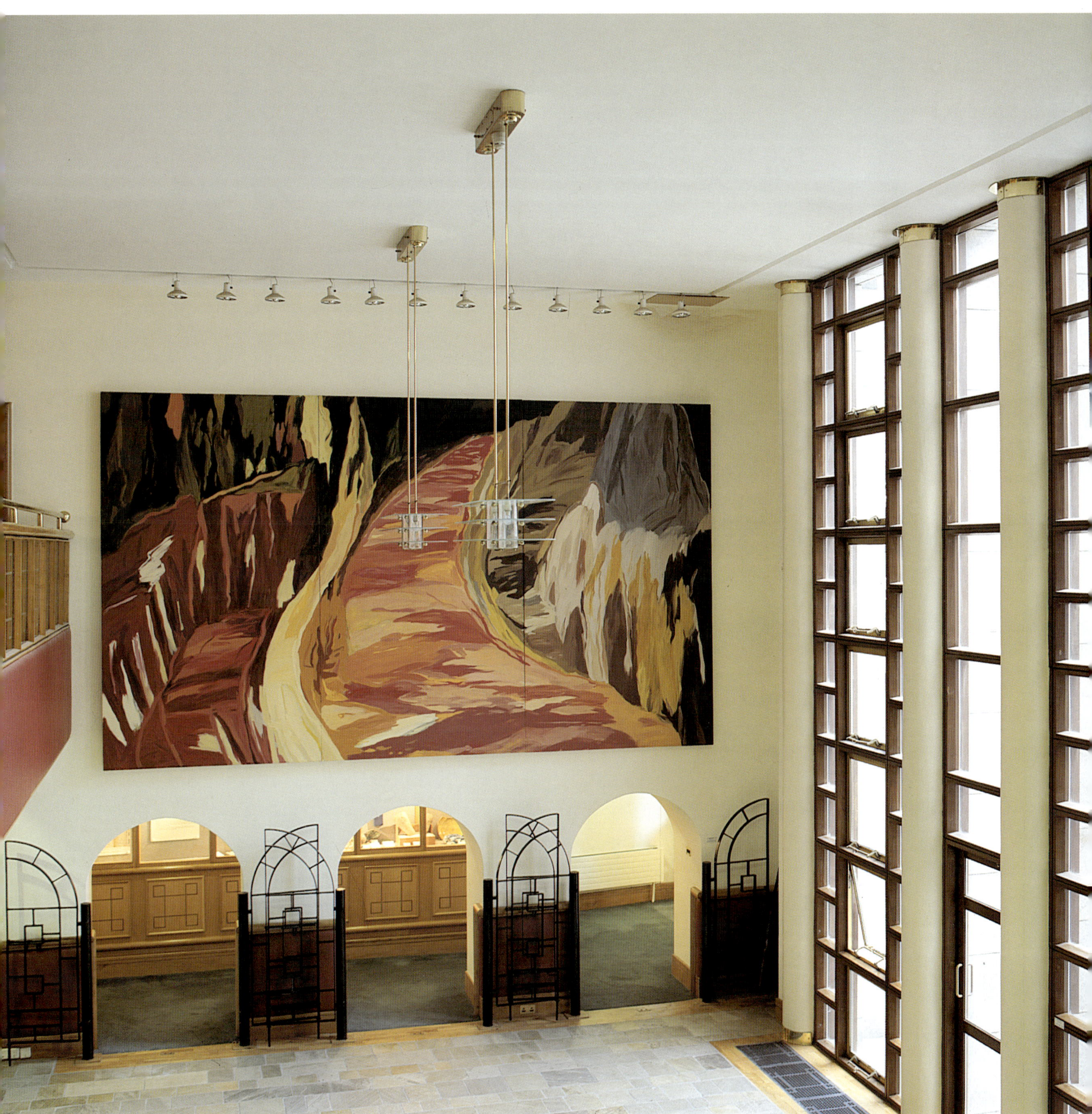

Felim Egan

Felim Egan was born in Strabane and studied painting at the Slade School, University College London. He lives and works in Dublin. He has a distinguished record of exhibitions, including solo exhibitions at the Irish Museum of Modern Art, and more recently at the Stedelijk Museum in Amsterdam. Although he is primarily known as a painter, Egan frequently incorporates sculptural elements into his two-dimensional work. Neon, steel, plaster and wood have been used. Apart from the work at Dublin Castle, he has received a number of important commissions for public spaces, including the atrium in the National Gallery of Ireland.

His work has gone through a number of phases but has remained primarily abstract, apart from a brief period in the 1980s when outlines of figures made an appearance. Classical mythology and landscape have provided some of his themes, but the abiding passion behind much of his work is music, as is the case in the Dublin Castle piece. The symbols and motifs which he uses can be linked to the rhythm and notation of music. They also grew out of Egan's interest in ancient Irish art.

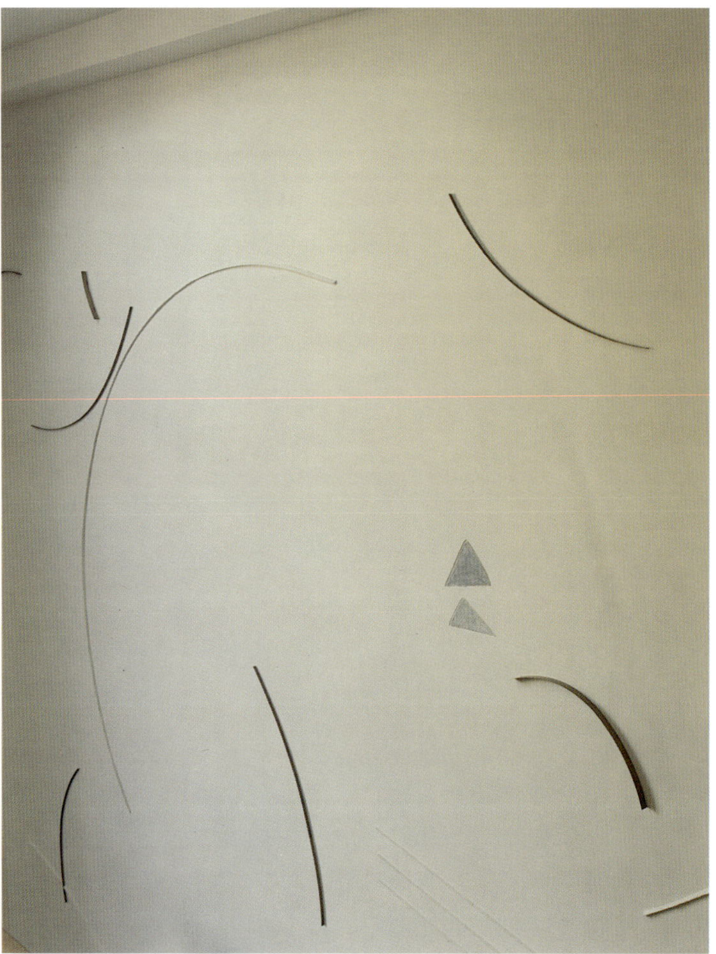

Gamboge Dance

1989, stucco, fresco and brass mural, 16 m

This work was selected from a number of submissions by different artists for the east wall of the conference centre – a huge area beside the staircase which spans some sixteen metres of wall space. It consists of arcs, straight lines and triangular forms, made of brass, plaster and fresco. One of the difficulties in making this work was the staircase itself, which, although it does not abut the wall, divides the space up so that one rarely sees the mural in its entirety. The abstract forms of Egan's work mean that the piece is effective even if seen only partially.

The mural has a subtle and playful quality despite its enormous scale. It appears like a large drawing made up of white plaster and brass lines, and floating triangles of blue, yellow (gamboge) and pink. The latter are made out of plaster which was cut away, replastered and then frescoed. They feature in much of Egan's work. He has said of their use in his paintings that they 'are a means of introducing colour into the work. They also generate direction and momentum, and they have playful associations that I like.' Here they help to orientate the spectator by giving a focus to the different parts of the mural as they come into view. They also anchor the other, less solid floating shapes, which seem to dance around them.

This piece is in direct contrast to Cecily Brennan's painting which hangs in the same space, and yet it is equally appropriate. It is sculptural yet subtle, compared with the dramatic painterly aspects of Brennan's *Garden Pathway*. Like Brennan's piece, it does not refer to the history of the Castle. It uses an international art language, and the musical and rhythmic quality of the forms provides an appropriate backdrop to the activities held in the conference centre.

PROVENANCE – Commissioned by the OPW for conference centre in 1988. Installed in April 1989.

LITERATURE

Art in State Buildings 1985-95 (OPW, Dublin, 1997) 105. ART 01135

COMPARATIVE LITERATURE

Aidan Dunne, *Felim Egan* (Third Eye Centre, Glasgow, 1984)

Aidan Dunne, review of exhibition in the Kerlin Gallery, *Sunday Tribune*, 6th May 1990

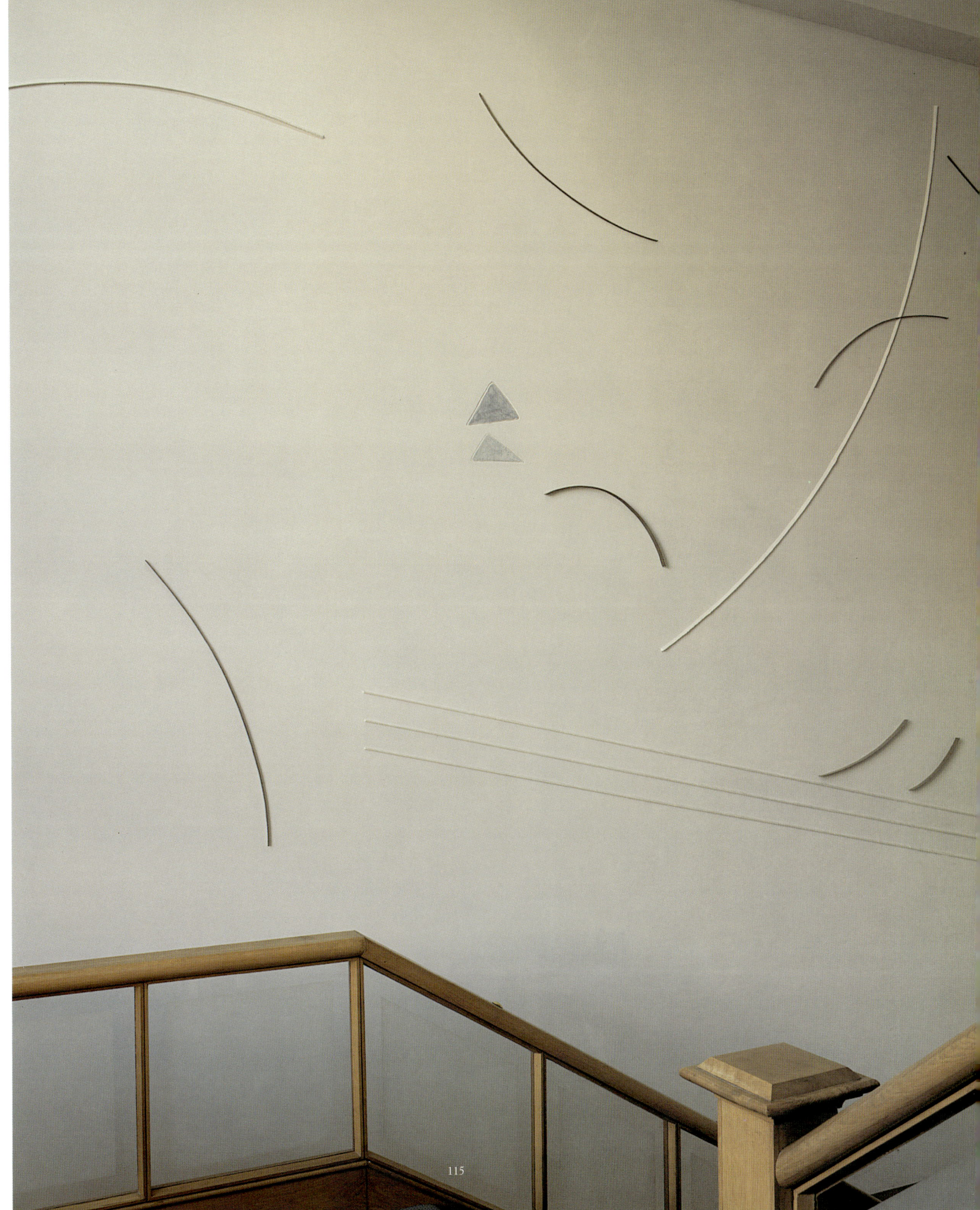

Eileen McDonagh

Eileen McDonagh is from Sligo and attended the Sligo School of Art & Design, from which she obtained a diploma in sculpture in 1978. She subsequently taught art in Dublin for a number of years before deciding to work on her sculpture full-time in the mid-1980s. She exhibits in Dublin, and has been involved in the commissioning of public sculpture in recent years.

Her work is characterised by an interest in traditional materials such as stone and wood. Aidan Dunne has described her work as showing 'an exemplary attention to detail and to bringing out the best in her materials'. Architecture is another important feature of her sculpture. She explores and uses the tensions and balance found in buildings in her combination and use of stone and wood. The Dublin Castle work was her first major public commission.

Incommunicado

1989, black granite, 366 x 183 cm

This work was chosen from a shortlist of six submissions for the newly constructed moat outside the conference centre. It consists of two megalithic-like structures made out of black granite, polished on three sides. The shape was initially inspired by a piece of Viking jewellery. The sculpture was to be made of limestone, but after experiments with this material, McDonagh realised it would change with time, absorb water and possibly become covered with algae. So she changed to the more expensive black granite, which contrasts more strongly with the surrounding granite and brick buildings. The artist, although initially interested in the historical context of the work, sees the setting of the piece within its contemporary surroundings to be of primary importance. The sculpture is deliberately minimal to contrast with the more elaborate style of the surrounding buildings. Its verticality unites the upper levels of space around the bridge, and the lower levels of the water and the surrounding courtyard. The piece is designed to be seen from both vantage points.

As with many pieces of public sculpture, subsequent changes to the site have affected the original intention of the work. When McDonagh was designing the piece, the moat was to be planted with waterlilies; the two semi-circular forms on the monoliths reflect the shape of their leaves. Another subsequent decision was the installation of a fountain at the base of the sculpture, which is at odds with its shape and its static quality. The artist had visualised the piece reflected in the waters of the moat, and saw the area as one of calm tranquillity. These changes were beyond the control of the artist and the architects who commissioned the piece. In spite of them, the piece continues to work well and to relate to its setting, providing a strong focal point to the moat and to the conference centre.

The title of the work, *Incommunicado*, evokes a human predicament. The two elements in the sculpture have an almost figurative appearance. There is a tension between the two granite forms which seem to face in opposite directions, one towards the Liffey and the sea, the other towards the Castle. In fact, McDonagh's working title for the piece was *In Communication*, the opposite of the final name. She saw the relationship between the historic and the modern as a key element to the meaning of the work, and this idea is presented in the sculpture. The polished granite exterior contrasting with the rough-cut side of the stone is a visual metaphor for the modern and the historic. The artist has stated that 'The stone will be left in its natural state on one face, giving the impression of both pieces splitting from each other. This symbolises the process of evolution – change and growth like the history of the Castle – the old merging with the new.'

PROVENANCE – Commissioned by the OPW (site specific). Installed in May 1989.

LITERATURE
Art in State Buildings 1985-1995 (OPW, Dublin, 1997) 106

COMPARATIVE LITERATURE
Medb Ruane, *Truss* (Project Arts Centre, Dublin, 1992)

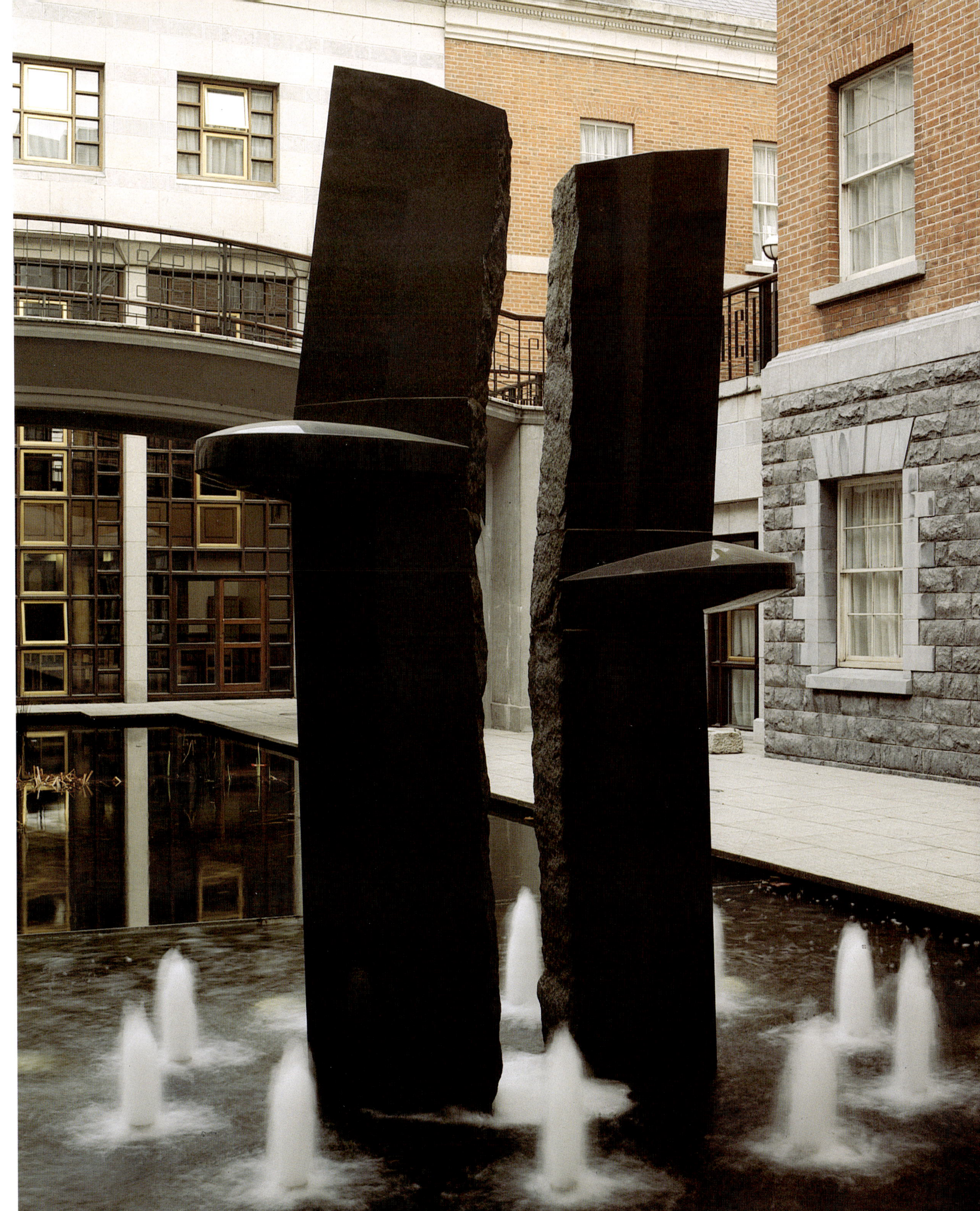

SHIP STREET RANGE

The Ship Street range of buildings, which is situated behind the State Apartments near the Ship Street entrance to the Castle, was practically derelict when the decision to rebuild it was made in the 1990s. It now houses part of the offices of the Revenue Commissioners. Formerly it was a barracks, and fortunately its exterior has been kept intact. In 1995 the Percent for Art scheme was used to commission a major piece of sculpture. The selected artists were able to discuss technical details of the siting of their planned work with the architects and engineers who were engaged on working on the site. Five artists submitted proposals. The artists were selected with the assistance of nominees of the Arts Council and the Artists Association of Ireland. The final choice produced one of the best known and most successful pieces of site-specific sculpture in the State collection.

Vivienne Roche

Vivienne Roche was born in Cork and attended the Cork School of Art, where she studied with the sculptor John Burke and, following his lead, worked mainly with steel. Her father was a structural engineer, and his profession had a major impact on Roche, encouraging her to see the potential formal qualities of steel in particular.

Not surprisingly, she has become increasingly interested in the connections between technology and fine art as her career has progressed. This has drawn her towards architecture, a discipline which ideally combines the aesthetic and the technical. Her interest in this began in earnest when she spent a year studying in the United States after graduating from art college. It can be seen in her work through her exploration of towers and bells, to more abstract forms which explore the dynamics of the steel or bronze from which they are made. Nature is also important to her work, and she has used glass and sailcloth, and incorporated kinetic elements.

Roche has made a large number of public or site-specific sculptures in Ireland, and was the co-author of a State-published report on public art in 1997. While examples of her work can be seen in locations around the country, a couple are within walking distance of the Castle. In 1988 she made a piece called *Liberty Bell* for St Patrick's Park, next to the cathedral. Another of her works can be seen on the pavement outside the cathedral on Patrick Street. More recently, she won the public art commission for the Lee tunnel in Cork. She has exhibited very widely in Ireland, and also in France, the United States, Great Britain and Scandinavia. She is a member of Aosdána, and a founding member of the National Sculpture Factory in Cork.

Plumbline

1995, painted steel, bronze, stainless steel, 14.5 x 3 x 3 m

The work is situated above a stairwell behind the reception desk of the new Revenue Commissioners' offices. It runs almost the entire height of the building – four storeys in total – and can be viewed from each level on walkways which open out onto the space. The piece is attached to an iron girder in the roof, and, apart from this, is suspended in space. It was made in three sections, and erected and fitted on site. It consists of an enormous 'line' of blue steel, which veers off into triangular sections, or 'elbows', at four points in its descent. In each of these sections is a plumbline – a bronze weight attached to a thread of stainless steel. This series of zigzags corresponds to the different floor and ceiling levels of the original Georgian interior. The natural engineering of the piece allows it to hang as a true vertical.

Roche has combined bronze and steel in a number of her other works. She sees bronze as rich and seductive, an obvious foil to the strength of steel, and in this piece the bronze weights are made to appear delicate and crafted. They provide a more human scale to the piece, and are positioned at the eye-level of a person standing on one of the balconies. The steel was painted blue by hand so that the variation of tone softens the structural nature of the material. This dynamic of a large structure being controlled by smaller elements relates very well to the surrounding space, which is basically the shell of a large Georgian building with offices facing on to it at different levels. The play on dimensions is even more central to the overall proportion of the work, which, although very long, is proportionately very narrow. The artist feels that the work reveals itself over space. It requires physical exploration, which also leads one to become aware of the space and dimensions of the building.

While Roche had used the idea of the plumb line in earlier works, it had been on a small scale. This commission allowed her to develop the idea, and it became the first in a series of large-scale works based on the plumb line. She later used two elements in her *Inclination* piece for the NMRC in University College Cork, and has also made a piece using three elements.

PROVENANCE – Commissioned by the OPW as part of Percent for Art scheme, 1995.

LITERATURE
Art in State Buildings 1985-1995 (OPW, Dublin, 1997) 107. ART 02915.

COMPARATIVE LITERATURE
John O'Regan (ed.), *Works 2 – Vivienne Roche* (Gandon Editions, Kinsale, 1991)
John O'Regan (ed.), *Profile 11 – Vivienne Roche* (Gandon Editions, Kinsale, 1999)

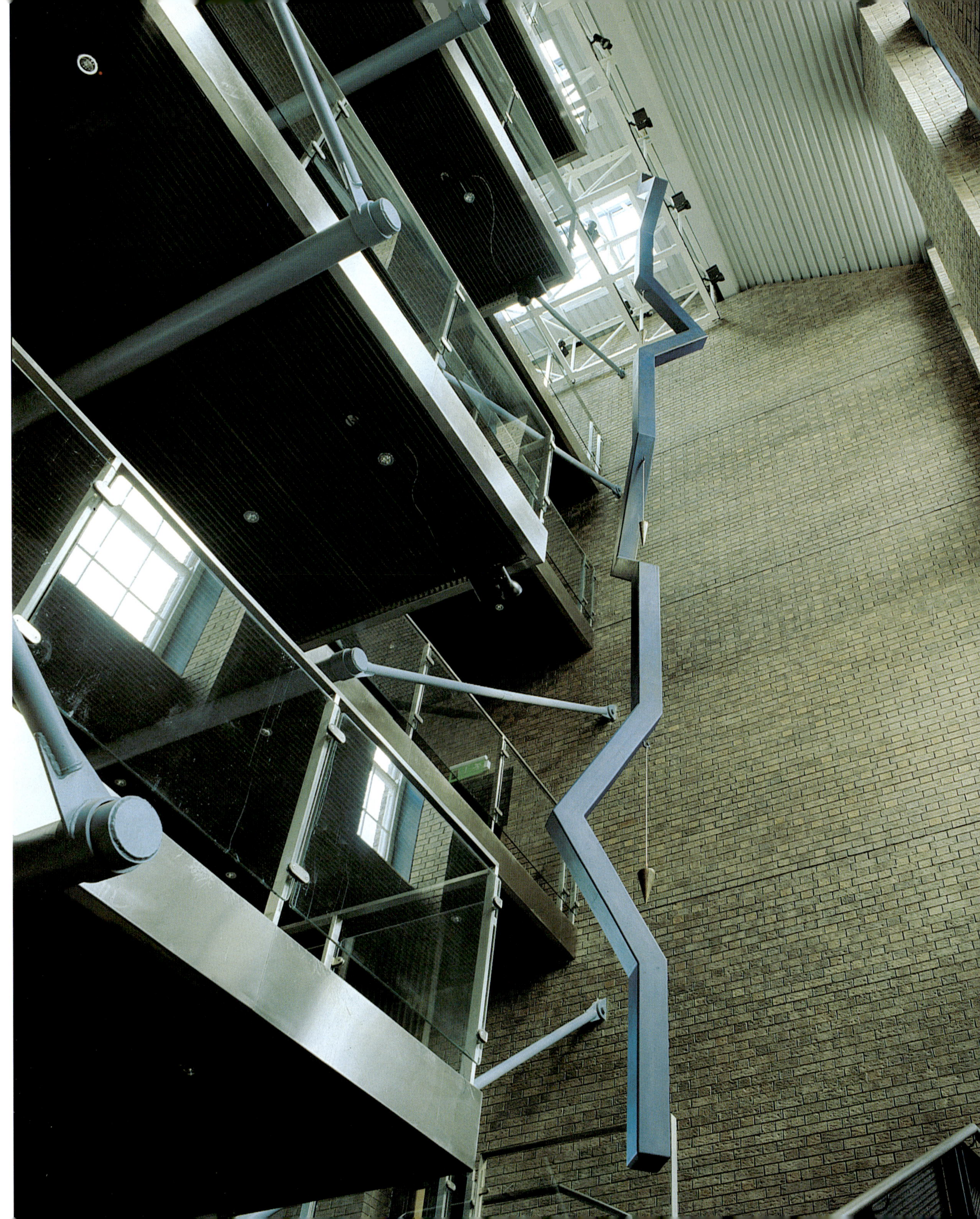

CLOCK TOWER BUILDING

This building, situated between the Ship Street range and the Dubh Linn Garden, directly behind the State Apartments, is the new home of the Chester Beatty Library. The original U-shaped block is marked on the 1843 ordnance survey as the Ordnance Office of the Royal Engineers. It dates to the early 19th century, and was used to store the munitions for the regiments housed in the Castle complex. After independence, this block was used for a time by the Revenue Commissioners. When the decision was taken to move the Chester Beatty Library from Ballsbridge into the city centre, this block was chosen as the ideal location. The courtyard around which the 19th-century buildings are ranged has been roofed in, and a new block has been added to the rear of the site. Two artworks were commissioned by the OPW in 1995 as part of the refurbishment of this building. Unlike the earlier commissions, these are much more functional and relate very closely to the building itself.

Rachel Joynt

Rachel Joynt has created a number of innovative pieces of public sculpture, including the now-famous bronze footprints (*Oileann na nDaoine*) on the traffic islands near O'Connell Bridge. The idea for this goes back to her NCAD degree show in 1989 when she sandblasted images of bricklayer's tools onto bricks in Fownes Street in Temple Bar. In both projects she used unobtrusive signs to connect the passers-by with their surroundings. She has also made installations using sifting sand at the Project Arts Centre (1993) and at Temple Bar Gallery (1999). Her work is always technically well thought out, and she relates it directly to the specific location in which it will be seen. In her public sculpture she brings an understanding of history, and is careful to choose subtle ways of allowing the public to connect with her ideas. One of her most memorable pieces is *Perpetual Motion*, which she made with Remco de Fouw for the Naas by-pass in 1995.

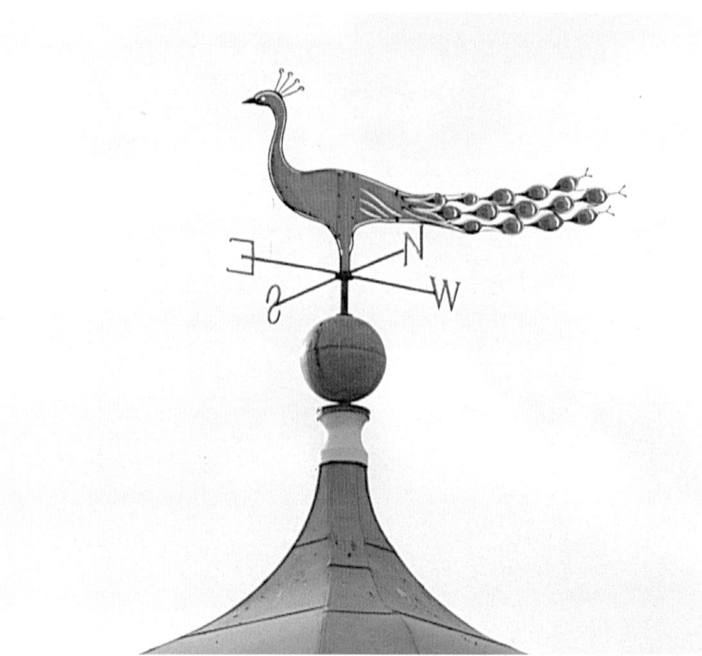

Peacock
1995, iron, patinated copper, blue glass, 150 cm (long)

When the Clock Tower building was being restored in 1995, it was decided to reinstate the original weathervane, although its arrow had long disappeared. Rachel Joynt was invited to design a suitable replacement. As the building was going to be given over to the Chester Beatty Library, Rachel decided to make a peacock for the weathervane. Her decision was based on the fact that while this would appear traditional – a natural replacement for the cockerel usually found on weathervanes – it is also an exotic motif. The peacock features prominently in Japanese-influenced art and design, and is associated with the Orient. It therefore draws attention to the oriental artworks contained in the building beneath it. The peacock, which is constructed of iron and patinated copper with a tail of blue glass discs, was made by Harry Page & Sons.

PROVENANCE – Commissioned by the OPW, 1995.

LITERATURE
Art in State Buildings 1985-1995 (OPW, Dublin, 1997) 106. ART 02907.

Jewel in the Concourse
1995, Mosaic pool, 633 x 133 cm

Having already made the weathervane for the building, Rachel Joynt was coincidentally selected to make a pool for the concourse of the Clock Tower. She chose to relate the design to the peacock on the roof. The piece is based on a gigantic peacock's feather made up of glass and Venetian enamels set into the slate floor of the museum's foyer, where it creates a focal point for the building. Like the weathervane, this is very oriental in feeling. When filled with water, pieces of gold and green reflect light back at the viewer.

PROVENANCE – Commissioned by the OPW, 1995.

LITERATURE
Art in State Buildings 1985-1995 (OPW, Dublin, 1997) 106. ART 02908.

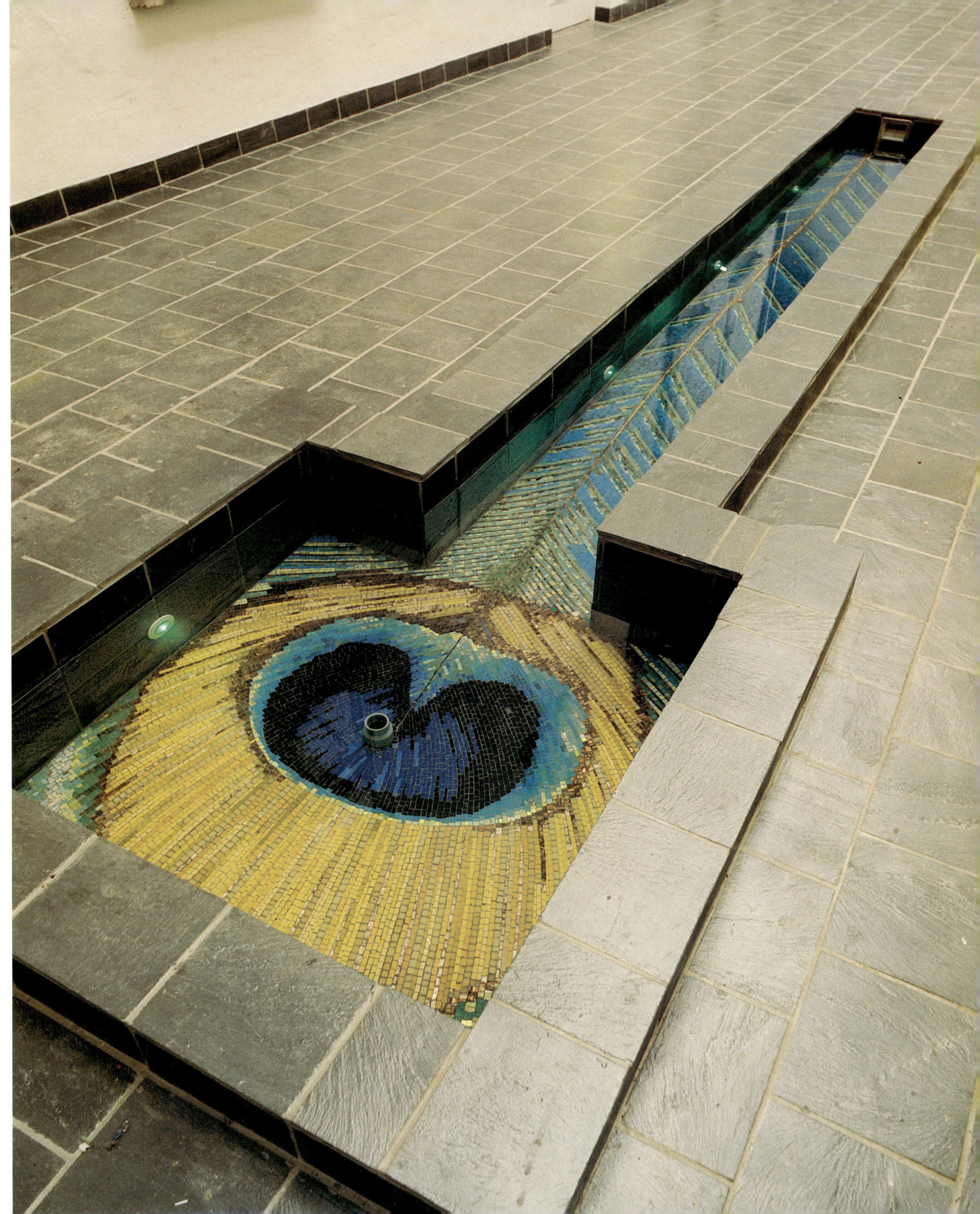

DUBH LINN GARDEN

The garden of the Castle, or the Pound, as it was known, had been a derelict patch of ground since the British administration had left. In the mid-1990s, because of the increasing use of the complex, the planned opening of the Chester Beatty Library, and the fact that Dublin Castle was due to host the EU presidency in 1996, it was decided to re-landscape the garden and create a proper helicopter landing pad. Ana Dolan, an architect with the OPW, came up with a new design for the area which incorporated the historical appearance of the garden with its new functions.

The garden had been circular for most of its history since it was first created in the 17th century. The decision was made to retain this shape, which is also suitable for landing helicopters. The ground was completely flattened, with the lawn laid onto a sand base designed to withstand heavy impact. The pattern on the lawn, which is designed to be seen from the air and from the State Apartments, came from 17th-century parterre gardens. The interlocking design is inspired by Celtic jewellery, and refers to the fact that the ancient Dubh Linn (Black Pool), around which the first settlers of Dublin lived, was sited here. It has been created using clay bricks with glass, in what appears to be the eyes and tails of the interweaving serpents. These were made by the artist Killian Schurmann. In the spaces surrounding the central lawn are a series of little gardens, each with a water feature. In each of these spaces, the OPW, with Designyard in Temple Bar acting as consultant, commissioned a suitable artwork. In addition, the artist Kathy Prendergast was commissioned to make new gates and railings for the garden. The seats around the edge of the lawn were made out of elm by Eric Pearce. Each of them has an Ogham letter inlaid in bog oak in its back. Like the work for the Clock Tower building, the pieces in the garden are functional rather than belonging purely to the realm of fine art.

Sarah Daly

Sarah Daly studied at Limerick School of Art & Design before joining Tileworks in Dublin in 1990. In 1993 she moved to Edinburgh, where she has set up her own company making one-off commissioned mosaics, and ceramic and glass. While working with Tileworks she was involved in several commissions for the OPW, including work at Government Buildings and Dunquin interpretative centre, Co Kerry.

Serpent Pool

1995-96, mosaic mural, 206 x 259 x 27 cm
Terracotta Garden

For her wall-mounted mosaic, the artist has used a central Celtic motif of a spiral made from the entwined bodies of three serpents, like the boss on a piece of prehistoric metalwork. The little fish which surround the central design of the mosaic are almost Roman in quality. The bright colours of the materials set against a small pool of water are deliberately Mediterranean in feeling, and the planting of lavender, rosemary, and other aromatic shrubs in the vicinity adds to this sensation. It is a piece which works particularly well in the summer months.

PROVENANCE – Commissioned by the OPW, 1994.

LITERATURE
Art in State Buildings 1985-1995 (OPW, Dublin, 1997) 105. ART 02912.

David Lambert

David Lambert is a founding member of the Blackstone Studios in Kells, Co Kilkenny, an educational studio which aims to provide the local community with access to employment and training in craft and design. He was born in Dublin and studied at Dun Laoghaire School of Art & Design. He has been involved in a range of sculptural projects, from community to public art. He works exclusively in stone, which he uses to create works which relate to the landscape, architecture, and the interior space. His work shows an awareness of nature and the environment, and these considerations are foremost in the artist's mind when he selects the shape and type of stone.

Bird Bath

1995-96, Kilkenny limestone, 61 x 91cm
Green Garden

This bird bath, or rainwater basin, was made to harmonise totally with its natural surroundings. The design of the two interconnecting forms is based on a solidified drop of rainwater.

PROVENANCE – Commissioned by the OPW, 1994.

LITERATURE
Art in State Buildings 1985-1995 (OPW, Dublin, 1997) 106. ART 02911.

bottom left
Sarah Daly, *Serpent Pool*

bottom right
David Lambert, *Bird Bath*

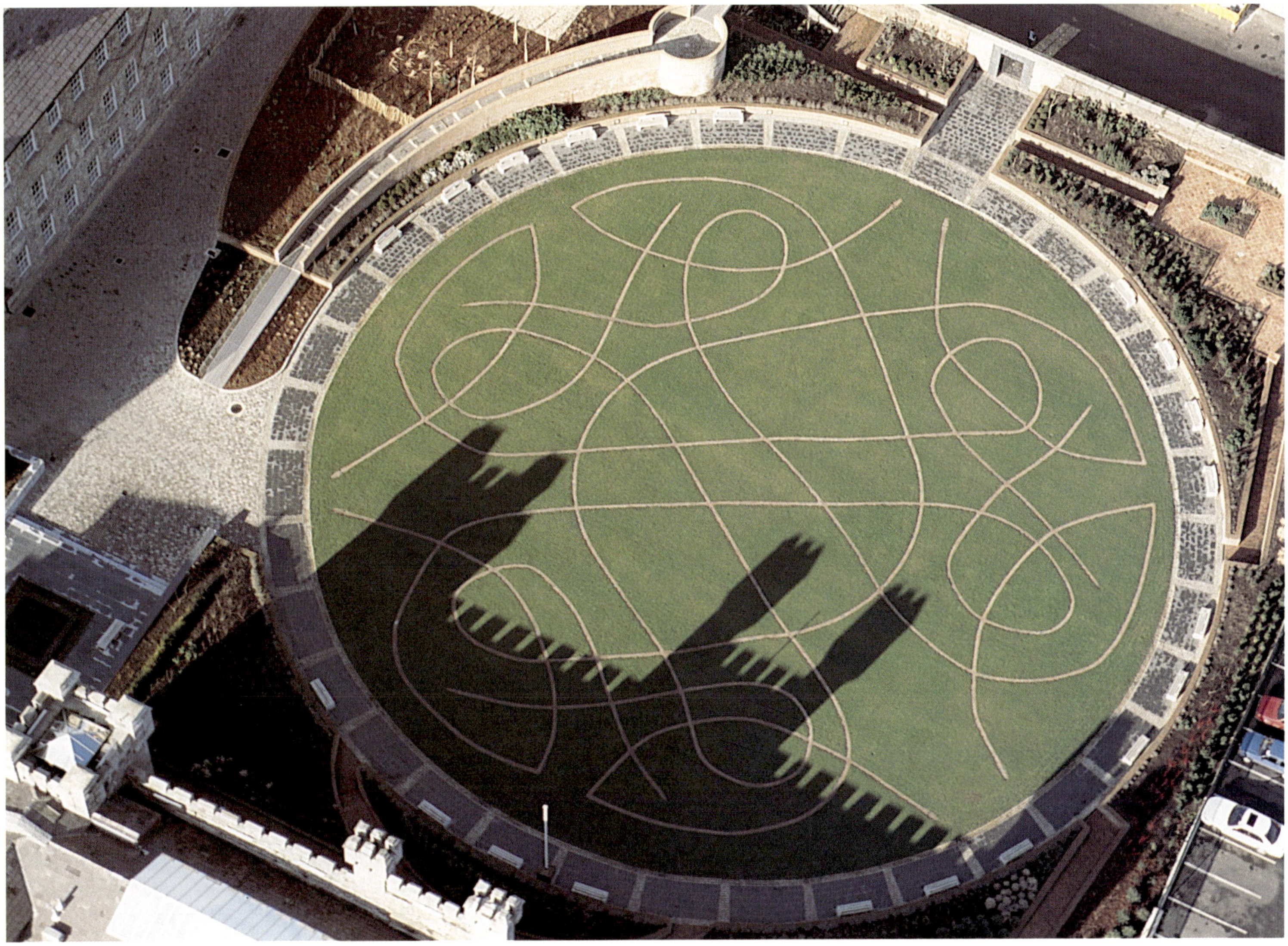

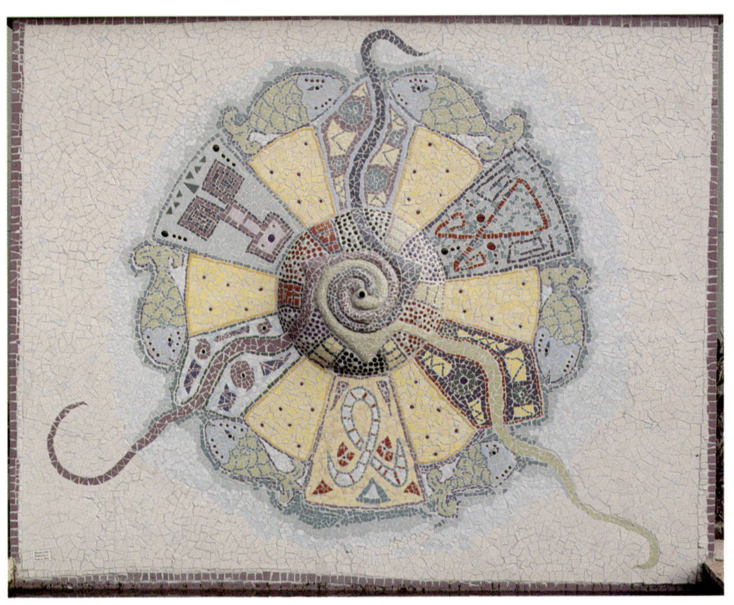

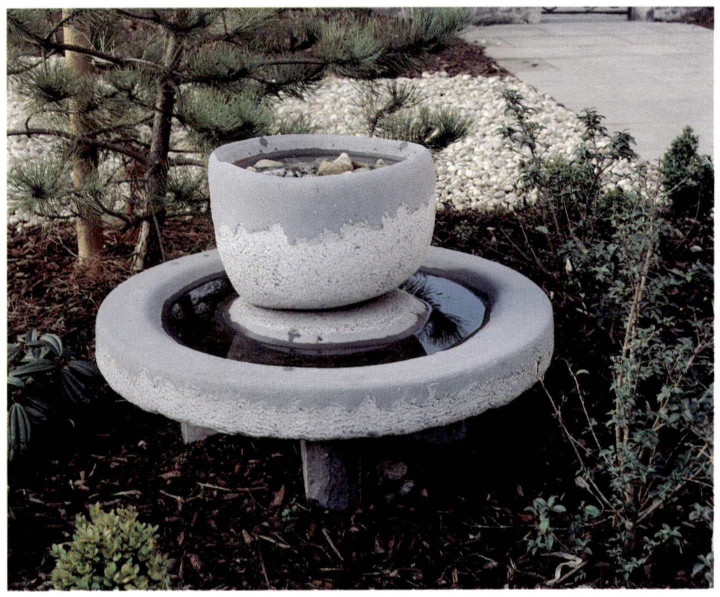

Killian Schurmann

Killian Schurmann trained in Germany as a glass-blower of scientific instruments. He first became interested in studio glass in the mid-1980s, and worked with the American glass artist Billy Bernstein in Germany, and in Bernstein's studio in North Carolina in 1986. After a number of years, during which he travelled extensively visiting glass workshops in Egypt, Mexico, Kenya, Czechoslovakia and elsewhere, he set up a studio in Dublin (1990). He has carried out major commissions for Kylemore Abbey and the Unitarian Church in Sallynoggin, Co Dublin.

Serpent Water Feature
1994, glass, 100 x 100 x 80 cm
Glass Garden

This sculpture is situated in a granite basin filled with water in the south-east corner of the Castle garden (near the Coach House and the garda offices). Like many of the other artworks in this area, it relates to the idea of the Black Pool. Two glass snakes are intertwined, creating a spiralling form of clear and blue glass, their heads facing in opposite directions. The site was chosen because it is in the direct path of the morning sun, which creates a jewel-like effect on the glass. Schurmann has a playful approach to his materials, using here big chunks of glass deceptively crude in appearance. He uses a technique called 'dalle de verre' in which the glass slabs are embedded in epoxy or cement.

PROVENANCE – Commissioned by the OPW, 1994.

LITERATURE
Art in State Buildings 1985-1995 (OPW, Dublin, 1997) 107. ART 02909.

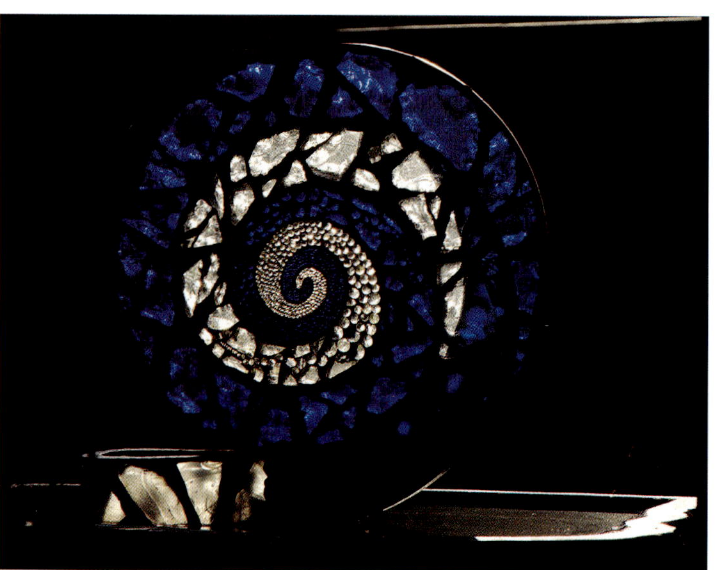

Kathy Prendergast

Kathy Prendergast is one of the country's most critically acclaimed artists. She lives in London, and exhibits in Ireland and internationally. Having graduated from the National College of Art & Design, Dublin, she studied at the Royal College of Art in London in the mid-1980s. Her NCAD graduate piece, *Waiting*, is now part of the collection of the Hugh Lane Municipal Gallery of Modern Art. In 1990 she had a solo exhibition at the Douglas Hyde Gallery, Dublin. In 1995 she represented Ireland at the Venice Biennale, and won the 'Year 2000' prize for the Best Young Artist at the show. Her ongoing project, *City Drawings*, in which the maps of all the capital cities in the world are meticulously redrawn in pencil so that their shapes create either careful or chaotic patterns, was shown at the Tate Gallery in London in 1997. Prendergast works in a wide range of materials, creating works which are often surreal in appearance and which open up questions of territory and possession. She is primarily known as a fine artist, but she has also undertaken projects which combine this with design. The wrought-iron gates of the Designyard building in Temple Bar, whose design is based on city maps, were made by Prendergast.

Railings and gates
1995, wrought iron
Dubh Linn Garden

Kathy Prendergast's work at Dublin Castle is indicative of the range of her ideas and capabilities. Rather than a fine-art piece, this work is completely functional. She used the theme of the spiral, which seems to have been central to all the artists' concepts of the Black Pool. But she has used the idea in a subtle and novel way. The design is inspired by 17th-century ironwork. The forms have an organic quality, in keeping with the garden behind them. These gates and railings were made by Harry Page & Sons to the design of the artist.

PROVENANCE – Commissioned by the OPW *c.*1995

LITERATURE
Art in State Buildings 1985-1995 (OPW, Dublin, 1997)

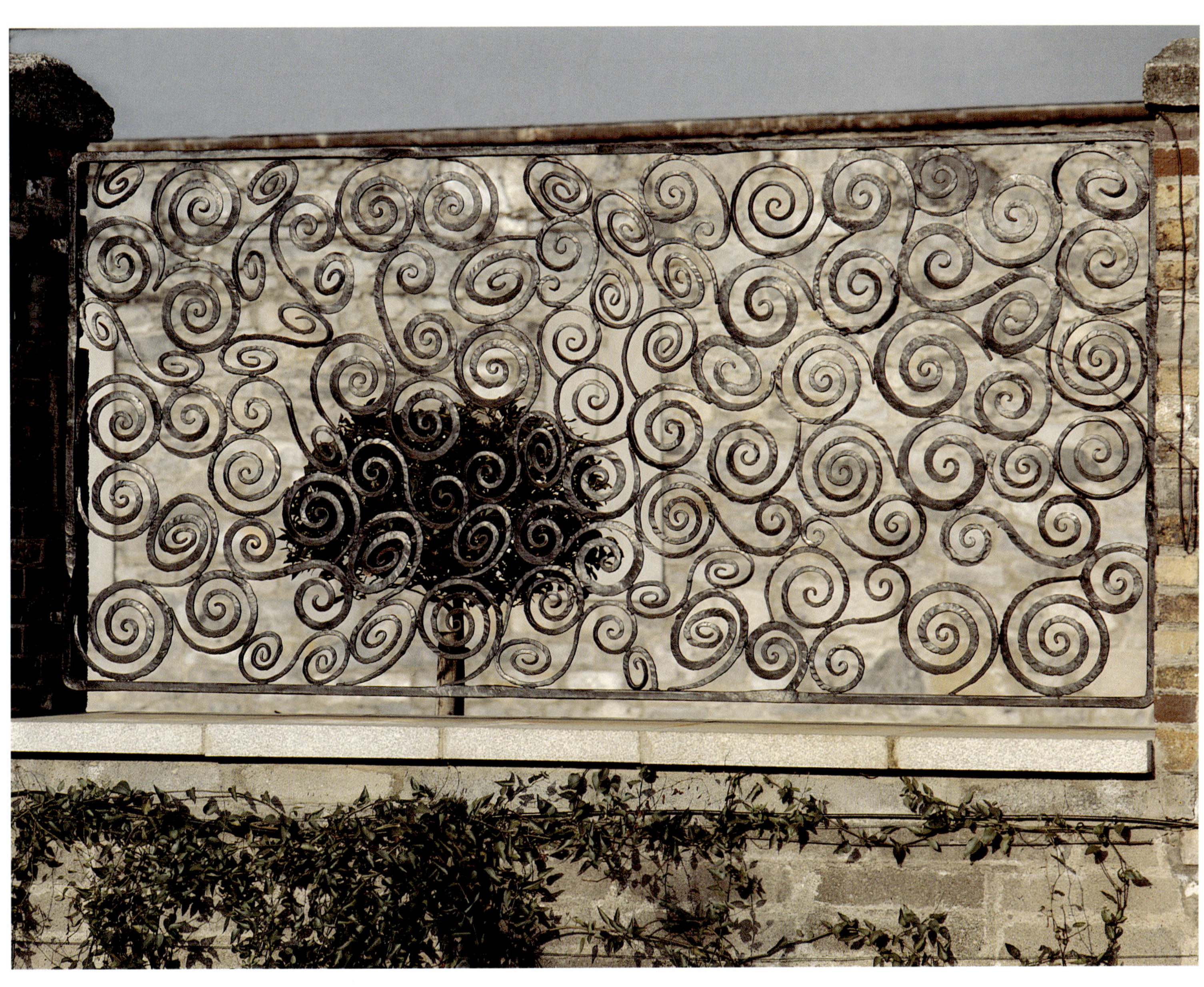

Kathy Prendergast
Railings and gates

THE COACH HOUSE

The Coach House is a castellated stone building which runs along the south side of the garden. It was designed by the architect Jacob Owen in the mid-19th century, and was used as a stables and coach house. In the 20th century, the OPW used it for storage; a number of works of art now on display in the State Apartments were once kept in this building. In the mid-1990s it was decided to restore it and use it for public functions. Very little new work was done to the interior, which still has the raw brick walls of the old stables.

The only piece of commissioned work was a specially designed reception desk, which is located directly inside the main entrance doors. This was made by Tileworks, a company set up by two graduates of the National College of Art & Design, Dublin, in the late 1980s. It is made of tiles, mirror and glass, and was envisaged by the OPW architects as a 'spectacular object contributing to a sense of arrival after walking across the new formally planned garden'. For each of the two main rooms inside the Coach House, a painting was acquired.

Michael Kane

Michael Kane is a well-established artist who began exhibiting in Dublin in the 1960s. He was a prominent member of the Independent Artists group, a group of artists who exhibited together in the 1960s, 1970s and 1980s, and whose members contributed enormously to the development of the visual arts in Ireland. Like the other prominent members of Independent Artists, Kane shunned the idea of following international trends for the sake of being fashionable, and worked in his own style. Throughout his career, he has been outspoken in his criticism of the art establishment in Ireland, which he, and many others, have perceived as elitist at certain periods. Kane is an accomplished printmaker, as well as a painter.

Kane has always been interested in Expressionism and in a figurative art which relates to real experience. Many of his paintings are autobiographical or relate to contemporary Dublin. The artist lives near the Baggot Street area of the city, close to the Grand Canal, which is known for its veneer of prosperity beneath which prostitution and a drugs culture thrive. While some of his early works have dealt with the negative aspects of life here, most of his paintings are about everyday experiences. In 1991, he stated that 'The ordinary, everyday, peaceful, almost always comical activities of people trying to live their lives as best they can have always attracted me in the making of images.' At the same time, he admits that the ordinary has always had another more 'disquieting' aspect to it.

The Diver

1988, acrylic on canvas, 276 x 240 cm

This large, colourful canvas is typical of the work Kane was doing in the late 1980s. This scene of someone bathing in the canal on a hot summer's day is a familiar one to Dubliners, as are the red brick buildings, and the bridge in the background of the painting. This is Baggot Street bridge, beside which is the bench now dedicated to the poet Patrick Kavanagh. Kane has often been linked with poets in his concern with capturing a kind of poetic experience of modern urban life, and indeed he writes poetry himself. (In 1987 Kane dedicated an exhibition of his work to Kavanagh.)

This image of someone diving headfirst into the waters of the canal is humorous and direct, and has a childlike quality. The paint is applied in thick strokes of strong primary colours which add to the exuberant atmosphere of the work.

PROVENANCE – Purchased from the Rubicon Gallery, Dublin, 1995.

LITERATURE
Art in State Buildings 1985-1995 (OPW, Dublin, 1997) 32. ART 01846.

COMPARATIVE LITERATURE
Henry Sharpe, *Michael Kane: His Life and Art* (Dublin, 1983)

Margaret Morrisson

Margaret Morrisson graduated from NCAD in 1989 and completed an MA at the University of Southern Illinois in Carbondale. She has exhibited regularly in Dublin since 1991, and has established herself as a serious and versatile painter. Her work is noted for its rich colour and texture. It frequently relates to exotic landscapes which she has visited, such as the Chichuahuan Desert and the Santa Elena Canyon in Texas. In more recent paintings, she has focused on established works of art such as Rodin's bronzes or Manet's *Dejeuner sur l'Herbe*. These works are more subdued in colour, and concentrate on the human figure. The OPW owns a number of her paintings.

Woman in a New Land

1993, acrylic on canvas, 192 x 216 cm

This work was first exhibited at a show in the Rubicon Gallery, Dublin, in 1993. It was one of five large canvases based ostensibly on gardens which, through the act of painting, are transformed into dramatic and sensuous landscapes. The artist sees this painting as marking a transitional moment in her personal and artistic life. It is one of the first paintings she made which contains a fig-

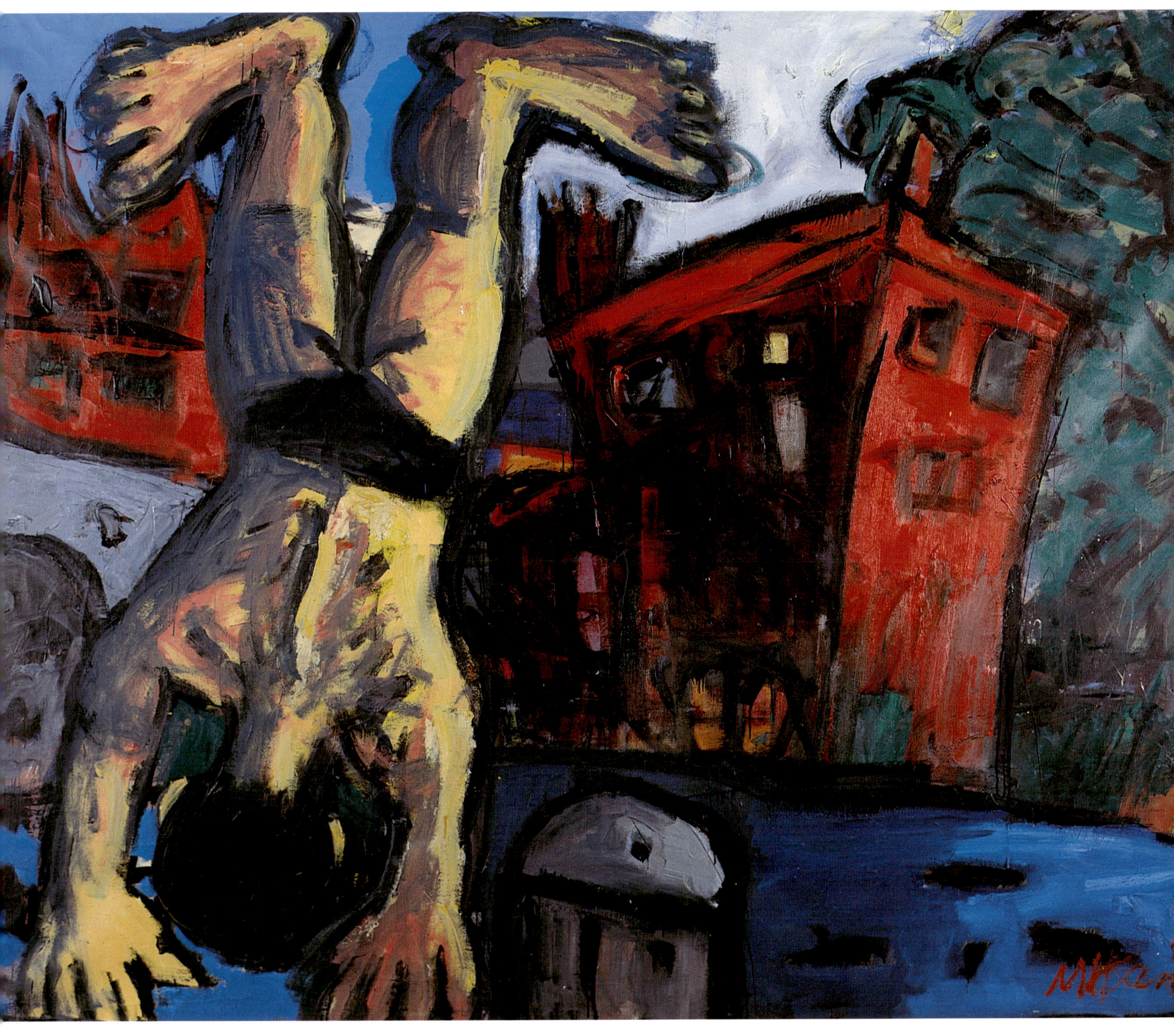

Michael Kane
The Diver

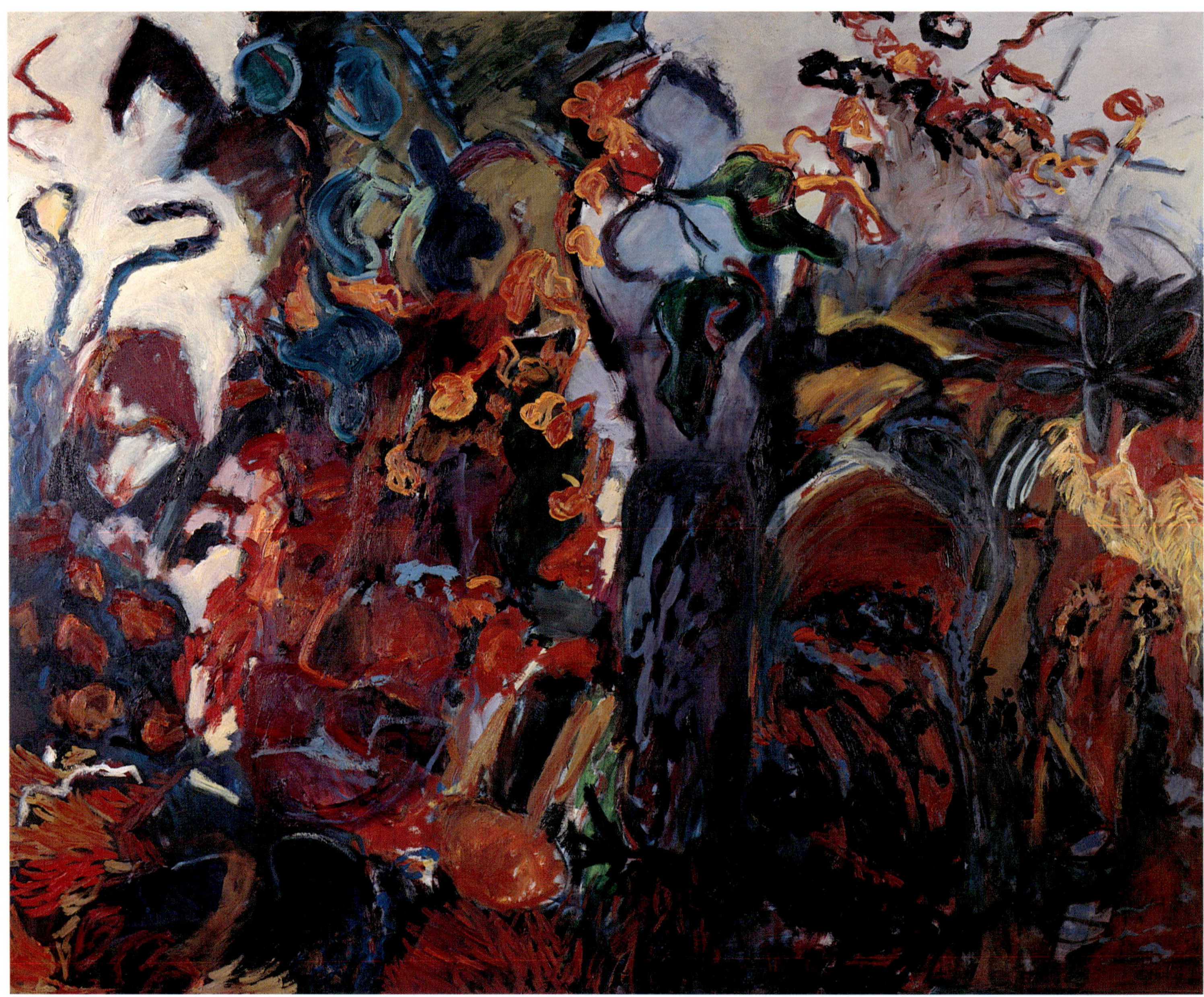

ure – a tall, sinuous, blue form in the centre of the composition. Around the figure is a jungle of exotic plants and flowers. The dramatic colours and vibrant use of texture and form was inspired by the artist's recent move to the United States. The almost biblical sounding title refers to this experience and to the adventure of exploring a new terrain.

PROVENANCE – Purchased from the Rubicon Gallery, Dublin, 1995.

LITERATURE
Art in State Buildings 1985-1995 (OPW, Dublin, 1997) 40. ART 01143.

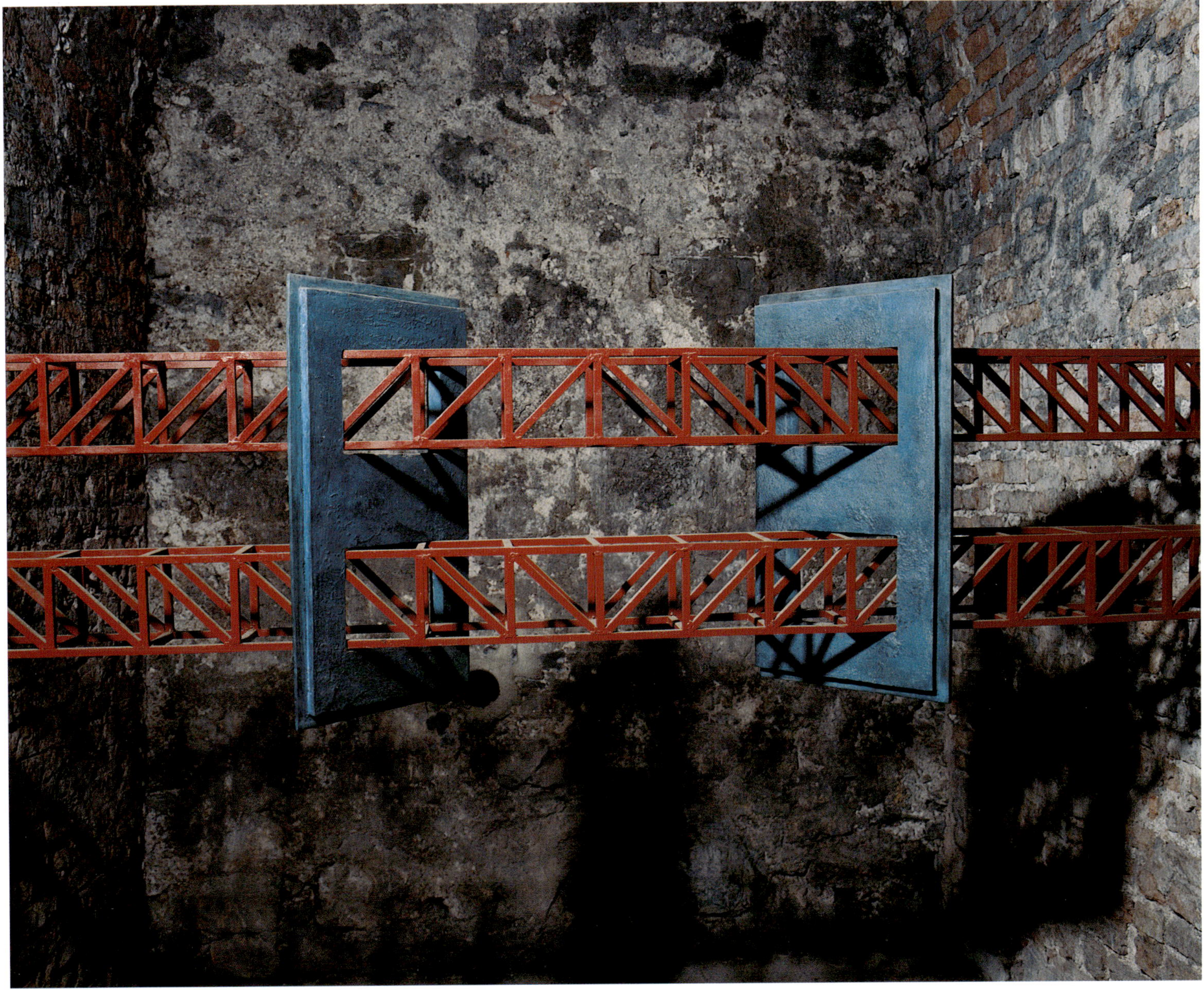

TREASURY BUILDING, THE VAULTS

The Treasury Building stands in the Lower Castle Yard opposite the Chapel Royal. It now houses the Office of the Comptroller and Auditor-General. This building was designed by the architect Thomas Burgh, and dates to the early 18th century. In front of the building is a large terrace with steps up to the doors leading into the building. This terrace contains a series of brick vaults which can be seen from the other side, opposite the shop and restaurant. These cell-like structures were presumably used for storage of some sort originally. (The Castle itself still has part of its vast network of underground rooms, in which wine and household goods were stored.)

In 1992 this block was restored by OPW architects who decided to spend part of the Percent scheme on commissioning two installations in the vaults, where they would be seen by the public. The situation of the vaults is extremely pertinent to the Castle itself. There has always been a dichotomy of public display and private undercurrents in the complex. There is also the geography of the buildings: due to the major architectural works of the 1980s, archaeologists had uncovered layers of human occupation on the site. Within a hundred yards of the vaults, one can visit the subterranean river and base of the medieval tower which came to light during this work. The two sculptors who won the commissions for the vaults both produced imaginative and enigmatic work which relates to these ideas.

Maurice McDonagh

Maurice McDonagh was educated at Waterford RTC and at National College of Art & Design, Dublin, where he completed his MA in Fine Art in 1991. He has been commissioned to do a number of site-specific sculptures, including one at Merchant's Quay in Temple Bar, and was the Irish representative at the European Sculpture Park at the Seville Expo in 1992, when he created a motorised structure on overhead rails called *Wall.* In 1995 he had a solo exhibition at the RHA Gallagher Gallery in Dublin, entitled *Round.* This consisted of twelve different painted steel sculptures arranged in a large circle. His work combines an interest in industrial materials with a concern with more 'spiritual' ideas of time and space, and indicates an appreciation of constructivist principles.

Secret History

1992, painted iron and bronze, 50 x 243 cm
(page 129)

Maurice McDonagh piece is based on a structural brace of red iron which appears to support the two side walls of the vault, preventing it from collapsing. The braces themselves pierce two bronze tablets, painted blue, which the artist intended to look like an open book with a cover and pages. In his initial plan, he proposed to place a sun at the centre of one and the moon at the centre of the other. In his proposal he gave the following explanation of the work: 'The piece spans the vault as if supporting the walls, and consequently those of the historic building above. The stylised book at the centre adds weight, both physical and metaphorical, to this support. It is pierced by the two bridges which are at once parallel and opposite, suggesting two paths in the historical process that encompass the official and the unofficial, the written and the unwritten.'

PROVENANCE – Commissioned by the OPW for the vaults in Dublin Castle as part of Percent for Art scheme, 1992.

LITERATURE
Art in State Buildings 1985-1995 (OPW, Dublin, 1997) 106. ART 01510.

Liadin Cooke

Liadin Cooke was born in 1958. She studied at the National College of Art & Design in Dublin, and later at Goldsmith's College in London, where she now lives. She has had a number of solo exhibitions in Ireland and has made a number of public sculptures, including one in 1997 for the Town Hall in Camden. The sculptural object is central to her work. She has said that 'Often what triggers off a piece of work is a found object, like a letter or something lying on the ground.' When she has selected this 'trigger', she sometimes spends years working on the ideas it generates. In this sense she sees her work as both conceptual and sculptural. As is evident from her piece at Dublin Castle, Cooke is interested in archaeology, and has worked on excavations in Spain and North America. In a more recent piece, *From Juliette* (1998), Cooke used a series of drawings of cross-sections of bone as the basis of an imaginative journey. These were influenced by archaeological drawings of finds.

Pouring the Black Pool

1992, patinated and polished bronze, concrete

Liadin Cooke's starting point for her installation was the idea of the Black Pool or Dubh Linn after which the city of Dublin takes its name. This was originally located where the present gardens of the Castle are. 'The name of Dubh Linn has always attracted me – the Black Pool. It conjures up something mysterious, slightly sinister and ancient.'

When seeing the vaults for the first time, Cooke was immediately struck by the 'strong sense of historical decay coming from them'. In her installation she has created something eerie and almost magical, which expresses her response to the site, and to its long history. Suspended from the ceiling of the vault is a strange bronze vessel with a long spout. Beneath it is the black pool, which is depicted as a dark circle slightly recessed into the floor of the vault (made out of stained concrete). The vessel casts an enormous shadow across it. Within the pool are two little objects made out of polished bronze – a tiny snake and a serrated form. The latter is like an artefact emerging from an excavation, partly uncovered. In this alchemical still-life, the artist has suggested that one can 'see the beginning of something – a city or an idea – or perhaps it is the end of something'.

The work's siting is crucial. The pouring vessel is attached to a shore in the ceiling from which water drips down onto it, causing the build up of a white substance on its surface. Water also drips down into the pool area below. The work is continually changing and developing within the shadows of the vault.

PROVENANCE – Commissioned by the OPW for the vaults in Dublin Castle as part of Percent for Art scheme, 1992.

LITERATURE
Art in State Buildings 1985-1995 (OPW, Dublin, 1997) 105. ART 01511.

COMPARATIVE LITERATURE
Peter Murray (ed.) *0044 – Irish Artists in Britain* (Crawford Municipal Art Gallery, Cork, 1999)

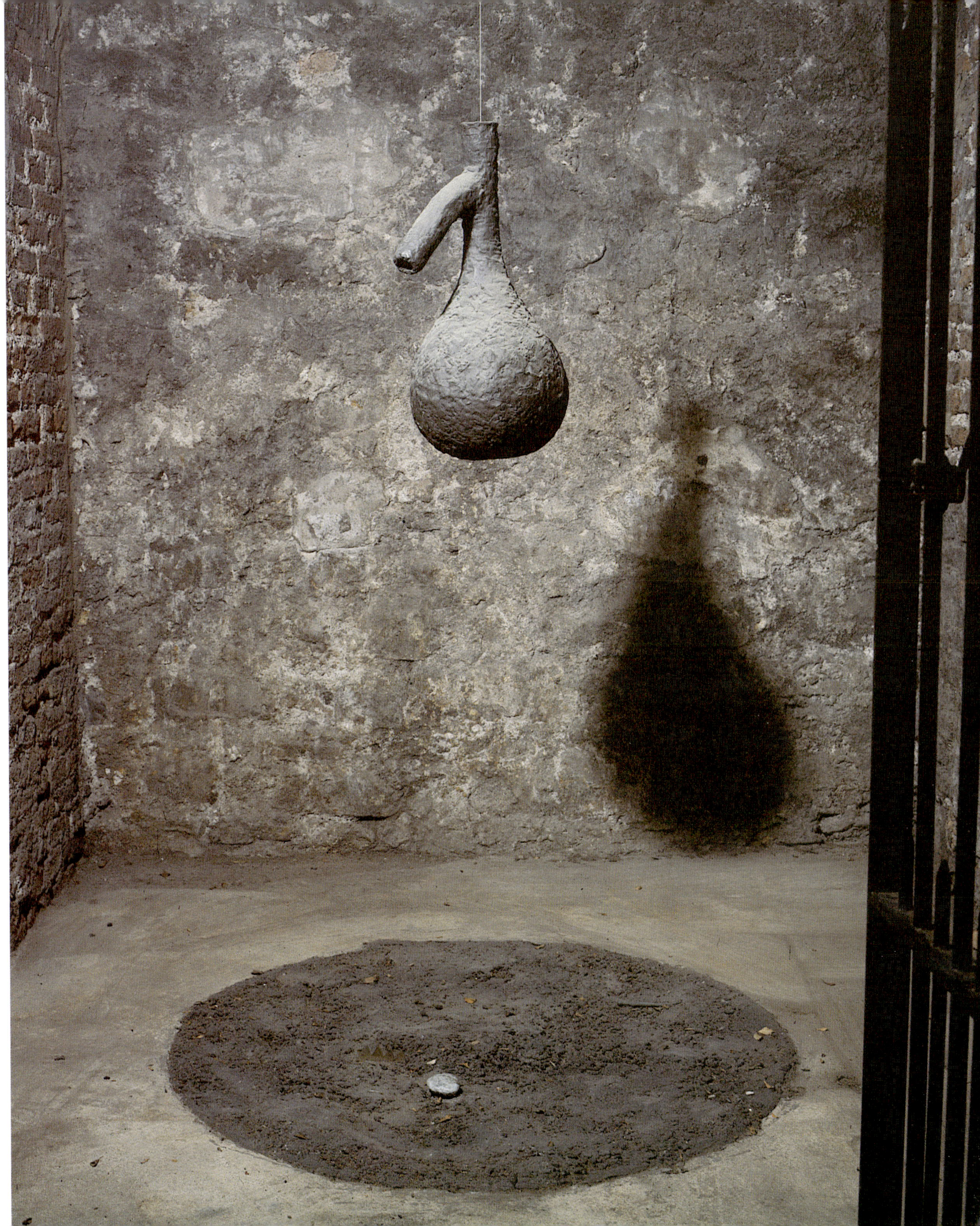

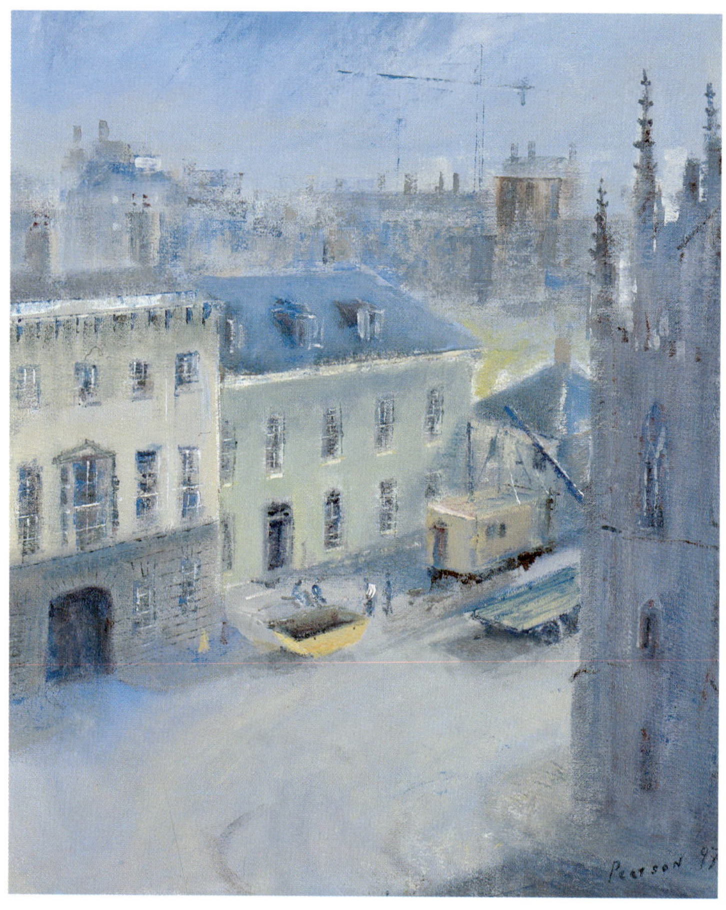

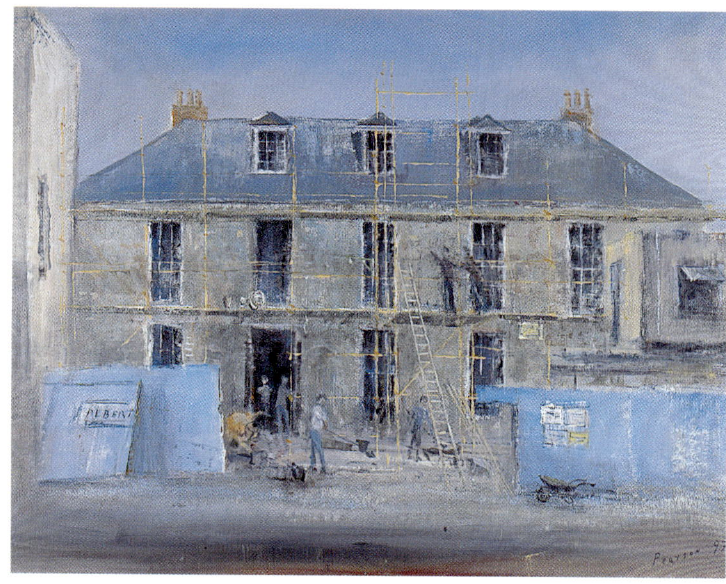

Peter Pearson
Refurbishment of National Drugs Unit
– The Old Armoury, Dublin Castle, under restoration

Peter Pearson
Refurbishment of National Drugs Unit
– Clearing up, moving the portacabin, The Old Armoury

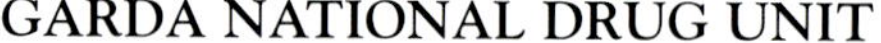

GARDA NATIONAL DRUG UNIT

The National Drug Unit has its offices in an 18th-century building behind the Chapel Royal. This building had been semi-derelict since the early 1980s, when the Dublin Detective Unit moved out. In 1997 it was refurbished by the OPW architect David Byers. A number of paintings were purchased for it, but perhaps the most interesting group were those specially commissioned by the architect. These record the building process itself.

Peter Pearson

Peter Pearson is widely known as a architectural conservationist and historian, with a passion for Dublin and its environs. He studied history of art at Trinity College, Dublin, after which he lived for a short time in Venice and spent a year at the Ecole des Beaux-Arts in Paris. His painting is strongly influenced and inspired by the architecture of Dublin, which he paints in soft glowing colours, enveloped in a misty veil. Some critics have claimed that he is indebted to the Venetian tradition of *veduti*, or view painting, in his approach to the subject.

Pearson has a particularly close affinity with Dublin Castle as he was responsible for the preservation of the Sick and Indigent Roomkeepers building, which is just outside the Palace Street entrance. He has painted many views of the buildings and rooms in the Castle; an exhibition of these works was held in the Castle itself in 1997. Given his attachment to the place, he was an appropriate choice for the commission of this group of paintings.

Refurbishment of National Drugs Unit

Clearing up, moving the portacabin, The Old Armoury
1997, oil on canvas, 65 x 55.5 cm, signed: Pearson 97

The Old Armoury, Dublin Castle, under restoration
1997, oil on canvas, 64 x 86 cm, signed: Pearson 97 (detail)

Five paintings were commissioned from the artist, of which two are included here. Pearson received the commission after he had an exhibition at Dublin Castle in 1997. In these works – painted in situ – he is recording the refurbishment of the building.

PROVENANCE – Commissioned by OPW, 1997.

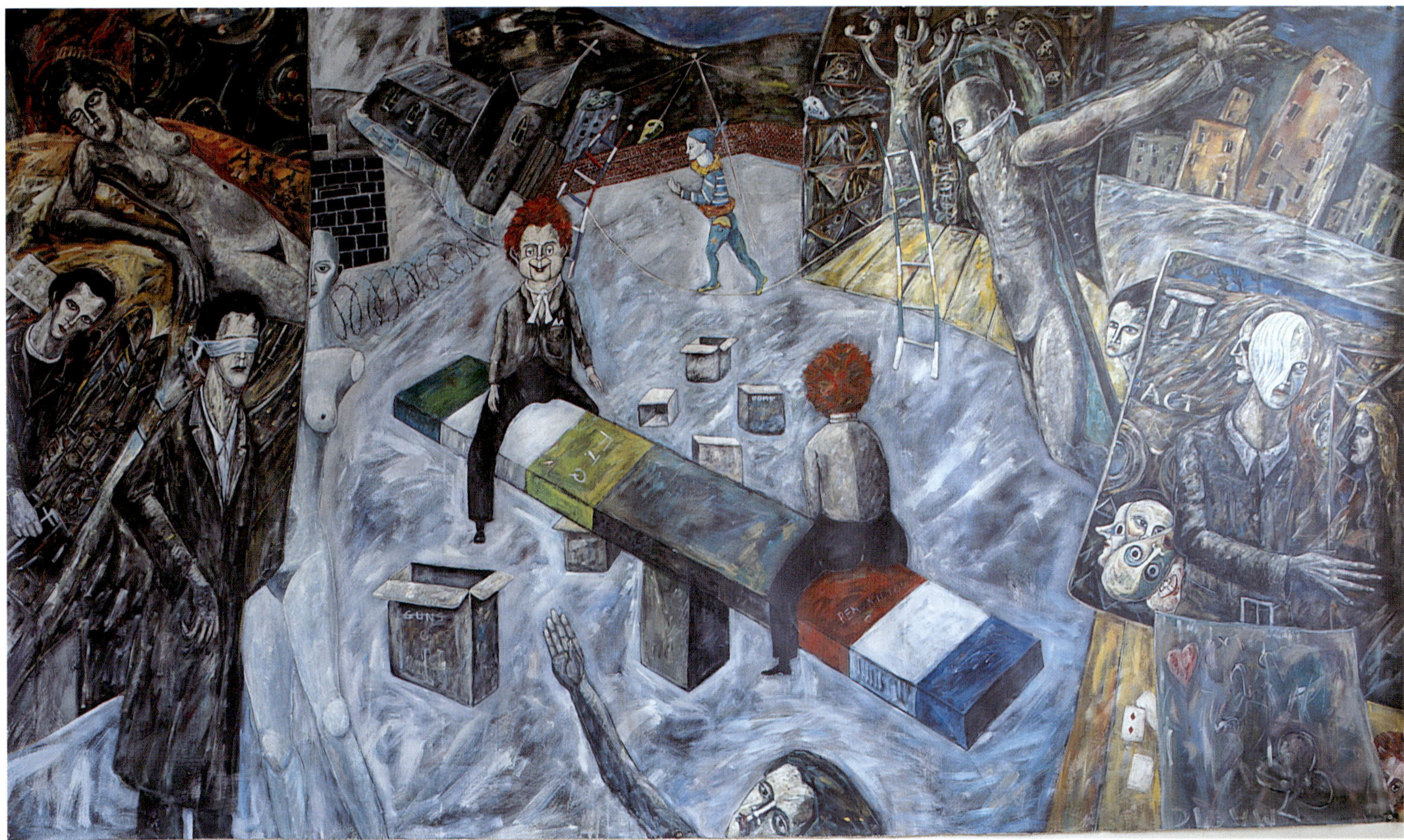

PURCHASE OF ARTWORKS FOR DUBLIN CASTLE

Apart from the above works, there are many other prints and paintings hanging in the numerous offices in the Castle complex. One of the most impressive examples is the enormous painting by Jack Pakenham which is currently hanging in the offices used by the Moriarty Tribunal. While much of what has happened in Dublin Castle has been of major consequence to the history of Ireland, this is one of the only works of art in the complex, apart from the ceiling of St Patrick's Hall, to deal directly with politics.

Jack Pakenham

Jack Pakenham was one of the first artists to engage with rather than merely respond to the political situation in Northern Ireland. He was born in Dublin in the 1930s, but after the early death of his mother, his Ulster Protestant family returned to the North of Ireland. He spent part of his childhood in a children's home in Co Down, and went on to study at Queen's University, after which he taught English for many years. When the Troubles in the North began, Pakenham, like many other artists, felt a need to respond to the anxiety of the situation. He began painting figurative works which contained claustrophobic images often connected with childhood or with play-acting. Masks and puppet-like figures often occur, in particular, a ventriloquist's dummy which he had bought as a present for his young son. These props are used to create nightmarish scenarios in which the protagonists are shown as playing out a kind of act or game over which they have no control. This has allowed Pakenham to deal with the themes of manipulation, innocence and corruption in a direct manner. His tactics are reminiscent of the German Expressionist painters of the post-World War I period, Max Beckmann and Otto Dix. As in their work, there are elements of humour in his paintings, but it is a black humour. Above all, he represents a world of chaos in which no one has the power or courage to escape.

Ulster Playground

acrylic on unstretched canvas, 213 x 365 cm approx

This painting is one of a series of sixteen works begun by Pakenham in the late 1980s. They are each enormous in size, and were painted after the artist had moved into a new and large studio. The works were shown at the Orchard Gallery in Derry and the Ormeau Baths Gallery in Belfast in 1995. In 1996, thirteen of them were exhibited at the Clock Tower building in Dublin Castle, where this work was purchased. They represent some of the strongest images produced by an Irish artist in recent years. In a statement which accompanied the Dublin show, Pakenham stated that the works were part of an attempt to deal with the experience of the North over the previous twenty-five years: 'I did not wish merely to make a visual record since it seemed to me the media did this much more successfully. What concerned me most was to get below the surface paraphernalia to the metaphysical and spiritual reality, in an attempt to portray and diagnose the malaise that made such things possible...'

In this work, Pakenham draws on his experience as a teacher. Many of his pupils ended up joining paramilitary organisations – frequently, it was those he would have least suspected. He was aware of their young minds being manipulated by politicians and paramilitaries. The playground is normally an innocent place, but here it is presented as a bleak concrete space surrounded by derelict buildings. Two identical children (based on the ventriloquist's doll) play on a see-saw which has been painted in 'tribal' colours. The harlequin figure in the background is attempting to walk a 'tightrope' between two painted ladders. He was partly inspired by a colleague of Pakenham's who became a target for the paramilitaries when he attempted to bring the two communities together. The rope on which he stands in not tight but slack, which makes it even more difficult to balance on. In one corner of the yard, a roll of barbed wire separates the children from an army surveillance post. The three large canvases in the foreground refer to Pakenham's own life, and to his role as an artist. The words 'ART' and 'ACT' are scrawled on two of them. Part of the imagery in these is taken from earlier works by the artist, including paintings that he made prior to the Troubles. Other images are linked to the theatre and to stage sets. In the work on the left-hand side is a priest holding a crucifix; next to him is a stained-glass window on which is depicted a scene of the crucifixion. Outside the canvas, on the opposite side of the playground, a real crucifixion is taking place. The following poem was written by the artist to accompany this work:

They balance each other
their grins fixed
loose bricks fall out of the walls
the hopscotch numbers slowly fade
games interrupted by the bomb.
They seek disguise
the highwire walker spins a coin
cannot decide which way to go
he walks the wire from lie to lie.
The guilty soldiers watch from towers
theirs is a secret world, they spy
they spy they spy
with their little eye
something beginning with D.

PROVENANCE – Purchased 1996

LITERATURE
Jack Pakenham – A Broken Sky (Orchard Gallery, Derry; Ormeau Baths Gallery, Belfast, 1995)

Selected Bibliography

Books

F.E.R., *Historical Reminiscences of Dublin Castle* (Dublin, 1901)

E. Fingall, *Seventy Years Young – Memories of Elizabeth, Countess of Fingall* (1927; reprinted by Lilliput Press, Dublin, 1991)

Peter Galloway, *The Most Illustrious Order of St. Patrick* (Phillimore & Co, Sussex, 1983)

Denis McCarthy, *Dublin Castle – At the Heart of Irish History* (Stationary Office, Dublin, 1997)

J.B. Maguire, *Dublin Castle, Historical Background and Guide* (Dublin, n.d., after 1965)

Jacquie Moore, *Art in State Buildings 1985-1995* (Stationery Office for OPW, Dublin, 1997)

Walter Strickland, *A Dictionary of Irish Artists*, 2 vols (Dublin, 1913)

J. Warburton, J. Whitelaw & R. Walsh, *History of the City of Dublin*, 2 vols (London, 1818)

Articles

Angela Alexander, 'A Firm of Dublin Cabinet-makers Mack, Williams and Gibton', *Irish Arts Review Yearbook 1995*, vol. 11 (Dublin, 1994)

John Cornforth, 'Dublin Castle Parts I-III', *Country Life*, 30th July-20th August 1970

John Gilmartin, 'Vincent Waldré's ceiling paintings at Dublin Castle', *Apollo*, xcv, January 1970

J.B. Maguire, Dublin Castle: Three centuries of development', *Journal of Royal Society of Antiquaries of Ireland*, cxv (Dublin, 1985) 13-39

Frederick O'Dwyer, 'The Ballroom at Dublin Castle: the origins of St. Patrick's Hall' in A. Bernelle (ed.), *Decantations – A Tribute to Maurice Craig* (Lilliput Press, Dublin, 1992) 149-67

Frederick O'Dwyer, 'Dublin Castle & its State Apartments 1660-1922', *The Court Historian: Newsletter of Society for Court Studies*, ii, 1st February 1997

Michael Wynne, 'Six Gaetano Gandolfi's in Dublin Castle', *Burlington Magazine*, cxli, no. 1155, June 1999, 252-54

Index